PREPOSITIONS +

PREPOSITIONS +

The Collected Critical Essays

LOUIS ZUKOFSKY

Foreword by Charles Bernstein

Additional prose edited and introduced
by Mark Scroggins

Wesleyan University Press

Published by University Press of New England
Hanover and London

Wesleyan University Press
Published by University Press of New England, Hanover NH 03755

This edition © 2000 by Paul Zukofsky, Sole Heir to and Executor of the
Estate of Louis Zukofsky and Celia Thaew Zukofsky

Foreword by Charles Bernstein and addendum to the 2000 edition
© 2000 by Wesleyan University Press

   Prepositions, first published by Rapp & Carroll, London, and Horizon
   Press, New York, © 1967 by Louis Zukofsky

   Expanded edition © 1981 by The Regents of the University of California; University of California Press, Berkeley and Los Angeles,
   California; University of California Press, Ltd., London, England

   "For Wallace Stevens," "With *Little/For Careenagers*," and "About the
   Gas Age," first published in the September 1974 issue of the *Journal
   of Modern Literature*, © 1974

   "Interview with Louis Zukofsky" conducted by L. S. Dembo. *Contemporary Literature*, Vol. 10, No. 2. © 1969. Reprinted by permission of
   the University of Wisconsin Press

Printed in the United States of America   5   4   3   2   1

CIP data appear at the end of the book

Contents

Foreword

By Charles Bernstein

American poetics of the late twentieth century is saturated with the terms and techniques developed in *Prepositions*, Louis Zukofsky's only collection of literary essays. As the title of this book suggests, these articles are both prefatory and relational, providing an active thinking field in which the propositions of any particular poem may interact.

The essays collected in *Prepositions* span from 1924 to 1971. The collection begins with three essays that define Zukofsky's poetics of "sincerity" and "objectification" and continues with tributes to William Carlos Williams, Wallace Stevens, and Ezra Pound, poets from the generation preceding Zukofsky's who were of utmost importance for him. In addition, the collection includes short notes on some of Zukofsky's own works as well as reflections on Marianne Moore, Hart Crane, William Blake, George Santayana, Spinoza, Charlie Chaplin, Lewis Carroll, Henry Adams, and "outsider" painter Dometer Guczul. The book ends with Zukofsky's own list of key words, an "Index to Definitions" that composes its own poem of motifs, as, for example, in the thirteen words that begin with *m*: mass, meaning, measure, melody, memories, metaphor, mind, modern, montage, morality, motion, mysticism, myth.

One of the most influential essays in *Prepositions*, "An Objective," is based on three essays Zukofsky wrote in 1930 and 1931, when he was in his late twenties, two of which were published in the breakthrough "Objectivists" issue of *Poetry* (1931), which Zukofsky edited. As a supplement to this edition of *Prepositions*, Mark Scroggins has assembled the original, far longer, versions of these essays, along with the most substantive interview with the poet, originally published in *Contemporary Literature* in 1969. Together with *Bottom: on Shakespeare* (1963), and *A Test of Poetry* (1948), this expanded edition of *Prepositions* provides the essential record of Zukofsky's published critical writings.

Zukofsky was born on January 23, 1904, in New York City, just a year after his mother had emigrated from what was then Russia and is now Lithuania (his father had come ahead a few years earlier). His

first major publication was "Poem beginning 'The'" in 1926, a trench-
ant response to Eliot's "The Waste Land" and a foundational poem for
Jewish American modernism. His twenty-four–movement long poem,
"A,"written over the course of his entire writing life, was published in
its first complete edition in 1978, the year of the poet's death. His
Complete Shorter Poems, an extension of the succintly titled *ALL,* was
published in 1991.

    Prepositions was constructed as a distillation or abstraction of
Zukofsky's poetic thinking. Since complex structure and elision were
Zukofsky's tools of the trade, it is not surprising that these essays reflect
the result of an historical process of "getting it down to the bare
bones," as he tells L. S. Dembo in the 1968 interview included here.
The objective of these elisions is to keep the essays open to active
thinking, to enable them to move into new historical and social and
poetic contexts all the while constantly transforming themselves. The
context-specific buttresses of earlier versions of the essays weigh the
pieces down into literary history; here the aspiration is for the words to
stand on their own. Precisely because of the fundamental amiguity of
many of Zukofsky's terms, his essays, in their final form, remain available to reinterpretation and therefore reintegration into contemporary poetic thought and practice. This achievement is both prescient
and exemplary.

    For all the technical and quasi-logical qualities of the first set of
essays in *Prepositions,* this is a work not of philosophy or aesthetics but
poetics. These are compositions, not explanations, where the sincerity
(care for the details) and objectification (structural solidity) of the writing take precedence over any putative argument. The image of an
objective lens, which Zukofsky uses in "An Objective," is illustrative of
the technique. The lens focuses the rays coming from an object, making the image ready for projection or microscopic examination. The
image in the lens remains virtual or immanent, available for use.
Zukofsky's poetics, like his poems, invites the reader's projection or
introjection, to fill in the blanks.

    Zukofsky was wary of philosophical abstractions and generaliza-
tions and his irritation with metaphysical poeticizing is evident
throughout this volume: he thought such theorizing a lot of "gas"
(169). For Zukofsky, concepts such as *reality* or *knowledge* are disembod-
ied and inert. Knowing, he insisted, takes place in particular acts of

perception: "No thought exists/Completely abstracted from action" ("A"-8). Moreover, Zukofsky rejected that much-cherished humanist idea of poetry as a source of a generalized human truth: "*Impossible* to communicate anything but particulars—historical and contemporary —things," as he puts it in "An Objective" (16). Specificity, detail, the concrete—these are, for him, the solid state components of any poetics. And indeed, Zukofsky's poetics of the particular were significant not only for his closest contemporaries—Charles Reznikoff, George Oppen, Basil Bunting, and Lorine Niedecker—but also were formative for the poetics of Robert Creeley, especially as articulated in *A Quick Graph* (1970).

Certainly, Zukofsky does call for a poetry that "can speak to all" (8), a formulation that is hardly particularistic; but the way to this objective is not through mythopoetic or thematic universalizing, nor through developing a theory of knowledge, but through the most concrete verbal attention humanly possible. When Zukofsky writes that "a case can be made out for the poet giving some of his life to the use of the words *the* and *a*" (10) he is being deliciously provocative. He is also defining the shape of his own body of work, from "Poem beginning 'The'" to "*A*" (eleven of whose sections begin with the letters *an*). The movement suggested here from the definite to the indefinite article is as telling as anything else in this poet's work.

In "An Objective," Zukofsky writes of a "Desire for what is objectively perfect" (12). Poetry is not the realization of such a utopia but, in contrast, what is *aimed at:* an aspiration grounded in the historical practice of the art of configuring words. These essays are neither theories nor theorems but "steps" in a process sounded as "stops" on an organ: recursive, recombinant, resourceful, even restless. "Rested totality" (13) is not the final stage at the top of the stairs but the *process* cast as "thing."

Several times in *Prepositions* Zukofsky notes that poetry approaches (or has as its "upper limit," as he puts it in "A"-12) the "wordless art of music" (18). The recourse to music emphasizes the thingness of poetry (its object status), the sound value of poetry (its song), as well as poetry's durational space (its temporality). Unlike music, however, poetry's sound is verbal. For Zukofsky sound, pitch, rhythm, and tone do not accompany meaning, neither are they arbitrary nor conventionally associated with meaning: they *make* meaning (17, 19). When words are heard as sound, the poetic mode of perception has taken hold. The result is not free verse but an acoustically charged poetry whose patterns are not derived from manuals but newly invented. "Technique" is stressed but as a matter of innovation not of finesse: the "immediacy" (78) of "invented technique" (72) is valued over the impression of received form (23).

For Zukofsky, "objectification" marks an insistence on "the detail, not mirage, of seeing" (12); the desire is to represent not the appearance of nature but its conditions—autonomy, completeness, self-sufficiency, particularity. Never words over world but words as world. In Zukofsky's poetics, "sincerity" is not an affect but the truth in the materials: "thinking with things as they exist (12), where things are not only objects but persons. To adapt the familiar Kantian phrase, neither sincerity nor objectification pertains to *the thing itself*, rather, they are means of grappling with the structures and conditions through which things come into perception and by means of which we come into contact with them and live alongside them.

Zukofsky's poetics intricately elaborate on a key tenet of William Carlos Williams's, quoted in "A Statement for Poetry": "A poem is a small (or large) machine made of words" (19). Zukofsky defines a modernist practice in which the poem is not an extension or expression of the self but an entity in itself, "another created thing" (20). The value of a poem—*conviction* is Zukofsky's word—is not measured in terms of the work's "attitudes and beliefs" (20) but by means of its style and technique. What matters is not the person standing behind the poem but the poem standing on its own prosodic feet, a construction set apart from the person who made it. The poem, that is, presents not the poet him or herself "but that order that of itself can speak" (8). In Zukofsky's lucid analysis in "Poetry/*For My Son When He Can Read,*" modernist composition is a constructivist practice involving the serial ordering of syllables, words, phrases, and lines, in which the articulation of a particular ordering defines the aesthetic of the poem ("the awareness of order," as Zukofsky puts it [8]).

In a constructivist poetics, the politics of a poem are exhibited as much by its composition as by its statement. For Zukofsky, belaboring the poet's piety or compassion compromises the sincerity of the poem's enactments—a view that put Zukofsky at odds, during the 1930s, with such journals as *The New Masses,* with whom he shared a left political perspective. Zukofsky's poetics challenged the socialist realism of his time, just as it challenges the multicultural populism of the present—not because of their socialism or multiculturalism but because of possible insufficiencies in this regard.

The longest—and earliest—essay in *Prepositions* is a montage of luminous passages taken from the writings of Henry Adams. The technique appears to anticipate Zukofsky's later, and far more intricate, use of quotations in both *"A"* and *Bottom: on Shakespeare,* and brings to mind the fact that Zukofsky, as much as Walter Benjamin, could envision a literary work composed soley of citations. In any case, Zukofsky's elected affinity with Adams, in which he casts Adams as poet in the cloak of historian, sets the stage for his use of Adams in "A"-8, where it might be said that he casts himself as historian in the cloak of poet. Zukofsky's imaginative identification with Henry Adams has affinities with several other poets' extensively citational studies in American affinity, such as Susan Howe's C. S. Pierce (*Pierce-Arrow,* 1999) and Paul Metcalf's Herman Melville (*Genoa,* 1965).

Like the theory of knowledge, the philosophy of history was a major preoccupation of the poet, and his writing weaves together public and private history, autobiography and politics, in a manner that addresses the interdependence of seeming contraries. Zukofsky touches on this in a statement he made for the publication of *ALL*: "In a sense *All* is an autobiography: the words are my life . . . The poet's form is never an imposition of history, but the desirability of making order out of history as it is felt and conceived." One might conjugate this, with a Wittgensteinian twist, to say: The facts compose a life as they do a history. The poet's form is never an imposition of facts, or autobiography, but the desirability of making order out of facts, and life, as they are felt and conceived. While Henry Adams's philosophy of history was an important influence on Zukofsky, as was Karl Marx's, it is Benjamin's "Messianic moment" that comes to mind when considering Zukofsky's aspiration, in his first statement of poetics, written six years after the Adams essay, for "rested totality" and "what is objectively perfect," suggesting as it does a desire for something beyond history's transitory instability and its inevitably partial (not to say *mis*-) representation. (Ron Silliman first suggested the connection between Benjamin and Zukofsky in *L=A=N=G=U=A=G=E.*)

An intriguing, but little discussed, essay in *Prepositions* concerns "BASIC" English, that curious 1920s and 1930s experiment of C. K. Ogden and I. A. Richards to create a simplified noun-centered English as a universal second language. Zukofsky clearly had an attraction for making English more concrete and this essays suggests a relation between this experiment and his own insistence on making every word count and on resisting verbal ornamentation. Indeed his own radically reductivist impulses played out in his poetic practice of condensation and elision. Zukofsky's interest in BASIC elucidates the fact that while his poems may appear rhetorical, verbally acrobatic, and suffused with intellect, he was aiming for an embodied language free of vague or ungrounded thought (even to the point of undervaluing the contingent imperfections that compose the everyday). Yet Zukofsky's at times hilarious send-up of BASIC shows how his commitment to complexity and specificity put him at odds with lexical essentialism and linguistic positivism, where the cure is worse than the disease. In "A"-8, he diagnoses the problem this way: "The simple will be discovered beneath the complex/Then the complex under the simple/Then again the simple under the complex." (For another perspective on the implications of BASIC, by one of Zukofsky's most immediate poet-contemporaries, see Laura [Riding] Jackson and Schulyer Jackson's *Rational Meaning: A New Foundation for the Definition of Words*.)

While the references to translation are brief in *Prepositions*, the topic is important in the light of Zukofsky's pervasive use of inventive translation in *"A"* and Celia and Louis Zukofsky's paradigmatic homophonic translation of Catullus. Zukofsky saw translation as a way of achieving objectification: translating oneself into a poem/object or personae, as he says in his essay on Pound (71). At the same time, he saw translation not as a means of assimilating a foreign poem into a fluent English but rather as a means to bring into English "unexplored poetic forms" (71).

These essays do not provide a skeleton key to Zukofsky's poems but, like the rest of this poet's work, are often complex and refractory. The idea that there is an underlying meaning to the poems, hidden from view but available by scholarly excavation, is rejected: "just read the words," Zukofsky advises (24). He shows that complexity and multiplicity of meaning are part of the experience of the work, not a veil to be lifted away. The structures and elisions of Zukofsky's poems often are made almost indiscernible, creating the particularly exquisite experiential richness in the perceptible unfathomability. While Zukofsky's work opens itself to, indeed inspires, elucidation through the use of source material, through the consideration of historical and social contexts, and through detailed structural and prosodic analysis, the objective of such critical interpretation is to be subsumed within the poem's affective elusiveness. Deciphering the codes may supplement the experience but it cannot explain it. Explanation is beside the point, beside the poem. Zukofsky's poems play to the ear; the truth of the work is in the music, not the underlying webs that produce it. As the poet says, talking about an ambiguous gesture by Charlie Chaplin that ends *Modern Times:* "what can the action of the shot mean but what is *does*—it *performs*" (64). And this is Zukofsky's point about his own poetry as well: it means by doing, it performs.

In his lifetime, Zukofsky's readers were small in number. He provided few hooks for the casual reader and chose to work in accordance with his own exacting standards rather than to assimilate his work to contemporary literary or market considerations. The result is a work remarkably durable, to use a word that Zukofsky applies, with admiration, to Wallace Stevens. This durability is currently resulting in a steady and accumulating interest in Zukofsky's work in the English-speaking world as well as in Europe. In France, his poetry is greatly revered by such poets as Claude Royet-Journoud, Emmanuel Hocquard, and Anne-Marie Albiach.

In the Dembo interview, Zukofsky quotes a line from Elizabethan poet George Chapman, "the unspeakable good liquor there," adding, "Obviously, the man who wrote that knew what it was to gargle something down his throat." The person who wrote this book knew what it was to write poetry *in*—and to write poetry *for*—the twentieth century.

"Poetry never exaggerates or destroys the things it is" (10), says Zukofsky, who tests this principle in every passage he writes. *Prepositions* is the work of a poet who created poetry not of attitude or ideas or moral views or lifestyle but as a bearing in and toward language, in and as language. In *Prepositions* he does not tell about poetry, he shows it. For "how else can the poet speak . . . but as a poet" (11).

New York, June 1999

Prefatory Note

The essays in this volume may be viewed as steps in the excursion of a poet who wished to imbue criticism with something of the worth and method of his craft. Time usually qualifies this aim with later information which dates an earlier feeling or insight, and the dates following the selections concede this fact. But the changes from the original drafts are few—mostly omissions. As the title *Prepositions* of this book may propose—the critic's constant intentions to the things he discussed directed, after all, such ways of speaking as: *for*, *with* and *about*. This final collection includes three addenda to the original publication of 1967.

L.Z.
1976

For

POETRY

For My Son When He Can Read

When you were 19 months old your ability to say 'Go billy go billy go billy go ba,' much faster than I could ever say it, made me take some almost illegible notes on poetry out of my wallet. The time had come for me to fill the vacuum I abhorred in my life as much as you had filled it in yours. Though I was not too agile then, I hope you will sense reading me why I had forgotten my notes—had stopped speaking while I was not writing poetry. Three months were to pass before the atomic bomb was used that ended the Second World War.

Sworn to drudgery, people parted in those months with everything in the spirit of a fool and his money. Yet as I heard your first syllables, no matter how blank the world was it again seemed possible. I saw why definitions of poetry rounding out like ciphers (abstract and like numbers on clocks that read only this century or that century and no other) should not satisfy either of us. For I hope that you as well as I will never want to live by them.

*

Poetry if anything has a sense for everything. Meaning: without poetry life would have little present. To write poems is not enough if they do not keep the life that has gone. To write poems may never seem enough when they speak of a life that has gone. The poet may visibly stop writing, but secretly measures himself against each word of poetry ever written. Furthermore, if he is of constant depth, he thinks of others who have lived, live, and will live to say the things he cannot say for the time being. People who do this are always working. They are not ashamed to appear idle. The effort of poetry is recognizable, as against a great deal of timely writing, despite the dress and respites of poets.

Poetry has not one face one day to lose face on another. A person would show little thought to say poetry is opposed to—since it is added to like—science. Poetry is readily explained except to those who refuse to learn or are insensible.

This translation of Confucius may not be all that one looking at a face one respects might want it to be, but the love one respects it for is clear: 'Education begins with poetry, is strengthened through proper conduct, and consummated through music.'

'Education begins with'—looked at either as process or structure, poetry apprehending, intense, disinterested, informs skills and the intellect. 'Is strengthened'—grows with integrity, an ability to select and relate what is worth knowing and to defend it for men's welfare. 'Consummated through music'—the aim of an order that might perhaps be communicated to all men.

The sage agrees with the history of technics: how things are made, why people live to make them, and live together by them.

Felt deeply, poems like all things have the possibilities of elements whose isotopes are yet to be found. Light has travelled and so looked forward.

How do we know? We look at the stars and because the light from them has travelled we see them shining tonight into tomorrow. With the same sense we look back and at once forward to 'The Pitcher' of Yuan Chen.

The time: 779–831, our era.

THE PITCHER

I dreamt I climbed to a high, high plain,
And on the plain I found a deep well.
My throat was dry with climbing and I longed to drink,
And my eyes were eager to look into the cool shaft.
I walked round it; I looked right down;
I saw my image mirrored on the face of the pool.
An earthen pitcher was sinking into the black depths;
There was no rope to pull it to the well-head.
I was strangely troubled lest the pitcher should be lost,
And started wildly running to look for help.
From village to village I scoured that high plain;
The men were gone: the dogs leapt at my throat.

I came back and walked weeping round the well;
Faster and faster the blinding tears flowed—
Till my own sobbing suddenly woke me up;
My room was silent, no one in the house stirred;
The flame of my candle flickered with a green smoke;
The tears I had shed glittered in the candle-light.
A bell sounded; I knew it was the midnight-chime;
I sat up in bed and tried to arrange my thoughts;
The plain in my dream was the graveyard at Chiang-an,
Those hundred acres of untilled land.
The soil heavy and the mounds heaped high;
And the dead below them laid in deep troughs.
Deep are the troughs, yet sometimes dead men
Find their way to the world above the grave.
And tonight my love who died long ago
Came into my dream as the pitcher sunk in the well.
That was why the tears suddenly streamed from my eyes,
Streamed from my eyes and fell on the collar of my dress.

The literal meaning of the translation, though informed with a sense of verse amounting to only adequate skill, runs through the intellect to dispose of an entire recent literature of dreams. The unsounded music of the Chinese I do not know leads me to project it—a pitcher I may be fortunate to drink from in the future. But now bolts and bars of the motto of Kansas, which by a coincidence too obviously literary I happen to think of, cast their shadows across the midnight stars that are anything but epigrammatic or verbal. Like these not fully known, of an order which I have not been accomplished enough to live, the words 'my love came into my dream as the pitcher' tend to weigh all written and unwritten poems (my own more than others because this moment I am either a poet or nothing) in a judgment as lasting as 'Dick the shepherd blows his nail.' Should I ever know the original of 'The Pitcher' the entire poem may judge every other actual or possible poem with the same implicit finality.

And Yuan Chen, whose sobbing woke him up, is for my purpose saying in not the best poetry in English :

By writing 'The Pitcher' in a language you may not find time to learn I am muted in a certain place and time, if you wish to say so and be vulgar. But after all you sense something of my meaning, and whether it is good or bad in my tongue, in English it is not too removed from all serious poets who lose their everyday lives in their poems so that these live; or not too removed from a suicide who saw a more complete time than he found one night looking at the stars above the earth, and whose last words to a friend might be :—live completely, love, feel all things with great constancy; live hundreds of years as it may seem; know all tongues; reach out with something you recognize as not lonely in a tree that has stood a long time and let the end be as the air as if it had never been disturbed around the tree :—the contradiction between the act of one hurrying his own death and these words need not materialize as a contradiction for you :—for I wish you long life so that you may grasp in the consistency of the living world this good-bye for the blossoming of your mind.

Someone alive in the years 1951 to 2000 may attempt a scientific definition of poetry. Its value would be in a generalization based on past and present poems and always relevant to the detail of their art. All future poems would verify some aspect of this definition and reflect it as an incentive to a process intended to last at least as long as men.

Though keyed at that time to avoid the ambiguity of our day's diplomacies, this generalization might, at rock bottom, not oppose in intention an abstract of a President's remarks of 1932 : 'Authorship is not only a means of clear thinking . . . It is the chief means for the dissemination of truth and fact, on which our system of life depends . . . I can think of no more happy task and of no nobler occupation than . . . honest and beautiful literary craftsmanship.' The skeptic—at best a scientist and a poet—will tacitly see beyond the more diplomatic words omitted from the foregoing remarks; not stop at 'our system'; ask if the division between truth and fact is fruitful of any definition; not resent simple acceptance of the true, the beautiful, and the just from which the remarks implicitly spring; but supplying his own mind to the interstices of the words point them, like bricks as it were, with Plato's generalization more sympathetic to him as a refinement of standards : 'If number, measure and weighing be taken away from any art, that which remains will not be much.'

The need for standards in poetry is no less than in science. The latter has been 'a subject of poetry' as in Lucretius. No measurement of science is so accurate as not to allow a margin of error to both observer and instrument. To the poet acting at once as observer and instrument the scientific standards of physical measurement are only the beginnings of images of poems. Good verse is determined by the poet's susceptibilities involving a precise awareness of differences, forms and possibilities of existence—words with their own attractions included. The poet, no less than the scientist, works on the assumption that inert and live things and relations hold enough interest to keep him alive as part of nature. The fact that he persists with them confirms him. When human beings 'vegetate' their existence covers at least an eosere for him. For if poetry can ever be contented it will be content only through a specialized sense for every unfolding. But poets measure by means of words, whose effect as offshoot of nature may (or should) be that their strength of suggestion can never be accounted for completely.

Still, the standard in a cadence or in the movement of a line of verse is always a quantity in proportion to the poet's susceptibilities as found in his words. In poems, as in works of science, the involved susceptibilities always function with respect to some concept of exactness of utterance. Those who say that the standards of science do not concern taste sometimes also say that the measure for judging a good song or a bad does not concern standards but one's taste or another's. Yet a measure of song would seem to be the work of consistently peeling away a marginal error from all legible and imaginable quantities to get at a standard of song. For if the thought 'no standard can be reached' gauges despair for song, the despair of science is sounded when whatever language or indicator that is its utterance is contemplated alongside the physical intricacies of fact. When poetry is defined as indirect or 'desirably' incapable of definition, symbols standing for sound, and words which are the semblances of the things, events or susceptibilities of science are conceived as echoes occurring out of nowhere. The choice for science and poetry when symbols or words stop measuring is to stop speaking.

To think clearly then about poetry it is necessary to point out that its aims and those of science are not opposed or mutually exclusive; and that only the more complicated, if not finer, tolerances of number, measure and weight that define poetry make it seem imprecise as compared to science, to quick readers of instruments. It should be said rather that the most complicated standards of science—including definitions, laws of nature and theoretic constructions—are poetic, like the motion of Lorentz' single electron and the field produced by it that cannot 'make itself felt in our experiments, in which we are always concerned with immense numbers of particles, only the resultant effects produced by them are perceptible to our senses.' Aware of like tolerances the poet can realize the standards of a scientific definition of poetry. They should embrace at least such action that informs skills and the intellect ordering events at once outside and in the head or whatever impinges upon it anatomically.

Utterance is but an extension or limit of this process. Poems are but phases of utterance. The action that precedes and moves towards utterance moves toward poetry. The scientist compelled to make order of a hunch, the architect building the house in which to live, the dancer telling others' eyes what it is to move, an historian shaping a sum of events to the second law of thermodynamics, an economist subsuming under a fiction of value a countless differentiation of labor processes, a weaver making the garment that will drape to a body, the painter, the musician, all who achieve constructions apart from themselves, move in effect toward poetry.

With respect to such action the specialized concern to the poet will be, first, its proper conduct—a concern to avoid clutter no matter how many details outside and in the head are ordered. This does not presume that the style will be the man, but rather that the order of his syllables will define his awareness of order. For his second and major aim is not to show himself but that order that of itself can speak to all men.

Singing like Gower even from his ashes, then, that order of itself may constantly intimate :

> Be attent,
> And time that is so briefly spent
> With your fine fancies quaintly eche :
> What's dumb in show I'll plain with speech.

How much what is sounded by words has to do with what is seen by them—and how much what is at once sounded and seen by them cross-cuts an interplay among themselves—will naturally sustain the scientific definition of poetry we are looking for. To endure it would be compelled to integrate these functions : time, and what is seen in time (as held by a song), and an action whose words are actors or, if you will, mimes composing steps as of a dance that at proper instants calls in the vocal cords to transform it into plain speech.

Moreover : granted that 'the business of every science is not to prove but to explain its subject, in order that men may know what it is with which the science is concerned'; and that the 'common speech' is that to

which 'children are accustomed by those who are about them when they
first begin to distinguish words'; and that, therefore, grammar which
springs from this is but a 'secondary speech';—those like us, son, 'to
whom the world is our native country' (as it was to Dante and Shakespeare) will declare (in substance with Gower's lines in *Pericles* that have
been quoted here) with Dante writing of the common speech, that 'the
exercise of discernment as to words involves by no means the smallest
labor of our reason.' 'Since we see that a great many sorts of them can
be found,' and that (anti-climactically) what he said 'on the pre-eminent
nature of the words to be used may suffice for everyone of inborn discernment.' For starting, simply, with Dante's intent to explain and
make plain—with 'combed-out' and 'shaggy' words, or as when breathing the new life he warned against metaphor whose discernment is lost
in the making—it appears that the scientific definition of poetry can
be based on nothing less than the world, the entire humanly known
world.

Like the theories of science which are valid because they explain
most, this definition will be valid inasmuch as it will be comprehensive.
One of its forms might be : that matters worthy of the 'highest common
speech—all that flows from the tops of the heads of illustrious poets
down to their lips'—properly embrace the whole art of poetry which
is 'nothing else but the completed action of writing words to be set to
music'—music being the one art that more than the others aims in its
reach to speak to all men. Beside this definition of poetry, all other
definitions of poetry would appear niggardly.

For the whole art may appear in one line of the poet or take a whole
life's work in which to appear. Close to this point of view the poet has
preferred in casual conversation a distinction between long and short
poems and avoided extant divisions of his art as belabored by logicians,
theologians, and masters of rhetoric. Always concerned with saying as
much as possible and speaking to the full, never lost in the overfall, he
steers from discourses on his art to a simple inventory of the poetry in one
line or so many lines, yet never presumes that identifying a poem by
length is more than a tag he uses while he sorts value. The question as to
whether a long poem is composed of short ones; or of stanzas (aside from
the fact that a stanza is nothing unless its form is in germ in the first
words, and indeed compelled by all the words, of the poem); whether
what he writes is epic, lyric, or dramatic;—seems to him as vain as the
question whether it is best to speak of inspiration, or felicitous speed,

or hard work. In his order of poetic intellect all clinical charts say almost nothing about the poetry. The poet wonders why so many today have raised up the word 'myth,' finding the lack of so-called 'myths' in our time a crisis the poet must overcome or die from, as it were, having become too radioactive, when instead a case can be made out for the poet giving some of his life to the use of the words *the* and *a*: both of which are weighted with as much epos and historical destiny as one man can perhaps resolve. Those who do not believe this are too sure that the little words mean nothing among so many other words.

The rhetoricians, however, need not find any special comfort in the last statement. Responsible for the rule that a clause introduced by the word 'that' is not preceded by a comma, whereas a clause introduced by the word 'which' is—they exist entirely in that frozen realm without crisis that Dante called the 'secondary speech.' In poetry one can sing without stopping and without commas of the redundant commonplace action of the species—

A dog that runs never lies down—and of the dog who if not mythical has rhetorical distinction, having been stopped by commas—

A dog, *that* runs, never lies down.

All this about dogs may be learned from a study of quantity and from the fact that both prose and poetry, if they are that, are meant to record and elate for all time.

In this connection, a scientific definition will probably find it unnecessary to distinguish between prose and poetry, though it may find considerable interest in gauging how much music made up of notes has qualities of poetry.

To record and elate for all time despite barriers . . . For if the customs, 'tastes,' and costumed men of this and that period are to order a scientific definition of poetry, poetry while remaining unaffected as matter will not come up from the shadows. In science a law is general till one fact disproves it. The law that replaces it must subsume that fact. In poetry, when bad taste sets in, if the sense of the correct thing to be done is not understood, all matter is bypassed.

*

Poetry never exaggerates or destroys the thing it is. It may border on the perilous or record the sentimental among other events and remain poetry.

Writing this, Paul, for a time when you can read, I do not presume that you will read 'me.' That 'me' will be lost today when he says good night on your third birthday, and not missed tomorrow when he says good morning as you begin your fourth year. It took all human time to nurse those greetings. And how else can the poet speak them but as poet.

1946

AN OBJECTIVE

I

An Objective: (Optics)—The lens bringing the rays from an object to a focus. That which is aimed at. (Use extended to poetry)—Desire for what is objectively perfect, inextricably the direction of historic and contemporary particulars.

It is understood that historic and contemporary particulars may mean a thing or things as well as an event or a chain of events: i.e. an Egyptian pulled-glass bottle in the shape of a fish or oak leaves, as well as the performance of Bach's *Matthew Passion* in Leipzig, and the rise of metallurgical plants in Siberia.

Omission of names is prompted by the historical method of the Chinese sage who wrote, 'Then for nine reigns there was no literary production.'

None at all; because there was neither consciousness of the 'objectively perfect' nor an interest in clear or vital 'particulars.' Nothing—neither a new object nor the stripping of an old to the light—was 'aimed at.' Strabismus may be a topic of interest between two strabismics; those who see straight look away.

II

In sincerity shapes appear concomitants of word combinations, precursors of (if there is continuance) completed sound or structure, melody or form. Writing occurs which is the detail, not mirage, of seeing, of thinking with the things as they exist, and of directing them along a line of melody. Shapes suggest themselves, and the mind senses and receives awareness. Parallels sought for in the other arts call up the perfect line of occasional drawing, the clear beginnings of sculpture not proceeded with.

Presented with sincerity, the mind even tends to supply, in further suggestion, which does not attain rested totality, the totality not always found in sincerity and necessary only for perfect rest, complete appreciation. This rested totality may be called objectification—the apprehension satisfied completely as to the appearance of the art form as an object. That is: distinct from print which records action and existence and incites the mind to further suggestion, there exists, though it may not be harbored as solidity in the crook of an elbow, writing (audibility in two-dimensional print) which is an object or affects the mind as such. The codifications of the rhetoric books may have something to do with an explanation of this attainment, but its character may be simply described as the arrangement, into one apprehended unit, of minor units of sincerity—in other words, the resolving of words and their ideation into structure. Granted that the word combination 'minor unit of sincerity' is an ironic index of the degradation of the power of the individual word in a culture which seems hardly to know that each word in itself is an arrangement, it may be said that each word possesses objectification to a powerful degree; but that the facts carried by one word are, in view of the preponderance of facts carried by combinations of words, not sufficiently explicit to warrant a realization of rested totality such as might be designated an art form. Yet the objectification which is a poem, or a unit of structural prose, may exist in a line or very few lines. The mind may conceivably prefer one object to another—the energy of the heat which is Aten to the benignness of the light which is Athena. But this is a matter of preference rather than the invalidation of the object not preferred. It is assumed that epistemological problems do not affect existence, that a personal structure of relations might be a definite object, or *vice versa*.

At any time, objectification in writing is rare. The poems or the prose structures of a generation are few. Properly no verse should be called a poem if it does not convey the totality of perfect rest.

It is questionable, however, whether the state of rest achieved by objectification is more pertinent to the mind than presentation in detail: the isolation of each noun so that in itself it is an image, the grouping of nouns so that they partake of the quality of things being together without violence to their individual intact natures, simple sensory adjectives as necessary as the nouns.

The disadvantage of strained metaphor is not that it is necessarily sentimental (the sentimental may at times have its positive personal qualities) but that it carries the mind to a diffuse everywhere and leaves it nowhere. One is brought back to the entirety of the single word which is in itself a relation, an implied metaphor, an arrangement, a harmony or a dissonance.

The economy of presentation in writing is a reassertion of faith that the combined letters—the words—are absolute symbols for objects, states, acts, interrelations, thoughts about them. If not, why use words —new or old?

III

The several definitions of *An Objective* and the use of this term extended to poetry are from the sixth movement of 'A'. The lines referred to read :

> The melody, the rest are accessory—
> . . . my one voice ; my other . . .
> An objective—rays of the object brought to a focus,
> An objective—nature as creator—desire for what is objectively
>   perfect,
> Inextricably the direction of historic and contemporary
>   particulars.

Assuming the intention of these lines to be poetry, the implications are that a critic began as a poet, and that as a poet he had implicitly to be a critic.

A poet finds the continuously present analysis of his work preferable to criticism so-called. Yet what other criticism exclusive of his poem seems permissible? In preference to the brands of circumlocution requisite to ponderous journals, a 'prose' criticism whose analysis follows without undue length of misinterpretation the more concise analysis of a considered poem seems permissible, if the general good demands such a prose. The direction of this prose, though it will be definition, will also be poetry, arising from the same source or what to a third reader might seem the same source as the poetry—a poetically charged mentality. Though perhaps gratifying to the poet whose poem is under observation—this prose, with all its poetic direction and right impetus, should, to the critic himself with his merely poetically charged mentality, seem secondary even tertiary and less; i.e. compared with that act which is a poem.

The graceless error of writing down to those who consciously want a something else from poetry—not poetry—as some stay for their own vanity; to 'sometimes' think that minds elaborately equipped with specific information, like science, must always confuse it with other specific information, like poetry. That may be the case with unfortunates. The point, however, would be not to proffer solemnly or whiningly confusions to the confused, but to indicate by energetic mental behavior how certain information may be useful to other information, and when the divisions which signalize them are necessary.

Such a process does not need to be accurately painful; rather it should be painlessly complete—as certain people are complete and ready to go anywhere but to the doctor.

Certainly the more precise the writing, the purer the poetry—and going back to the critic, he should know what pure poetry is. Or we shall never know how to dispose of our sensations before we begin to read poetry, or how to raise them to honesty and intelligence—as well as— those of us who are precisely afflicted—to that precision of style, we should do well to cultivate.

A poem. A poem as object—And yet certainly it arose in the veins and capillaries, if only in the intelligence—Experienced—(every word can't be overdefined) experienced as an object—Perfect rest—Or nature as creator, existing perfect, experience perfecting activity of existence, making it—theologically, perhaps—like the Ineffable—

A poem. Also the materials which are outside (?) the veins and capillaries—The context—The context necessarily dealing with a world outside of it—The desire for what is objectively perfect, inextricably the direction of historic and contemporary particulars—A desire to place everything—everything aptly, perfectly, belonging within, one with, a context—

A poem. The context based on a world—Idle metaphor—a lime base—a fibre—not merely a charged vacuum tube—an aerie of personation—The desire for inclusiveness—The desire for an inclusive object.

A poem. This object in process—The poem as a job—A classic—

Homer's *the wet waves* not our *the wet waves* but enough association in the three words to make a context capable of extension from its time into the present. Because, there is, though meanings change, a linguistic etiquette, a record possibly clear to us as the usage of a past context— The context as it first meant—or if this may not be believed—an arrived-at equilibrium—or at least the past not even guessed by us arrived at an equilibrium of meaning determined by new meanings of word against word contemporarily read.

A poem : a context associated with 'musical' shape, musical with quotation marks since it is not of notes as music, but of words more variable than variables, and used outside as well as within the context with communicative reference.

Impossible to communicate anything but particulars—historic and contemporary—things, human beings as things their instrumentalities of capillaries and veins binding up and bound up with events and contingencies. The revolutionary word if it must revolve cannot escape having a reference. It is not infinite. Even the infinite is a term.

Only good poetry—good an unnecessary adjective—is contemporary or classical. A standard of taste can be characterized only by acceptance of particular communication and concerned, so to speak, whenever the intelligence is in danger of being cluttered, with exclusions —not with books but with poetic invention. The nothing, not pure nothing, left over is not a matter of 'recencies,' but a matter of *pasts,* maybe *pasties.*

It would be just as well then dealing with 'recencies' to deal with Donne or Shakespeare, if one knew them as well as a linguistic usage not their own can know them. And yet contexts and inventions seem to have been derived from them.

One can go further, try to dissect capillaries or intelligent nerves— and speak of the image felt as duration or perhaps of the image as the existence of the shape and movement of the poetic object. The poet's image is not dissociable from the movement or the cadenced shape of the poem.

An idea—not an empty concept. An idea—its value including its meaning. The desk, i.e. as object including its value—The object unrelated to palpable or predatory intent—Also the meaning, or what should be the meaning of science in modern civilization as pointed out in Thorstein Veblen.

No predatory manifestation—Yet a manifestation making the mind more temperate because the poem exists and has perhaps recorded both state and individual.

The components of the poetic object continued : the sound and pitch emphasis of a word are never apart from its meaning.

In this sense each poem has its own laws, since no criticism can take care of all the differences which each new composition in words is. Yet criticism would hardly be different if musical notations or signs were used instead of words. Example : any piece of original music and the special criticism it produces.

The components of the poetic object continued :

Typography—certainly—if print and the arrangement of it will help tell how the voice should sound. It is questionable on the other hand whether the letters of the alphabet can be felt as the Chinese feel their written characters. Yet most western poets of consequence seem constantly to communicate the letters of their alphabets as graphic representations of thought—no doubt the thought of the word influences the letters but the letters are there and seem to exude thought.

Add—the core that covers the work of poets who see with their ears, hear with their eyes, move with their noses and speak and breathe with their feet. And yet lunatics are sometimes profitably observed : the core that is covered, the valuable skeptic knows, may in itself be the intense vision of a fact.

Intention must, however, be distinguished from accomplishment which resolves the complexity of detail into a single object. Emphasize detail 130 times over—or there will be no poetic object.

Or put the job of explanation up to cabinet-making : certain joints show the carpentry not to advantage, certain joints are a fine evidence; some are with necessary craftsmanship in the object. The first type— showing the carpentry not to advantage—is always present in a great deal of unnecessary writing; the second and third are rare; the second —which is a fine evidence—is rare to this time; the third—which with necessary craftsmanship is hid in the object—is, whenever craftsmanship is present, characteristic of this time.

'Recencies?' No more modern than a Shakespearean conceit which manages to carry at least two ideas at a time. Or Dante's literal, anagogical and theological threefold meaning referred to in a letter to Can Grande.

In contemporary poetry three types of complexity are discernible : 1 —the swift concatenation of multiple references usually lyrical in movement—almost any poem by Donne, for example; 2—the conceit— Shakespeare's 'when to the sessions,' his working out of love as bookkeeping, or Donne's 'Valediction,' his 'two twin compasses'; 3—the complexity of the epic—Byron's *Don Juan*, or most of it.

The word *complexity* is perhaps misleading. Ultimately, the matter of poetic object and its simple entirety must not be forgotten.

I.e. order and the facts as order. The order of all poetry is to approach a state of music wherein the ideas present themselves sensuously and intelligently and are of no predatory intention. A hard job, as poets have found reconciling contrasting principles of facts. In poetry the poet is continually encountering the facts which in the making seem to want to disturb the music and yet the music or the movement cannot exist without the facts, without its facts. The base matter, to speak hurriedly, which must receive the signet of the form. Poems are only acts upon particulars. Only through such activity do they become particulars themselves—i.e. poems.

The mind may construct its world—this is hardly philosophy—if the mind does construct its world there is always that world immanent or imminently outside which at least as a term has become an entity. Linguistic usage has somehow preserved these acts which were poems in other times and have transferred structures now. The good poems of today are not far from the good poems of yesterday.

1930, 1931

A STATEMENT FOR POETRY

Any definition of poetry is difficult because the implications of poetry are complex—and that despite the natural, physical simplicity of its best examples. Thus poetry may be defined as an order of words that as movement and tone (rhythm and pitch) approaches in varying degrees the wordless art of music as a kind of mathematical limit. Poetry is derived obviously from everyday existence (real or ideal).

Whoever makes it may very well consider a poem as a design or construction. A contemporary American poet says: 'A poem is a small (or large) machine made of words.' The British mathematician George Hardy has envied poetry its fineness of immediate logic. A scientist may envy its bottomless perception of relations which, for all its intricacies, keeps a world of things tangible and whole. Perhaps poetry is what Hideki Yukawa is looking for when, with reference to his latest theory of particles that possess not only charge and mass but also dimensions in space, he says: 'This problem of infinity is a disease that must be cured. I am very eager to be healthy.'

'Poetry is something more philosophic and of graver import than history.' (Aristotle, *Poetics* 9.) True or not this statement recalls that poetry has contributed intense records to history. The rhythmic or intoned utterance that punctuates the movement of a body in a dance or ritual, aware of dead things as alive, as it fights animals and earth; Homer's heavenly singer who gave pleasure at a feast in a society accomplished in husbandry and craft, whose group beliefs *saw* the Muses presiding over the harmony that moved the words; the dry passages of Lucretius forced by his measures to sing despite their regard for abstract patterns of thought, beginnings of atomic speculation: the stages of culture are concretely delineated in these three examples.

Poetry has always been considered more literary than music, though so-called pure music may be literary in a communicative sense. The parts of a fugue, Bach said, should behave like reasonable men in an orderly discussion. But music does not depend mainly on the human voice, as poetry does, for rendition. And it is possible in imagination to divorce speech of all graphic elements, to let it become a movement of sounds. It is this musical horizon of poetry (which incidentally poems perhaps never reach) that permits anybody who does not know Greek to listen and get something out of the poetry of Homer : to 'tune in' to the human tradition, to its voice which has developed among the sounds of natural things, and thus escape the confines of a time and place, as one hardly ever escapes them in studying Homer's grammar. In this sense poetry is international.

The foregoing definition of poetry has been, for the most part, cultural in its bearings. But what specifically is good poetry? It is precise information on existence out of which it grows, and information of its own existence, that is, the movement (and tone) of words. Rhythm, pulse, keeping time with existence, is the distinction of its technique. This integrates any human emotion, any discourse, into an order of words that exists as another created thing in the world, to affect it and be judged by it. Condensed speech is most of the method of poetry (as distinguished from the essentially discursive art of prose). The rest is ease, pause, grace. If read properly, good poetry does not argue its attitudes or beliefs; it exists independently of the reader's preferences for one kind of 'subject' or another. Its conviction is in its mastery or technique. The length of a poem has nothing to do with its merits as composition in which each sound of a word is weighed, though obviously it is possible to have more of a good thing—a wider range of things felt, known, and conveyed.

The oldest recorded poems go back to the Egyptian *Chapters of Coming Forth by Day*, some of whose hieroglyphs were old by 3000 B.C. The human tradition that survives the esoteric significance of these poems remains, as in these lines praising the sun :

> Millions of years have passed, we cannot count their number,
> Millions of years shall come. You are above the years.

It is quite safe to say that the *means* and *objects* of poetry (cf. Aristotle's *Poetics*) have been constant, that is, recognizably human, since ca. 3000 B.C.

I. The Means of Poetry : *Words*—consisting of *syllables*, in turn made up of *phones* that are denoted by *letters* that were once graphic symbols or pictures. Words grow out of affects of

A. Sight, touch, taste, smell
B. Hearing
C. Thought with respect to other words, the interplay of concepts.

II. The Objects of Poetry: *Poems*—rhythmic compositions of words whose components are

A. Image
B. Sound
C. Interplay of Concepts (judgments of other words either abstract or sensible, or both at once).

Some poems make use of—i.e. resolve—all three components. Most poems use only A and B. Poems that use B and C are less frequent, though C is a poetic device (invention) at least as old as Homer's puns on the name of Odysseus: 'the man of all odds,' 'how odd I see you Od-ysseus.' (cf. also the earlier, homophonic devices of syllabaries.)

A. *Image*. Composed groups of words used as symbols for things and states of sight, touch, taste and smell present an image. For example: Homer's 'a dark purple wave made an arch over them like a mountain cave'; the image of Hades evoked by the eleventh book of *The Odyssey;* or the landscape and journey which is all of *The Odyssey*—the homecoming of Odysseus.

cf. Weight, grandeur, and energy in writing are very largely produced, dear pupil, by the use of 'images.' (That at least is what some people call the actual mental pictures.) For the term Imagination is applied in general to an idea which enters the mind from any source and engenders speech, but the word has now come to be used of passages where, inspired by strong emotion, you seem to see what you describe and bring it vividly before the eyes of your audience. That imagination means one thing in oratory and another in poetry you will yourself detect, and also that the object of poetry is to enthral, of prose writing to present ideas clearly, though both indeed aim at this latter and at excited feeling.
[Longinus (213–273), *On the Sublime* XV, 2.]

B. *Sound*. Besides the imitation in words of natural sound (the sound of the sea in Homer, the sound of birds in 'Bare ruined choirs where late the sweet birds sang'), the component of sound in poetry, as conveyed by rendition, comprises sound that is

1. Spoken (e.g. 'and we'll talk with them too,
       Who loses and who wins, who's in,
         who's out,'—*King Lear*)
2. Declaimed (e.g. Milton's *Paradise Lost*)
3. Intoned or Chanted (e.g. words used in a liturgical monotone)
4. Sung (to a melody, i.e. a musical phrase or idea. Some of the best examples in English are Campion's poems, Shakespeare's songs —which have been set to music by Purcell, Johnson, Arne— and Burns' songs written to folk tunes.)

C. *Interplay of Concepts.* This component effects compositions in which words involve other words in common or contrasting logical implications, and to this end it employs sound, and sometimes image, as an accessory. The elements of grammar and rhetorical balance (v.s., Shakespeare's 'who's *in*, who's *out*') contribute to this type of poetry. (Examples: most of Donne's poems, Andrew Marvell's *The Definition of Love*, George Herbert's *Heaven*, Lord Rochester's *Ode to Nothing*, Fitzgerald's translation of *Rubaiyat*, Eliot's *The Hollow Men*.)

From the preceding analysis of the components of poems it is clear that their forms are achieved as a dynamics of speech and sound, that is, as a resolution of their interacting rhythms—with no loss of value to any word at the expense of the movement. In actual practice, this dynamics works out standards of measure—or metres. The good poems of the past have developed the 'science' of prosody in the same way that the effective use of words has developed the logic of grammar. But poetry, though it has its constants, is made in every age.

Prosody analyses poems according to line lengths and groups of lines or verses as vehicles of rhythm, varieties of poetic feet or units of rhythm (analogous to a measure in music) *and* their variants (e.g. unexpected inversions of accent, unexpected 'extra' syllables), rhymes *and* their variants (e.g. consonance, assonance, perfect rhyme—i.e. the same sound rhymes with itself, etc.), rhyming patterns, stanzas or strophes, fixed forms and free verse. No verse is 'free,' however, if its rhythms inevitably carry the words in contexts that do not falsify the function of words as speech probing the possibilities and attractions of existence. This being the practice of poetry, prosody as such is of secondary interest to the poet. He looks, so to speak, into his ear as he does at the same time into his heart and intellect. His ear is sincere, if his words convey his awareness of the range of differences and subtleties of duration. He does not measure with handbook, and is not a pendulum. He may find it right to count syllables, or their relative lengths and stresses, or to be sensitive to all these metrical factors. As a matter of fact, the good poets do all these things. But they do not impose their count on what is said or made—as may be judged from the impact of their poems.

Symmetry occurs in all the arts as they develop. It is usually present in some form in most good poetry. The stanza was perhaps invented in an attempt to fit a tune to more words than it had notes: the words were grouped into stanzas permitting the tune to be repeated. But existence does not foster this technique in all times indiscriminately. The least unit of a poem must support the stanza; it should never be inflicted on the least unit. As Sidney wrote in his *Apology* (1595): 'One may be a poet without versing, and a versifier without poetry.'

The best way to find out about poetry is to read the poems. That way the reader becomes something of a poet himself: not because he 'contributes' to the poetry, but because he finds himself subject of its energy.

1950

FOR WALLACE STEVENS

Tho I never met Wallace Stevens I was interested in him very early. I wanted to read all of him, but did not get around to it till I was told I would be giving the Wallace Stevens Memorial Lecture. I have been at it for three months to the neglect of my own work and the occasional reminder of my wife's common sense, *well you know it will last only an hour, how much do you have to do.* But I went on reading him and jotting notations, tho having stopped writing criticism, I did not intend an essay. I felt myself speaking to Stevens for three months. It's really as simple as that.

The contingency of one poet reading another if he gets interested the way I do: I'm not lush about things—I try not to read into things, I try to read, which means that if the page doesn't have it any imagination on my part as to what I might read into it has no significance. I hope everybody would read me the same way—that is, not wonder whether I was afraid of a draft as I am at the moment, but just read the words. This activity is a kind of mathematics but more sensuous, and it has little to do with learning, it has something to do with structure. But I won't go into that aspect—simply say, the contingency of one poet reading another that way makes for a kind of friendship which is exempt from all the vicissitudes and changes and tempers that are involved in friendship.

I balk at speaking about *an identity.* I don't think there is any such thing or state of things, but sometimes a word impels, well, an impersonal thing—a feeling of duration, best defined I think as

An edited version of a tape of my talk on the occasion of the Eighth Annual Wallace Stevens Memorial Program and Awards to young poets, sponsored by the Department of English of the University of Connecticut at Storrs and the Hartford Insurance Group, April 29, 1971. —L.Z.

Spinoza defined it, an indefinite continuance of existence. It is not a temporal thing, may be felt only an instant, but that instant call it love, eternity, infinity: whatever you *want*—that's it. Stevens describes that feeling. It *dures* Stevens might be saying. He always picked up an archaic word, tho I don't find this one in him. But what *dures* or endures as impersonal friendship when one poet reads another is a reading removed from yet out of time, without actual mutual influence or conscious awareness of tradition, literary handbooks or chronometers. Both poets may not be contemporaries, only one of them actually alive—the other, legend like Shakespeare or Homer.

A strange case of this feeling of duration recently happened to me. I was again reading Luis De Leon's book called *The Perfect Wife*, which I had read about 1944 not particularly impressed then. He lived about the time of Shakespeare. But now the parallels were uncanny: his first Luis like my first name; the patrilineal De Leon like my Hebrew surname. I don't feel like a lion, but for some reason in Hebrew the word lion repetitiously precedes the sense of my given name. His interest in *The Song of Songs* and *The Book of Job* recalled my own; the Inquisition he went thru to translate them into Spanish, my lesser trial to sound their Hebrew in English. I felt very close to him. I don't know enough Spanish or any Spanish for that matter to say that Luis ever influenced me, but we were together. As I said, both poets don't have to be contemporaries. If they are they don't have to be aware of each other; it may take years for one of them suddenly to become aware. One of them must be actually alive, I take it you'll grant me that. But in effect when the sense of duration is felt the legend on the page at that time literally reads the reader, makes his existence while he reads the legend's existence. Stevens explicitly realized this contingency thruout his work, especially in two poems of *Transport to Summer*, published in 1947. I quote only a few lines from the one that is frequently anthologized:

> The house was quiet and the world was calm.
> The reader became the book; and summer night
>
> Was like the conscious being of the book.

.   .   .

The words were spoken as if there was no book,

.   .   .

The quiet . . .
The access of perfection to the page.

.   .   .

. . . the reader leaning late and reading there.

I quote the other poem, a variant of the same idea, in full:

The Lack of Repose *

A young man seated at his table
Holds in his hand a book you have never written
Staring at the secretions of the words as
They reveal themselves.

It is not midnight. It is mid-day,
The young man is well-disclosed, one of the gang,
Andrew Jackson Something. But this book
Is a cloud in which a voice mumbles.

It is a ghost that inhabits a cloud,
But a ghost for Andrew, not lean, catarrhal
And pallid. It is the grandfather he liked,
With an understanding compounded by death

And the associations beyond death, even if only
Time. What a thing it is to believe that
One understands, in the intense disclosures
Of a parent in the French sense.

And not yet to have written a book in which
One is already a grandfather and to have put there
A few sounds of meaning, a momentary end
To the complication, is good, is a good.

Let the poem speak for itself. I would feel rather foolish to read into
it that this might be Stevens reading Mallarmé, or maybe he's
thinking of today's prize winner reading Stevens.

In quoting "The Lack of Repose" I intend what I believe
Wallace Stevens intended, an instant certainty of the words of a

*Reprinted from Wallace Stevens, *The Collected Poems of Wallace Stevens*, © 1969,
with the kind permission of Alfred A. Knopf, Inc.

poem bringing at least two persons and then maybe many persons, even peoples together. Whether in the poverty of history the latter happens or not to both in their singleness it does not matter whether the reader is the book or the book is the reader or if the grandfather is the forebear of the grandson or the grandson the forebear of his grandfather. The instant certainty of the words is all that exists for one become two. Maybe the certainty is mysticism, but after many years both Stevens and I decided, I think, if only like mist it also exists or existed. No, it exists at least in the reading and will in every rereading, tho we don't know much about it except that it was a little part of life or created or ever creating nature. That instant of certainty affirms what the eyes see and the ears hear at least until proved wrong, when it is particularly hard not to feel the actual shocks of seeing and hearing. The mind then tends to believe or as Aristotle put it we haven't a leg to stand on, or as Stevens reads somewhere, *X understands Aristotle instinctively.*

In his poems Stevens exists as the many-worded faculties of a body, and as for its honest self rather more uncertainly as the mind of a body: that is, all his poems affect being involved in the old philosophical bugbear of a theory of knowledge, a question as to what (quotes) "really" exists. To be sure his most often gay, lovely skepticism doubts its own skepticism and becomes the only kind of skepticism true to itself. Unassuming it does not risk missing any rare insight of lesser philosophers than Aristotle that may lead to richer observation or listening or faculty of thought in the poems. But philosophy is not their end, tho they seem to be philosophizing. Along about 1936 impatient with his and most anybody's use of the words *reality* and *imagination* I deferred reading the greater part of his work after admiring the early poems of *Harmonium*, and it is this neglect that I wish to set right today. Reading him for the last three months I felt that my own writing, without my being aware of it, was closer to his than to that of any of my contemporaries in the last half century of life we shared together. Let me particularize this because as a kindred nature I shall always feel it intensely and not merely as a case of, to quote *The Book of Joel, young men see visions and old men dream dreams.* I should like to particularize by calling out the dates when there might have been a mutual activity. It was only once that we came close, at least I hoped that we had come close to meeting, but as I have said it never happened.

He was born in 1879 and I was born in 1904, so that there is a quarter of a century between our birth years. By 1914 he had had three years of Harvard, had been admitted to the New York Bar, and won a prize from *Poetry* (Chicago). In 1914 I was ten. If you want to find out about me, you won't find much for the personally curious in my book *Autobiography*. It's the music that's important. *Autobiography* does not say that crazy—intense—things happened then on the lower East Side of New York, nor that I owned an illustrated Shakespeare, and my English teacher was offering a prize to everyone in his class who would read all the Plays and answer his questions about them—pretty stiff questions. I read all the Plays—that was at about the age of eleven. The prize I got incidentally if you're curious and since we're speaking was a book called *The Boy Electrician*; but the athlete of the school got a book I wanted. I think it was Thackeray's Major Pendennis or *Pendennis* rather. If my story has a point regarding Stevens it is as devious as, perhaps I had something in common with Shakespeare: one of my first impressions on reading Stevens would be how much some of his lines recalled Shakespeare. Not imitating Shakespeare, Stevens' work has that kind of passion. It might not be evident to everybody, but it has.

By 1916 he was with the Hartford Accident Indemnity Company, probably travelling for them. I know very little about his life. I have read the *Letters*, but as with my own life tend to forget all but the impersonal detail. He may have been living in New York. The renaissance so-called of American poetry had already started with the publication of the first issue of *Poetry: A Magazine of Verse*—I guess, in 1913. There was also the *Others* group in New York that included Williams, Stevens' lifelong friend, tho there again one was too busy doctoring and the other was probably being too serious an insurance man doing his job for them to meet often. For all I know a few years later we may have walked—I forget where Stevens lived in New York, I think it was 9th Street near Fifth Avenue—and walked the same streets, past each other unknown.

By 1920 his early poems, *Sunday Morning* and the plays *Three Travelers Watch a Sunrise* and *Carlos among the Candles* had appeared in *Poetry*. The plays fascinated me, a new kind of theater for the amateur theatrical producer, but not new to poets I suppose. Theater depends on its words. If it isn't in the words you can't have action, unless it's all pantomime. Stevens was interested in the words.

Sunday Morning for a 16-year-old might not have been a completely lucid thing insofar as its so-called matter was concerned, the lady trying to be very Christian on a Sunday morning, thinking of paradise and so on, in her dressing gown surrounded with all the nice things which are distasteful only to her reverie of walking on the waters and the seraphic paradise that might follow: a conflict which bothered Stevens all thru his poems. For all I know it was the conflict that bothered all of us at the turn of the century. There had been Darwin and obstinate rationalists whose atheism or agnosticism became a religion. They wanted to impose it on everybody, and Stevens felt it. It carried over to trouble or deepen his poems. I freed myself of the problem sooner because of the 25 years difference between us in history. I suffered it maybe from the age of 10 to 13 and no more.

Alright—I read Stevens' plays and wrote poetry in high school—no matter. What *mattered*, perhaps, was that, even before I read Stevens, growing up with the kind of theater that interested him I finally walked out of the East Side, it seemed then for miles and miles, to find this place called Greenwich Village and the Provincetown Playhouse. I expected palisades of course as pictured in the early Dutch history of New York. I was disappointed. Still it was a new world.

Harriet Monroe's anthology *The New Poetry*, which I had saved for, contained a considerable portion of Stevens' work published in the early '20ies. He was one of the few poets I know of never in a hurry to be published. The editor of *Poetry* might ask for a poem, but he urged her to wait till he had a better one.

Remembering what was happening to me at the time, I imagine he was reading a good deal of philosophy. I was reading Henry Adams, and had heard of Wittgenstein. I was fortunate to have one of the finest professors of philosophy who, despite disabling asthma, acted his thoughts in his lectures. He did not write very much—respected for one concise slim book called *The Purpose of History*—a man named Homer Woodbridge. Dewey had something else for me. It's how he inflected his voice that mattered—stressing active-*ing* or a passive-*ed* that made the point of his course—sometimes as he sat on the radiator, and when it was hot of course he moved away. His educational philosophy did not interest me. The preoccupied man did. And a year or so later, there's no use denying it, they still exhume it as one of the best things I've written tho I've never reprinted it, something of mine appeared in *Poetry*.

1923: *Harmonium.* I had a copy of it, I cannot imagine whose copy it was because I couldn't afford it. In any case I had a copy and read it constantly. He had begun his vast work about existence thru all the seasons. The interest in haiku those days—its seasonal effect, the mention of flowers, and so on—may have prompted Stevens. But he did not take the easy way out of collecting unrelated short impressions. *Harmonium* as a beginning is epic in proportion, the sense and thought of the separate poems intricately interwoven into musical sequence. I understand he was to call the longer final work *The Whole of Harmonium.* He went on from the implicit *spring* of his first book to his later titles with their explicit references to *summer* and *autumn*, and the last poems I suppose are *winter*. For me the lovely course of his whole work is the constancy of its song. I suppose it comes from the Lutheran church of his youth, the Lutheran Pennsylvania lineage, maybe some Pennsylvania Dutch element. Also the name Stevens I take it is Welsh, attesting to the bardic and choral disciplines of the Eisteddfod.

Coming to his whole work late, I am moved by the fact—as I would wish it in my own work—that his music thruout has not been impaired by having philosophized. *The Role of the Idea in Poetry*—gentle irony plays in these words, the title of a late poem (1950)—is finally defined by the sound of its last line:

"I am the greatness of the new-found night."

It is the old man . . . / Who reads no book and *Without evasion by a single metaphor*, postponing division between *The physical pine* and *the metaphysical pine*, to *see the very thing*, that the music of "Credences of Summer," perhaps his most "classic" poem, brings to life: a life aware of and attuned to the force of a century of music that starts with Telemann, goes on to Haydn and to Mozart. As to the innovative range of forms that Stevens permitted himself he once summed up his intent: "The essential thing in form is to be free in whatever form is used. A free form does not assure freedom. . . . So that it comes to this, I suppose, that I believe in freedom regardless of form." Or as he wrote elsewhere, *not doctrinal in form tho in design*. The poet's design is his work. I may be doctrinal for myself in design but never wish to be doctrinal for anybody else. If I feel that form does not burgeon from an original inventive impulse it has no use for me. Now, speaking positively, I may do a regular form which nearly every reader of poems will recognize as the most irregular thing under the sun, while a doctrinal minority of practicing poets finds it painfully regular. I must trust myself then as poet, and like Stravinsky accused of imitating Mozart, answer (at least to myself) *no, I stole Mozart*.

1927: we'll call out the years and go faster. As a poet I had to make some kind of living. I was fortunate to get a minor job with a very noted firm—the National Industrial Conference Board—and somehow advanced to writing papers on industrial relations. But such jobs never hold out, and a friend suggested there might be something at Hartford, the Hartford Indemnity Accident Company, and gosh yes I met their personnel man at Grand Central and I recognized him by his tie and he recognized me by my hat—what intrigued me was maybe I'd meet Wallace Stevens. I don't know what it's like today, but there was this vast foyer almost a feeling of the interior of the Duomo and in a corner the black receptionist, a most cordial receptionist, no trouble at all as to what he was—a human being as you might expect in the state of the Charter Oak. I hear now it's legendary, but there it was. I didn't get the job, but that's of no consequence. Before leaving I asked the receptionist if Mr. Stevens was in and he went back to ask and Mr. Stevens was away. I hope he was away on a claim somewhere, maybe Florida— content that he had done his job by Hartford Indemnity Company, and spending what he called in "Hibiscus on the Sleeping Shores" a *stupid afternoon*.

I appeared in print more frequently, again of no consequence except I sometimes wonder whether Stevens read me. Thru the years 1928, 1929 I looked for his new work in periodicals, but very little appeared after *Harmonium*. His second book, *Ideas of Order*, was not published until 1936. By then I was involved in something else. I did know Bill Williams. And when we decided, with very few others, no one will publish us, let's publish ourselves, we launched Bill first. I guess it was my fault they called it the Objectivist Press and I've never heard the end of it, but we published William Carlos Williams' *Collected Poems, 1921–1931* with a preface by Wallace Stevens in 1934. Now I have absolutely no recollection whether I wrote Stevens for the preface—I don't think I would have—or whether Bill asked for it himself. We were all very grateful for the preface, except Bill. Stevens had used the word *anti-poetic* to praise his friend, but Williams was offended for almost 30 years. Their metaphysics did not matter to me. Williams had come out and made the second page of the *New York Times Sunday Book Review*. I can't tell you how wonderful our bit of practical sense seemed in those days.

1936: I collected the poems and comment for my comparative anthology *A Test of Poetry*, published, after the usual lag, in 1948. I needed Stevens' permission to include what I used of his, and approached his publisher. I prefer formalities to intrusions. I understand Stevens was something like that. Permission came gratis. I had selected his poem "Another Weeping Woman" (c. 1917) and presented it preceded by two passages from *King Lear* (*Poor naked wretches . . . just. / And the creature run from the cur? . . . so.*)—without further comment, except for one word in the chronological chart at the end of my book that summed up my consideration in comparing them: *duration*. I sent Stevens a copy of the book, and of course I got a courteous answer, a very comforting answer. I think that was about all the correspondence we ever had. He wrote: "The contents pick up a particular interest." I was especially comforted by the word *particular* because it could have been *general*.

After 1948, I suppose Stevens' life and my own could be summed up as having lived thru two world wars—in his instance, even if one is a vice-president with the Hartford Indemnity Company, after 18 years. But why not—and I really love this statement to the *Times* interviewer in 1954 on the publication of his *Collected Poems*:

I'm . . . not a poet part time, business man the rest. This is a fortunate thing, considering how inconsiderate the ravens are. I don't divide my life, just go on living.

Anyway, here I deal with surety claims—claims on surety bonds. Poetry and surety claims aren't as unlikely a combination as they may seem. There is nothing perfunctory about them, for each case is different.

His care for *particulars*, the wars etc., spurred one of his clearest inductions in the opening lines of "Connoisseur of Chaos":

> A. A violent order is disorder; and
> B. A great disorder is an order. These
> Two things are one. (Pages of illustrations.)

(That is: A. The particulars elate or hurt / B. If you don't expect too much from the universe maybe it's an order. / Both A. and B. are only propositions *about* a singular activity whose particulars are countless.) My inferences in parens are offered merely in support of my feeling that very little skeptical philosophy has paid off as well as Stevens' three lines have in poetic intellect.

Along with all the elegance of intellect a grass roots or local, often barbaric voice in Stevens' poems makes him in their pored-over image of American landscape the genius of its soil: at one with the eccentric native genius of *the Arkansaw* in his poem "The Jack Rabbit." Shunning doctrine, dogma, the shows that teach ignorance, it has somehow suffered the history of the Americas— the continuing portions of all history whatever the scholarly gaps. Reading him I am led to hope that my own poems, tho different, sound that native and kind. If it's Florida, if it's the Caribbean, Uruguay, or wherever Stevens' landscapes exist without imposed shouting and spouting: indigenous like Winslow Homer's palm tree in a Florida wind, tho Stevens is never after describing a painting. In sound—words or waves—whatever takes place exists. As he said, along about the '50ies, *poetry is the subject of the poem*.

I must now limit the incidents—or shall I spell it i-n-c-i-d-e-n-c-e of my reading Stevens, referring as the geometers do to partial coincidence or community of elements between two figures (since the thought occurs to me that if Stevens were alive we might both be smiling over the great unwilled *natural* modesty in every man always "willing" so to speak to be distracted from what he thinks he intends saying)—to at most three or four more. There is our use of horses and donkeys thruout our poems. Checking their chronology with regard to these creatures I found that his earliest use for them ("Primordia—4," 1917) preceded mine in "Poem Beginning 'The' " by about nine years. But in later years my interest in horses, etc. ("*A*"-7, 1928) appears to precede his "Owl's Clover," 1936. I had never read "Primordia—4" until a month ago. I don't know if he ever read "*A*"-7 published in *Poetry*, February 1931. Not to multiply cases of object matter that compelled us, any reader is welcome to read Stevens' "The Sick Man" (1950) and my "Poem 14" (1926) and "Song 18" (1932) in *55 Poems* together and guess as to influence; tho with respect to vapors I prefer to settle for *this most excellent canopy, the air, look you*. Having read Stevens, I am sure he would too. I understand he was generous to younger poets, and Marianne Moore on her 75th birthday (1962) my wife recalls for this occasion told her that Stevens had been interested in my writings. If so, I can't say now that I heard Miss Moore say it, intent as I was atavistically wishing her health towards the proverbial Mosaic 120th birthday—*eye . . . not dim . . . nor . . . natural force abated*. Thinking back while reading Stevens' last poems I remembered that in 1950 the magazine *Imagi*, published in Philadelphia, included a poem of mine in an issue celebrating a mid-century of new American poetry and it occurred to me at once that Stevens too must have contributed. He had: the poem "A Discovery of Thought." I had read it then and it had completely slipped my mind. It should not have—if only for its larghetto, the words *an infancy of blue snow*, and the genius of *The gathering of the imbecile against his motes*. The printed page when desirable offers more certainty than memory against the motes—or the mind?

> Who can adjudge stages
> Or write wisely
> Where cycles started or ended,

Without stories to drag them— . . .
So my song with an old voice is whole:
        ("*A*"-12, 1950)

. . . not to have reasoned at all,

     .   .   .

To be stripped of every fiction except one,

The fiction of an absolute—Angel,
Be silent in your luminous cloud and hear
The luminous melody of proper sound.
(Stevens' "Notes Toward a Supreme Fiction,
    It Must Give Pleasure VII," 1947)

The parts of this poem are titled: (1) *It Must Be Abstract*, (2) *It Must Change*, (3) *It Must Give Pleasure*. (I glossed again in my reading: (1) yes, all words are abstract, post-*solids* or other *actual states*— things *after the* things, only relatively that one word is 'concrete,' another 'conceptual'; (2) whatever is written changes, in the way Stevens and I are transmuted in my reading—what is constant, as he says toward the end of the poem, *Pleased that the irrational is rational*; (3) how fine, it does.)

The test of poetry is the range of pleasure it affords as sight, sound, and intellection. . . . criticism probes only my own considerations. I believe that desirable teaching assumes intelligence that is free to be attracted from any consideration of every day living to always another phase of existence. Poetry, as other object matter, is after all for interested people.
                              (L.Z., *A Test of Poetry*, 1936)

In the 1954 interview I referred to previously Stevens also said: "There's nothing to that saying that poets are born. They're not born in particular. Everyone is born. Some of those who are born are interested in poetry, that's all."

"Interested"—one more gloss before we get on to the prizes. About 1950 I bought *The Century Dictionary* for $7—for my son then six or seven. William Dwight Whitney was its editor—professor of comparative philology and Sanskrit at Yale. That's near enough Hartford. I wondered searching for Stevens' old and rare words in *The Century* whether he had ever used or owned its ten volumes. My hunch was he had—that he perhaps read it at random, delighted when looking up some particular word to let his eyes stray to the very one to which I now sought the clue: *Gubbinal*—one of his gay titles. I suspected it might be Italian—Gubbio, the city, or *gubbia*, a cart drawn by 3 beasts made little sense with his poem. No French word—I believe French was a second language to him—remotely resembled *Gubbinal*. I looked for it in *The Century Dictionary* and found: *gubbin*, a kind of clay ironstone (Staffordshire), a paring (cf. *gubbings*, the parings of haberdine; also any kind of fragments)—an English word. John Taylor, 'the water-poet,' in 1630 wrote,

> All that they could buy, or sell, or barter,
> Would scarce be worth a gubbin once a quarter.

That made sense with Stevens' poem, granted he had turned *gubbin* into an adjective. Perhaps some scholar has come closer to the meaning, but I was not unhappy with my scholarship, rather content to look no further than the poem.

One of the poems I shall read later carries the title "From the Misery of Don Joost." Obviously one can easily read Don Juan for Don Joost—but the tragic sounds (as out of Lear) that ensue clash with the title, which suggests only a wry smile: *Joost*. The volumes of *The Century* are heavy; their white refractive leaves were meant to last. Not much darkened, still unfoxed, page 3243, volume IV yielded *joust, jouster* see *just* etc.; the etymology of *just, joust*, early modern English, *giust* after the Italian, *bring together, come together, touch, strike with a lance, tilt*, an Old French spelling *joste*, close enough to Stevens' *joost*; and back to the Latin to an asserted but unverified form of *jugis* meaning *continual* (cf. Lewis & Short, *perennial, perpetual, always flowing*). It seemed then as to influence that the very paper of *The Century* had brought us together. There had been the tilting knight. As I read his poem, *my body, the old animal* (surely no later than 1923), *the stinging / Animal* ("*A*"–11, 1950) returned to me as my own. So you see how I came to read him. Well, I guess we're almost ready for the prizes.

[*Remarks on presenting them*:] This is a first in all senses. I've never had to be so generous in my life, hand out prizes for poems which I haven't read. I refused to read them. I don't want to be a judge. But I hope it all turns out happy for everyone. We are all—as Stevens says Andrew Jackson Something. I'll be reading the prize poems—without rank attached—by myself, and maybe the winners will look at mine.

Well if I may put all this together, I'll feel more in my element doing what I originally intended to do if I had not been asked to do more: simply read six poems of Wallace Stevens first, followed by six selections of my own—the sequence of Stevens' poems suggesting an antiphonal sequence in mine.

1. From the Misery of Don Joost
2. Of Bright & Blue Birds & the Gala Sun
3. Extraordinary References
4. The Planet on the Table
5. Puella Parvula
6. Song of Fixed Accord

1. 'An' song beginning "*A*"–15: (An hinny . . . hide any)
2. *Catullus* 31
3. from "*A*"–21: Rudens III 6 (*Voice off*): (A concept . . . felicity)
4. from *Bottom: On Shakespeare*, part 3: "Continents," pp. 155–6: (*où tópos* . . . the secret studies)
5. 'An' song beginning "*A*"–22: (An era . . . initial)
6. from *Little*, chapter 22: (What were you doing . . . more than the words say)

Finally to return to Stevens: (part of a speech accepting a prize from The Poetry Society of America, 1951):

The other day, in the middle of January, as I was taking a walk in Elizabeth Park, in Hartford, I saw at a little distance across the snow a group of automobiles that had pulled up on one side of the road. A dozen people or more got out of them. They took off their coats and threw them together in a pile on the asphalt. It was then possible to see that this was a wedding party. Often in the summer, particularly on Saturday mornings, one sees such parties there. They come to have photographs taken in the gardens. But these people had come in January. The bride stood up in white satin covered with a veil. An ornament in her hair caught the sunlight and sparkled brightly in the cold wind. The bridesmaids were dressed in dark crimson gowns with low necks. They carried armfuls of chrysanthemums. One of the men stood in the snow taking pictures of the bride, then of the bride surrounded by the bridesmaids, and so on, until nothing more was possible. Now, this bride with her gauze and glitter was the genius of poetry. The only thing wrong with her was that she was out of place.

What is the apt locale of the genius of poetry? As it happens, she creates her own locale as she goes along. Unlike the bride, she recognizes that she cannot impose herself on the scene. She is the spirit of visible and invisible change. . . . she has herself chosen as her only apt locale in a final sense the love and thought of the poet, where everything she does is right and reasonable. Her power to change is so great that out of the love and thought of individual poets she makes the love and thought of the poet, the single image. Out of that which is often untutored and seemingly incapable of being tutored, insensible to custom and law, marginal, grotesque, without a past, the creation of unfortunate chance, she evolves a power that dominates life, a central force so subtle and so familiar that its presence is most often unrealized. Individual poets, whatever their imperfections may be, are driven all their lives by that inner companion of the conscience which is, after all, the genius of poetry in their hearts and minds. I speak of a companion of the conscience because to every faithful poet the faithful poem is an act of conscience.

August 13, 1971

With

GOLGONOOZÀ?

Scene: the summer house of William and Catherine Blake, No. 13 Hercules Buildings, Lambeth; a living room for all purposes except squalor. The lasting Northern light of an English sun plays everywhere: 'a fierce desire as when two shadows mingle on a wall.' Working Mr and Mrs Blake are naked. There has been a knock on the door, but they do not look up. In the conversation that follows Mrs Blake says nothing, appears as though the changing light spoke for her.

The Visitor, passing over the threshold almost before he knows, stands lovingly respectful—not in the least embarrassed. His attitude may be: 'Some people dream and dread, and some dream they dream and do not dread.' All that Blake says here has been attributed to his actual conversation or comes from his writing. But his responses are also the Visitor's own sorry hindsight that Blake had anticipated him 'somewhere.'

B. Come in! It's only Adam and Eve, you know. I never stop for anything. A vision of Milton . . . came to ask a favor of me. Said he had committed an error in *Paradise Lost,* which he wanted me to correct in a poem or picture. I declined. The error was *That carnal pleasures arose from the Fall.* The Fall could not produce any pleasure.

V. (*helping himself to tea things*) Will you both? Thanks. How good of this bun to bolster the exactitude of your logic, it nearly escapes (you called them) forests of solitude, cold floods of abstraction. I should feel best if you could stare at a knot in a piece of wood without being frightened. Why did you say *frightened*? I am not sure in resolving your contraries of hurting and not hurting you were unlike Spinoza. Unknown to you? He might have taught Voltaire, who fashionably despised him, how to read *Genesis* and saved the Enlightened man from the stupidity of sounding rationally Encyclopedic. I take it not all the books reach England in good time. Spinoza might have led you—and Milton—to read *Job* faster. You'll remember that Satan disappears after the second chapter of that book, and his Jehovah after all turns out to be Job.

B. (*looking towards Catherine*)

... every kindness to another is a little Death In the Divine Image; nor can Man exist but by Brotherhood (*as V. anticipates*). The Prophets Isaiah and Ezekiel dined with me . . . Ezekiel said: '. . . we of Israel taught that the Poetic Genius (as you now call it) was the first principle and all the others merely derivative . . . tributaries of the Poetic Genius. It was this King David desired so fervently and invokes so pathetically, saying by this he conquers enemies and governs kingdoms . . . From these opinions the vulgar came to think that all nations would at last be subject to the Jews.'
. . . I also asked Isaiah what made him go naked and barefoot three years. He answer'd: 'The same that made our friend Diogenes, the Grecian.' I then asked Ezekiel why he ate dung . . . He answer'd, 'The desire of raising other men into a perception of the infinite : this the North American tribes practice, and is he honest who resists his genius or conscience only for the sake of present ease or gratification?' *Devils are False Religions.*

V. Your genius or conscience was always honest, and casts off your idiot Questioner. But 'For the soft soul of America' who is sure what the North American tribes practiced, or practice today? Sacks or baskets of soot of your chimney sweepers piling their coffins, and from our incinerators tons of the same on our heads. *The Song of Los* and *The Human Abstract* are our times : 'Pity would be no more/If we did not make somebody poor.' (*fumbling a cigarette*)

B. Want Matches?
Yes! Yes! Yes!
Want Matches?

V. No!

B. (*solus*) Like dreams of infants . . . the golden springs/Where Luvah doth renew his horses? . . . skull riven into filaments . . . eyes into sea jellies . . . I saw the Covering Cherub/Divide Four-fold into Four Churches . . . Paul, Constantine, Charlemaine, Luther . . .

V. Gibbon laughed at all the useless research into *filioque.*

B. Joys impregnate. Sorrows bring forth. Excess of sorrow laughs. Excess of joy weeps.

V. (*quoting B.*) 'Knowing and feeling that we all have need of but- ter . . . That the delicate ear in its infancy/May be dulled'—they do read you besides their Science, Hazard and Harold and Geoffrey and John Middleton—

B. Jellicoe ... Johnny, Bob and Joe—

V. 'Happy people' (hopefully) in their industry of critics, scholars and teachers, sometimes lauding or quarreling among themselves, but with reverence for you. It is not easy for Five Senses to explicate your fable of history in which life sneezes seven times before the eyes open—that is too quick for every child to hear when he rather skips most of Gulliver. Both of you somewhere lose the guileless, he less in the names made as if human tongues first fabled them, you in Los' hammering tongue roaring down epic with Reason. Golgonooza, 'awful name.' If you stressed the last syllable I could believe you. Pronounced Golgonoozà!

B. Softly lilling flutes ... Timbrels and violins sport ... A moment equals a pulsation of the artery ... a hard task of a life of sixty years.

V. And if Hazard has no name for your engraving which appears on the end papers and dust jacket of his book—graces? dancers? an abstract of drawing and painting that America's ratio first tangles to see again—

B. ... sweet moony night ...

V. And if John Middleton says, Blake was 'not concerned to be an artist'—

B. While I, looking up to my umbrella,
Resolv'd to be a very contrary fellow,
Cry, looking quite from skumference to centre :
'No one can finish so high as the original Inventor.'

V. And if they punctuate your songs, explicating systems where you did not—

B. ... obstruction ... without fluctuation ... adamant ... Degrade first the Arts if you'd mankind degrade ... Give high price for the worst, leave the best in disgrace ...

V. I like Geoffrey best—with the fewest words he shows me (if only) 60 plates of your Illuminated books.

B. When you look at a picture. you can always see
If a man of sense has painted he.
No real style of colouring ever appears,
But advertising in the newspapers.

(*Now sings compassionately, making up his own tune as he was known to do as an old man for his intimate friends*)

I rose up at the dawn of day—
'Get thee away ! get thee away !
Pray'st thou for riches? Away ! away !
I have mental joy, and mental health,
And mental friends, and mental wealth ;
I've a wife I love, and that loves me ;
I've all but riches bodily.

V. *(imagines he sees Mrs Blake smiling aimlessly in the sunlight and takes it for a sign to leave, sotto voce)* 'And none can tell how from so small a centre comes such sweet

... The citizens of New York close their books ...

1965

WILLIAM CARLOS WILLIAMS

I

A CITATION

Dear Bill,

This is, as you will find out, for The Nation. Or, as you have found out, for several nations. What for? A celebration of their life and poems.

I have been asked to say what we have meant to each other, what we did, how we met, and so on—to sum up, in short, 30 years at a week's notice.

I could begin with old Hume who wrote 'My Own Life'—in my edition of *The History of England from the Invasion of Julius Caesar to the Abdication of James the Second*—in just less than 13 Roman numbered pages. It is the tersest autobiography I know—and the funniest. From what you keep on saying at 75 I know you will find his last page good enough for a laugh, despite our habitual inclination to want to cut a word here and there :

'. . . were I to name a period of my life which I should most choose to pass over again, I might be tempted to point to this later period. I possess the same ardor as ever in study, and the same gayety in company. I consider, besides, that a man of sixty-five, by dying, cuts off only a few years of infirmities; and though I see many symptoms of my literary reputation's breaking out at last with additional lustre . . . It is difficult to be more detached from life than I am at present.

'To conclude historically with my own character : I am, or rather was, (for that is the style I must now use in speaking of myself, which imboldens me the more to speak my sentiments;) I was, I say, a man of mild disposition, of command of temper, of an open, social, and cheerful humor, capable of attachment, but little susceptible of enmity, and of great moderation in all my passions. Even my love of literary fame, my ruling passion, never soured my temper, notwithstanding my frequent disappointments. My company was not unacceptable to the young and careless, as well as to the studious and literary; and as I took a particular pleasure in the company of modest women, I had no reason to be displeased with the reception I met with from them. In a word, though most men, anywise eminent, have found reason to complain of Calumny, I never was touched, or even attacked by her . . . and though I wantonly exposed myself to the rage of both civil and religious factions, they seemed to be disarmed in my behalf of their wonted fury. My friends never had occasion to vindicate any one circumstance of my character and conduct; not but the zealots, we may well suppose, would have been glad to invent and propagate any story to my disadvantage, but they could never find any which they thought would wear the face of probability. I cannot say there is no vanity in making this funeral oration of myself, but I hope it is not a misplaced one; and this is a matter of fact which is easily cleared and ascertained.

April 18, 1776'

Let anyone who wishes guess at the relevance to my life and yours that prompted *that* quote. Lives declare their same differences some hundred or some hundreds of years later on the other side of that or this pond.

As for the invariant Bill Williams:

Blue at the prow of my desire.

An early line—and for that reason I suppose uppermost in my mind, there is a difference of only twenty years between our ages—its character owns all the phases of your later work, the catastrophic and gentle in its characters, in their signing hieroglyphics.

The good memories are never recollected. It is as Hamlet says: *If it be now, 'tis not to come.* They are here, not to be written *about* and not in a hurry: but as the years have it, the earliest with the latest—*if it be not to come, it will be now.*

Ezra, early in March (your month you have said) 1928—'Re/ private life: Do go down an' stir up Bill Willyums, still the best human value on my murkn visiting list.'

Your Easter letter of that year asks me, 'Was the Matthäus Passion well sung?' I had begun 'A' for which, 30 years later, having as you say an idea, you have just presented me with a foreword—when I thought you were working on *Paterson V*. There were projects then about which you were 'less volatile . . . I have gotten older . . . after 70 perhaps . . . perhaps it will crystallize soon.' Not a bad prophecy. But my satisfaction is that I seem then to have been 'ubiquitous' (*you say*—how could I have been?) and with a few friends we did get things done: *The Descent of Winter* issue (*Exile 4*); *A Novelette and Other Prose* (To, Publishers); your first *Collected Poems* (The Objectivist Press).

The names of our presses were my ideas: *To*—as we might say, a health to—*To*. I have this that you said about it: 'I never knew *To* was a noun gosh all hemlock. I'll have to look that up. Anyway it's not a bad name for publicity—nobody can understand it or keep from thinking about it once they see it.' And as for the *Objectivists* (who I suspect any century now are to make the exegetical anthologies) Charles Reznikoff ingenuously condensed my longish prospectus into 'writers publishing their own work.'

It involved an unremitting exchange of letters, your blanket orders to shorten, emend and correct anything in your manuscripts that would clean them up and save pennies—a conceptive impatience on your part sometimes that offered the editor the poor consolation of thinking. Not that your talk is not always rich with some concept—though you have often refused to believe it. But like Puck, whose pointed ears you've inherited, after yielding to the human and worse humane maze you must also fly from it, putting a girdle round about the earth, as he says, in forty minutes: to the attic under the gable, the car, the roses in your back yard, the oak dining room or the typewriter in your doctor's office.

The visits to your home entailed crossing the Hudson by either of two ways: taking the old bus in an alley behind the Hotel Astor, or the ferry to the Erie Railroad—somehow always with your 'Wanderer' in mind. I preferred the Erie route: perhaps for the historical associations—and the change after the direct breeze of the ferry—the iron girders and vaulting of the station, the scene of C. F. Adams' chapter of 'An Erie Raid'; perhaps for the fact that the same journey afforded a contrast of finance, as murky as when Aristotle first wrote about the unnatural evil, and the American robin's egg blue covers of your *Spring and All*. I had earned it as a bonus and sometimes carried it with me. The colored paper covers have crackled; it has been my favorite of all your books—dated April 11, 1928.

I suppose a citation ought to carry gifts with it. They happen to be yours—three extracts I once jotted down from your letters: 'Floss going back to plant 30 new plants and expecting miracles of bloom in the spring.' (That would be after the four of us had walked in the rose garden in Bronx Park during the worst of the war in 1941. The next is about Paul playing his quarter-size just about ten years ago.)

Dear Louis & Celia :

I told mother this afternoon of Paul's playing of the violin. She was highly amused and interested, could hardly believe it true. I had to show her the size of the fiddle and show her how he stood and bowed. She was very much taken by the story. Finally she said, My compliments to the father and mother. So that's what I'm sending you.

Best,

Bill

(The next is dated Oct. 22/35.) I can't stand the full restraint that X even in his wildest ravings is willing to acknowledge. Maybe that makes him a better man than I am. My only answer to that is there aint no such animal. No one is 'better.' Anyone is only relatively perfect. It is this tolerance which I apply to others as well as myself which alone keeps me going . . . to a man with some sort of pride of spirit—if you call it that—I remain only a half educated barbarian. That goes deep. Deep in me where hell will break loose. I deny . . . every tenet that can be called tenable, every scientific trend, every philosophic stab . . . Every physical grasp of facts establishes *that* sort of tradition as false—empty. That's what I wish to avoid, to destroy. That's, for instance, the real underlying ground in my imagination of the character of Washington—or Shakespeare. There is something there, underneath the dynamo of intelligence —of life itself that is crude, rebellious—the lack of which, or the denial of which . . . makes an ass.

Yours,

Louis

1958

II

Aristotle knew that 'the argument of the *Odyssey* is not a long one.' And Chapman spurred by the job of rendering summed it up as 'A man,' or perhaps just 'man.' The friendliest reader for the time being forgets, still scampering through Williams.

It is in complexities that appear finally as one person that the good of a life shows itself—ringing all together to return the world to simplicity again . . . like a good picture : a sharp differentiation of good from evil—something to look at and to know with satisfaction, something alive—that has partaken of many things, welcoming them indiscriminately if they seemed to have a value—a color—a sound to add still more to the intelligent, the colorful, the whole grasp of feeling and knowledge in the world.

A man writes or makes or criticizes or teaches by something like the order of this passage from *Raquel Hélène Rose* : if not for eternity, with a foregone conclusion, as Williams says somewhere else with the same different words, that 'The province of the poem is the world.' Which is to say a man is 6,000 or 20,000 years old—or what age have you for young or old animal *man*—always repeating but measuring up to himself with a difference.

And his *horse* when man re-creates him does the same—until what time he might be replaced by a new species, which is a permissible question, since it may be imagined to happen. When it does only then will a psychoanalysis of him according to the new criticism have some completeness. But till then he is the horse of man's 'whole grasp of feeling and knowledge in the world.' Like Williams' :

> The horse moves
> independently
> without reference
> to his load
>
> He has eyes
> like a woman and
> turns them
> about, throws
>
> back his ears
> and is generally
> conscious of
> the world. Yet
>
> he pulls when
> he must and
> pulls well, blowing
> fog from

his nostrils
like fumes from
the twin
exhausts of a car.

Which is to say the horse is measured by Cro-Magnon ochre, and
Phidias' stone, and Picasso's design, and by the twin exhausts of a car,
and the pulse of verse—among an imponderable number of other
things. Or what other horse can you evoke today after his many trials
leading to his rarer appearances in the streets, reined in by a policeman.

'If politics,' as Williams says, 'could be the science of humanity.'
And so his art.

Art means standards, recurrences. True enough with a difference in
each instance—of medium, person, place, material, time, whatever the
residues that wear : but leaving the recurrence, 'made by man.'

It is not a matter of influence when Williams' Sam Patch frozen in
a cake of ice is 'like' the woman in the transparency of iceberg of Apol-
linaire's *Couleur de Temps*. Or it is—who cares, except for the standards. There is or there isn't a bit of Gris in Williams, of Klee, Demuth,
Sheeler, but there is of every painting of his time that re-made things
into a picture. And of Lucretius' 'Spring goes on her way and Venus,'
and the same new life that followed later in Dante, and some Villon,
and Chaucer's own rooster, and Anonymous English, and Shakespeare
('the clatter and true sound of verse'), and, well, the Jamesian perception of Williams' 'The Jungle.' But all this is not to be pointed up
for the sake of dullness.

As Gertrude Stein (one of Williams' interests) remarked :

I get pretty angry with it all. I met a man the other day who said he was
a professor of how to use scientific textbooks. They all have to be told. Our
life is so organized . . . Our universities are run by regents rather than
professors . . . Knowledge is a thing you know and how can you know
more than you do know . . . Before that in all the periods before things
had been said been known been described been sung about, been fought
about been destroyed been imprisoned been lost but never been explained.
So then they began to explain. And we may say that they have been explaining ever since. And as I say we are still in the shadow of it.

There is also the other side of the same coin minted by Einstein :

'Everything should be as simple as it can be, but not simpler'—a scientist's defense of art and knowledge—of lightness, completeness and accuracy. The modern of all times to whose energies *byplay* is never *playboy*.

Aristotle? 'An herb peddler,' as Williams has noticed of one aspect of the grammarian's better insight with his 'simple . . . the certain nature . . . produces motion as being loved' and 'the things for whose existence we are more zealous than for the existence of the ideas' (and we are in *Paterson's* time) and his Stein-ish definition of substance 'a this.' *This* is Williams' contribution to culture.

1948

III

Writing with a sense of the history and destiny of The United States —as in the Earlier Discoveries of *In the American Grain*—William Carlos Williams with *A Voyage to Pagany* impels Americans towards a Beginning. The curious as to history may find it convenient to draw a parallel between this later effort of sensitized American intellect and the earlier effort of Henry Adams in his *Mont St Michel and Chartres* (1904).

As there has been no actual contact of subject matter the parallel can be no more than metaphor. It points the fact that two minds, with approximately a quarter of a century between them, have reacted as Americans, along different lines, toward what might be termed the European unchanging—in the words of Williams, 'the ancient springs of purity and plenty.'

Both writers come to Europe : Adams to the cathedrals of France to see the Virgin; Williams among other places to Paris, 'a stitched-up woman hunting a lover.'

'It must be a lover. He must come of machines, he must break through. Nothing will subdue him.' So they come as lovers, both from machines. They must break through to get at what they want, since neither will walk on Nothing. But there is a difference of twenty-four years.

Son of his New England family Adams voyaged, a mind replete with education—the heart as though trip-hammered with its in-effectualness—to preserve intact the spirit which in the past had preserved his family; in the end a mind surfeited, prodigal to family, the lover in humility, submitting (perhaps he did not know) to his own superstructure over French Gothic mind; the spirit mortified, but somehow complete. In summary he said of it :

Of all the elaborate symbolism which has been suggested for the Gothic cathedral, the most vital and most perfect may be that the slender nervure, the springing motion of the broken arch, the leap downwards of the flying buttress—the visible effort to throw off a visible strain—never let us forget that Faith only supports it, and that, if Faith fails, Heaven is lost.

The new voyage to pagany (pagany meaning Europe) is steered near Adams' original route. Again what was launched is not the machine, but instinct. 'One thing about the man, he never argued with his instincts.' After twenty-four years, it is still the machine which persists. But no need to be mortified. Wary one must be, of course—always the check upon the instincts; America has raised one that way; but one can approach, like the Indian, circle around, and then attack. Attack at least with the precision of the machine become instinct.

The Ancient Beauty, yes. At Santa Croce one is 'purified past the walls of any church,' but not subdued : purified for oneself, for one's own Beginning and the Beginning of one's own (*Spring and All*). Europe, Venice of Waters, the Pagan underneath the Christian, Giotto, Cimabue, the world's 'shell of past loveliness,' meet it with distrust! Learn, yes, be penetrated, become clear on all levels as with the clarity of Williams' Viennese doctors, but 'close the eyes sharply to, at the height of enjoyment, at the peak of understanding. He had strengthened his understanding of what he had long since discerned. He carried his affirmation away in his pocket—with his time-table.' Like an American. Old Europe may not like it.

What this change means to the writing is clear. The *Mont St Michel and Chartres* of Henry Adams in submission attains an imaginative completeness, a clarity originally foreign and resolves into unity. What might have been a tiresome itinerary becomes a celestial Baedeker, the plan of the book chastened as the nervure of the Gothic arch. What was intended to be impersonal has the element of the personal diffused through design. The struggle of American mind for the ciborium not its own casts the spell of tragedy through the calm of structure.

The recalcitrance of William Carlos Williams in *A Voyage to Pagany* makes for anything but tragedy. What is intended to be a novel becomes in structure an animated itinerary. There is practically no design, since the aim impelling the book is—to move on to the Beginning. There can be no lingering for what is final, for what resolves into unity. Fact—impels from incident to incident, because the Beginning comes only with the finish of what is Past.

Intellectualism is a by-product of this itinerary and teases the imagination. The author of that perfect piece in *Spring and All,* 'The pure products of America go crazy,' might have remained on his own ground and implied in a novel of the defeat of those 'pure products,' farmers, migrant laborers, substrata of These States, the defeat of intellectualism itself. The poet's nature compelled him otherwise. For one concerned with the Beginning, a portrait of what is closest to oneself to begin with is indispensable; it makes for honesty—the welcome absence of premature sentiment with regard to America's 'peasantry'—rare in recent fiction.

What is good in *A Voyage to Pagany* breaks through—despite the hazards of intellect—sees through incident, surrounds and fathoms objects. The principal character Dev, a constantly impressionable fellow, irritates himself into thought :—'What does anybody find in anybody? Something he can't get except through that somebody'; the words, 'What is it, dear?' making the natural keystone of a perfect love scene; 'Carcassonne, a rock ruined by tears'; 'the tan and grime wrestling the hair stuck together at the ends, growing from the scaly scalps, from poor soil——'; the Arno 'river getting broader and going about its business'; 'music a presence which you feel occasionally during the playing'; of Bach's *St Matthew Passion*—'I heard him agonizing, I saw him *inside*, not cold but he *lived* and I was possessed by his passion.'

Americans might do no better than to emulate the Europeans, and consider the portrait of what is at least their own Beginning—carefully.

1928

THE EFFACEMENT OF PHILOSOPHY

Anyone who reflects generously on Santayana's debt to Spinoza will be disposed to sympathize with the affective quality of his naturalism or intelligent materialism of his *Dominations and Powers*. As he says, his book is a departure from Plato and Aristotle, who spoke for an ancient city in its decline; they hardly considered non-territorial powers, such as universal religions, nor the relation of the state to the non-political impulses of human nature :

Sometimes, in exceptional and reflective natures, the distraction and the triviality of life, even of healthy life, become oppressive, and a sympathy with the goods pursued by contrary moralities renders one's own morality pathetic and almost remorseful. . . . Victory or prosperity for one's own people or one's own civilization will no longer seem an ultimate or unqualified good . . . only manifesting, in one arbitrary form, the universal impulse in matter towards all sorts of harmonies and perfections. Then all the other harmonies and perfections, not attainable here, perhaps not attained anywhere, will come crowding to the gates of our little temple. And the spirit will be tempted to escape from that particular sanctuary, to abdicate its identity with the society that bred it, and to wander alone and friendless, to be the lover of all climates and the friend of all friends.

But the lover of all climates is in effect the lover of none and no one, if nature works so privately in 'each cataloguer of human virtues' as 'to soften almost to sadness the vital necessity of being oneself'. Sadness does not compel vital necessity, rather vital necessity compels sadness. We do not admire, said Spinoza, the architect who planned a chapel so much as the architect who planned some great temple. He also said, to perceive a winged horse is to affirm it, and there cannot be too much merriment.

Whether one can plan or how one knows may form the dispute of the summer student. It has been forestalled by the hymn of creation in the Rigveda : before the void there was neither non-being nor being, after it came warmth and desire, and sages looked with thought in their hearts for the kinship of what is in what is not.

What one acts and speaks about are inescapable to the materialist, but precisely what the sages looked for. Perhaps the fortunes of the Greek word *ruthmos* may elucidate this matter : first it meant *shape*, then *rhythm*, now *proportion* or *style*. The mathematician or the statistician is probably better equipped than the philosopher to draw the conclusion that history, especially written history, works cyclically in expressing material phenomena. The unmathematical philosopher will probably be quick to see simply that in all times a proportion or style is mixed with story and with heart-beat. Different times seem to favor one or another of these phases. If it can be proved that they follow one another cyclically, he who likes story and is fated to style had at best make as much story of it as he can to be free in a materialist sense.

Aristotle zealous for things scolded Plato for his Ideas, never noticing that the whorl of the spindle of Necessity in *The Republic* was like the whorl on earth, and Aristotle took over Plato's Ideas without knowing it. The point to the materialist is, will nature or the time or oneself permit one to make a temple or a lesser thing. Spinoza may be said to be the last great Western philosopher. He based his *Ethics* on a single definition that was integrated in the manner of Bach's *Art of Fugue*. Materialist philosophers of history may do well to think about Bach's remark : The order which rules music is the same order that controls the placing of the stars and the feathers in a bird's wing.

Santayana's book is philosophy of history, written after Vico, Marx, Adams, with a political cast. For the purposes of studying politics he presupposes that the forces of nature effect 'dominations' and 'powers,' respectively fatal and favorable to whatever is driven by desire, and express themselves in time, as moral orders that are 'generative, militant and rational.' There are 'Virtues,' too, 'having only a vegetative or lyric life, perfect in themselves and not addressed to exercising any influence over other beings,' and also 'the hope that the reader may feel them always silently hovering over the pages.' They do hover but not with tolerable order, through scattered soliloquies and formal essays. Like the modern composer, if he has expounded all harmony it needs a new ear to hear it. Yet the words are not new, not even discordant. Philosophy seems to be effaced by the matter of its study that once unified its attention: man, his intellect and his works. The analogies between man and the animals are gratuitous like old wives' tales or the stories of very old actors. Spinoza for all his resignation to geometry could still write and save animal faith and skepticism:

... many errors consist of this alone, that we do not apply names rightly to things . . . When men make mistakes . . . if you could see their minds they do not err; they seem to err, however, because we think they have the same numbers in their minds as on the paper. If this were not so we should not believe that they made mistakes any more than I thought a man in error whom I heard the other day shouting that his hall had flown into his neighbor's chicken, for his mind seemed sufficiently clear to me on the subject.

Santayana takes the title of his book from *Colossians*, but Paul writes of wisdom and singing with grace in your hearts. If by his own confession Santayana is not proselytizing why should he write:

... a cosmopolitan middle class, like the Jews, already diffused through-out the world and dedicated to commerce, may rise to the top, and may undertake to subordinate all nations and religions to international co-operation and prosperity. In rising to the top, this cosmopolitan middle class takes over the arts and sciences and the literary activities native to the older societies and often manipulates them cleverly, with an air of superior enlightenment; but this is merely the subjective superiority of the incurable foreigner, who has no roots in the society he studies and has cut himself off from his own roots.

'Where they sin against nature,' says Santayana in his preface, 'nature will take her revenge.' Many years ago nature casually turned him over to Spinoza who said: 'The superstitious, who know better how to reprobate vice than to teach virtue, have no other intention than to make the rest as miserable as themselves.'

1951

MODERN TIMES

Mark Twain (over the embalmed Egyptian): 'Is he dead?'

Impersonal, faster than the audience knows, international Chaplin in *Modern Times* is found at the head of a demonstration, the red flag of DANGER in his hand. Not by chance, because *the scene is in the film*. What Mr Charles Chaplin (himself) thinks should be nobody's business.

A long time ago, Charlie achieved a perspicuity of style, or a readiness for being imparted. For years the little Americans of nickleodeon days laughed alone. The fathers who could not catch up with *the clown* frowned to keep the laughs in. They preferred books on the interiors of Ibsen to the English music hall. Be that as it may, Charlie had let go in a make-up and dance raising American acting to a world position, soon to offer comparisons with the histrionic poetry of the Japanese Noh.

There were differences. Instead of allowing him to say in concise Japanese verse, 'I am going on a journey down the road, it will lead me past' etc., and poising him graciously on the property, celluloid permitted him only movement and silence. The result was the composition of action on the screen : his back ambled off into the open. Drama was brought into the actual air.

The historian of the film will helpfully interpose that everybody at the time was doing it. Art does not rise out of thin air. Certain conditions existing, the thought (e.g. the art) which reflects them in the topographic air will make it alive with relations of method embodying them. The *Survey of the Film in America* circulated by the Museum of Modern Art has shown that a cinematic technique of handling material objects was common to the films of the time. What happened to these objects in action signalizing existing conditions as reeled in the different pictures was various.

The style of Charlie's acting was similar enough to Ben Turpin's to permit them to pair in Essanay comedies. Yet the abstracted motion of the dummy kissing the lady's hand as part of the whole pattern of the visual rhythm—a manikin dancing—is the literal, never figurative, *Clever Dummy*, Ben Turpin's picture made in 1917. Take him as the human dummy, 'that man, the dummy,' and he is meaningless. He is art to his own prescription, and different from Chaplin. Charlie's minutes of choreography, dancing in and out of double sliding doors and final wedging of his counterweight between them, are not forgotten. Nor his visual variations on dropping food on a table, till at last the ice cream falls into the Lady Opposite's lap. And whatever sentiment of bereaved affection in the *Gold Rush* started his Oceana Roll—two forks stuck into two bread rolls—they became little Dutch shoes which danced of themselves as no feet could ever dance in them. The Oceana Roll was the perfection of dancing shoes, without interpretive feeling throttling the lilt : their feeling such as one might get listening to the music of Byrd's *Wolseys Wilde*, the tenor of the music dancing in the sixteenth century notation. But even here the elementary starting point of eating and the folk, country people, dancing, are likely to be overlooked. For the physical needs have been brought into free relation with the equally valid exhilarant of art making its demand in existence.

Start with an obsession of eating, like the surréalistes, and what exists is obsession, a razor blade consuming an eyeball, as in Dali's *Le Chien Andalou,* and congealing all movement. Frank Powell directing *A Fool There Was* in 1914 anticipated and knew better. The surréaliste's obsession of Lilith in the bodily form of Theda Bara stultified all human representation and the putrescence of moral gag meant to be conveyed, but she herself moved in a design. There is at least that much motion in her even today, while the stupidity of a morality of absolute good and bad is laughable as an inert joke in which a dead time forced her to take part. The 'scientific' data and shock of the surréalistes become more and more inert, remain for the most part just data, and their explicit or implicit comment complicates a ridiculous morality.

Thomas Ince, in 1916, filmed, in *The Fugitive* with Bill Hart, the equivalent of a descent from the cross *lap-dissolving* into a mound of stones in the Western desert. The desert in today's films is not felt as then, though much more reel is covered with it. Cocteau, who has praised Ince, probably admired the force in his seeing things in relation, did *Le Sang d'un Poète* to fill a gap. But even the nervous tension of something like capillaries sensitive to the moral weight of dramatic vision cannot replace the historic dimension of events actually happening.

For the most important art, an attitude toward history is not enough. Pervading the work of René Clair is the attitude of a synthetic judgment of the times, disturbing the movement of the films at their best. Because of the general discussion like it in the air, the judgment of the French director seems more personal than if he were present to speak with his own gestures. The most complete moments in Clair are history of the manners of different strata of society presented without the overemphasis of his attitude : rather than the myopic professor officiating over his text while the winds of money blow through the scrambling crowd in *A Nous La Liberté*, the queen picking up a magazine or the night watchman in the bank, tipping his hat when he hears his financier-boss over the phone, in *Le Dernier Milliardaire*. Whereas in Chaplin's films it is usually not even a question of *strata* of society (the layers of drawing room comedy) : but of people in the masks they portray among actual events determining them or imagined events which they make possible dramatically.

An escaped prisoner, a soldier, a policeman with heavy eyebrows, a stagehand, a waiter, a pawnbroker, a drunken millionaire ready to commit suicide, a girl waif of the streets : their situation or lack of it, not their pleasurably stratigraphic registration by a director like René Clair, realizes them as products of the economics of working day life or a holiday and presents them as people of impulse. The rapidity with which they move as of themselves it would seem from incident to incident in the crowding number of events in each Chaplin film compels sequence, and concentrates their cinematic action many times that of the single historical meaning in the personal continuity of attitude of René Clair. The foregoing reaction is sharpened by Charlie's use of Clair's trimness of machinery in *Modern Times*, in which a mechanical face-wiper enlivened by insistent movements becomes a sequence of terror.

A half-baked idea like humanity has become mechanized by civilization does not animate a face-wiper. Charlie's devices and 'types' live with material thoughtfulness and thus historical meaning. It was some years ago that people began to see satire in Charlie, as distinguished from comedy to which rhetorics have tagged one definition or another and decided it ends well. *Satire:* emphasizing insistence of intelligence

in men affected by obverse events and driving to a new physical reality
—as when Swift has the Laputans build from the roof down, or pre-
scribes how gloves can be made from the hides of Irish babies. The
impetus of Chaplin's films is more or less of that order of insistence at
different times, plus a sense of sportsmanship deriving from a detailed
recording of actual things in relation. Charlie the actor never revealing
his natural self is also Charlie in the set, an intelligence working itself
out in the concrete. So that a new idea in a new Chaplin film is not
merely a notion, a general sense of today, or an understanding of politics,
art, life or whatever, but inventive existence interacting with other
existence in all its ramifications: sight, hearing, muscular movement,
coordination of all the senses acting on the surrounding world and
rendering it laughably intelligent.

One remembers that a white bearded Jew, the pawnbroker in *The
Pawnshop*, looks benignly patriarchal, while the poor lank fellow with
black mustache not successful at pledging his alarm clock to a scrutiniz-
ing clerk is turmoils away from the eternal forgivingness of the white-
bearded face. *Behind the Scenes*, in which Charlie scabs on his fellow
stagehands and wins the girl according to pedestrian expectation,
reaches the end with Charlie kissing her. Yet the very last shot is Charlie
winking at the audience—*close up*, and *irised out*. In *Shoulder Arms*,
Charlie embodying a transformation in Ovid camouflages himself into
a tree. The metamorphosis which Charlie poetically senses is not his
sole achievement. He becomes the man-tree to destroy the human foe.
In the same film the soldiers and the candles floating on the waters of
the trench are not merely a fantastic limbo, but the limbo of war to
overworked nerves reenacting it in sleep. Once *Easy Street* is cleaned
up, the threatening, thick eyebrows of the villain become kind. In *A
Dog's Life* a dog acted with human discipline till its doggishness was
value around ash cans.

A herd of sheep, driven, and their appointment is the pen or the
slaughterhouse. Evaluated in this opening shot of *Modern Times*, taken
from above, in the sportsmanship of the montage—the cinematic
equivalent of material thoughtfulness—are the backs of sheep bulg-
ing. They urge each other out of the picture. The satire of nerves and
their obverse—events—follow. People fill a subway entrance and
crowd the screen; then, a street; and the inside of the factory in which
they work at the conveyor belt appears. The rest is the active sentience
of continuity which includes a simple but strong plot, so effective it can

be seen again and need not be told since as story it is like everyday's newspaper. Useful as a frame of reference it includes a multitude of things, material as well as fantastic things made possible : the screen action holding together in the timing, the sound devices, and the light. The elements of opposition in these cinematic effects and their emotional absorption into relations of the story further the historical validity of the screen by inventing out of the actual world of the spectator.

A sign over an escalator, in the department store episode, reads, *This is a moving stairway.* Does Charlie leave nothing to the imagination—as the Elizabethans did when they posted a sign in proxy for a set, or the Noh when it suggested a journey in a line of verse, or the Chinese actor who straddled a whip substituting for the breathing horse? Is the meaning in the obvious clutter of Charlie's set the hoax of an inclusive consciousness: that people ride on escalators so mechanically they do not know they move from floor to floor; that the head today expanding way above the feet's movement does not know when they stand or ascend? Charlie synthesizes concretely by proceeding to move up and down the escalator as part of his plot.

Sharpening this venturesomeness of physical movement which seeps with intelligent conflict, concentration on anatomical details develops a sequence of terror. A flash of the film, directing sight to a propulsion of gullet, makes the throat cognizable after years of just swallowing—and especially 'terrible' when it is that of the minister's wife. In the wider design of the plot—a movement continuing and never let down, as a theme developed in pricksong—there is the terror of Charlie's face being brushed by a mechanical wiper, and later the cumulative terror of Charlie lovingly wiping the face of a machinist caught in a machine. The spectator may refuse to be convinced that the director's intention was terror, but by the time that shot in the film is reached laughter is somehow involved in the lacrimal.

Tears, said a master of the Noh, are justly not wrung out of one. In Chaplin they remain finally in the satire and the movement. His direction, encompassing his acting, sees all around as well as arouses. The *sportsmanship* of the montage has been referred to in passing. The phrase reduces itself to the fact that nothing is fair on the screen unless shown in a relation (or a strained relation) that has the amplitude of insight impelled by the physical, to be found in actual events themselves.

The girl whose father has been shot down in the demonstration is shown in *close up*, grieving with the air around her. The satire, if one wishes to bring home a point, is that any director would have shown the close up of a star and omitted the air. The city in which the girl's father has been shot is not named in the film. But if the spectator sees more than one thing at a time he sees 1. the girl 2. the air around her 3. the fact that it was filmed in America.

World interaction of events today forces peoples to think in relation instead of discretely, and the speed of interaction on the part of an audience with the facts conveyed in a film is more immediate than whatever quibbling as to the director's 'real' intention. Mr Chaplin (himself) may have purposed nothing more palpable than to make people laugh. But pictures do not need to be translated like books which lean on the crutch of analysis. It is to Mr Chaplin's credit as director that his co-star, Paulette Goddard, is always the waif in *Modern Times* and that the air around her is America's, whether he meant it that way or not.

In the *close up* of the girl Charlie does for the air of the United States what Pudovkin in *Life is Beautiful* does for the soil of the Soviet, in a shot showing the hand of a man, most of whom has already walked out of the frame, over the land on which he will work. In the mass scenes of *Modern Times* moving with the newsreel immediacy and swift timing of Jakob Blokh's *A Shanghai Document*, the direction realizes : the strike, the hunger demonstration, the unemployed crowding the gate to get a job in the factory. To have filmed these things for the facts they are would seem to be a more difficult job than the one Eisenstein faced in *Ten Days that Shook the World*—his documentation and his cast already backed by the conviction arising from events of past history. Charlie also has his past pat : a stuffed model of Buffalo Bill sits in the corner of the department store while the hobos driven to loot its liquor befriend Charlie over drinks. As it happens he is only looking for a place to sleep. The montage of this scene might pass almost unnoticed, the amplitude of its insight in relation to history and to the tradition of Chaplin's previous films is so adequate.

Perhaps the one scene in *Modern Times* that will not bear seeing again is Charlie skating alone, blindfolded, over the unfenced mezzanine, while the girl looks on in terror. The feeling is that Charlie is not doing so well here as he did in *The Rink*. And it is significant in that the cinema is not a one-man show, or the tired symbolism (if that was intended?) of man always skating over the edge. Charlie cannot, in 1936, go back to a dance that he *did*, or to a sentimental spectator's idea of what his dancing might be, but must continue to develop the cinema. And D. W. Griffith in *The New York Hat* (1912) realized the kernel of that development when he showed not Mary Pickford his star reflected in a mirror, but a character and the sideview of a mirror.

'Adornment,' says Dante, (and he might have used the word *technics*) 'is the addition of some suitable thing' . . . 'everything which is suited to us is so either in respect of the genus, or of the species, or of the individual, as sensation, laughter, war'; (*De Vulgari Eloquentia* II, 1). '. . . it must be observed that, as man has been endowed with a threefold life, namely, vegetable, animal, and rational, he journeys along a three-fold road; for in so far as he is vegetable he seeks for what is useful, where-in he is of like nature with plants; in so far as he is animal he seeks for that which is pleasurable, wherein he is of like nature with brutes; in so far as he is rational he seeks for what is right—and in this he stands alone . . .' (II, 2). 'Everything that moves, moves for the sake of something which it has not, and which is the goal of its motion; . . . Every-thing that moves, then, has some defect, and does not grasp its whole being at once.' (Letter to Can Grande, 26).

Chaplin's *technics* developed with respect to his work as individual, alongside of other technics invented to suit the need of the species, now embraces a tradition of the film, as much as any one man can who moves to grasp its whole being at once in the present.

There exists probably in the labors of any valid artist the sadness of the horse plodding with blinkers and his direction is for all we don't know filled with the difficulty of keeping a pace. Charlie in the past yoked himself to the world, and now lives and works in this age of gears. What distinguishes Charlie from film technicians of lesser calibre is that he is usually not taking his career as a standstill for a display of personal sensitivity, charm, or whatever. In a significant shot in *Modern Times* Charlie films the false athleticism of the poor in mind plunging into the shallow fact and returning, limping, the *bourgeois gentilhomme* find-ing it impossible to swim in his poverty.

Having developed with the cinema, Chaplin now uses sound and sings. His variations on the theme of 'Hallelujah I'm a Bum' are musically competent. Yet they are rightly never heard for themselves. His music counterpoints his action, as in the climactic sequence of his upright waiter's hand carrying a tray above the heads of the churning crowd of dancers. The music might have bolted the action just as the tray carried high might have failed as a feat. Moving intrinsically, and against each other, both come through together.

Singing, Charlie concocts his words internationally. The result is the effect of words conveying a familiar feeling of being spoken without the least affectation. Singing for the first time on the screen, Charlie would almost seem to be providing for an emergency in case his voice will not carry as part of his action, of which his dance introducing his song is also a part.

A few titles bearing the signature of the artist's previous achievement in the history of the film resolve themselves into its present development: into the interaction of the shots including modern times.

Similarly, certain words in Joyce's *Ulysses* might be imagined as spoken for their cinematic value in a continuity and not lose the formal energy of words conveying a situation—people in a time.

(*Corley to Stephen*): *Not as much as a farthing to purchase a night's lodgings. Where on earth (can I) get something, anything at all to do.*

In a shot in *Modern Times*, placing the romanticism of *going out to find work* against the rest of today's situation, Charlie is extravagantly and pathetically heroic when the beam of a crumbling shack falls on his head. To yoke oneself to the world of the facts and to keep apace is of an altogether different order of decision than trying to swim in one's poverty. Finally and despite odds, Charlie and the girl decide to go off together in the film, and their arms bend up at the elbows, their fists are clenched, too powerfully fast for the spectator to speculate what Mr Chaplin means. If the spectator is intent on the film and not on his own thought, what can the action of the shot mean but what it *does*— i.e. *performs.*

1936

LEWIS CARROLL

When asked whether 'The Hunting of the Snark' was a political satire, Carroll had but one answer, 'I don't know.' As for the genesis of writing, in an essay 'Alice on the Stage' (1887), he distinguished between times when the Muse had to say something and times when she had something to say. Of the genesis of *Alice* and the *Looking-Glass*, he said they 'were made up almost wholly of bits and scraps, single ideas which came of themselves,' and he desired no higher praise to be written of him than 'He gave the people of his best; the worst he kept.'

The dream world of Carroll's *Alice in Wonderland* and *Through the Looking-Glass* has never offended predatory interests because they are too callous or too stupid to notice that the guilelessness of his nonsense exists on a tangent departing at some point on the periphery of sense. Carroll ultimately refused to commit himself as to whether his nonsense had any overt meaning. But the nonsense recorded its own testimony.

When the insistence of the Queen of Hearts that the sentence be given before the verdict makes Alice's dream too terrible to go on, the entire fantastic court—a pack of cards—rises into the air and Alice as defendant—not witness—wakes. The Hatter who kept hats to sell, but had none of his own—'what with the bread-and-butter getting so thin' —is also remembered.

And:

Plato makes his characters display at once their blind acquiescence in their instructor's opinions, and their utter inability to express themselves gram- matically. But the writer . . . proceeds from questions to demands, 'give me (of) the bread'; and here the conversation abruptly ceases, but the moral of the whole is pointed in the narrative : 'she gave him a box on the ear.' This is not the philosophy of one individual or nation, the sentiment

is, if I may so say, European; and I am borne out in *this* theory by the fact
that the book has evidently been printed in three parallel columns, English, French and German. (*A Broken Spell*, 1856)

Next we went to the Treasury and saw thrones, crowns and jewels—
until one began to think that those three articles were rather more common than blackberries. On some of the thrones, etc. the pearls were
literally showered like rain.

Königsberg. On our way to the station, we came across the grandest
instance of the 'Majesty of Justice' that I have ever witnessed—A little
boy was being taken to the magistrate, or to prison (probably for picking
a pocket). The achievement of this feat had been entrusted to two
soldiers in full uniform, who were solemnly marching, one in front of the
poor little creature, and one behind; with bayonets fixed of course, to be
ready to charge in case he should attempt an escape.

Ten and one-half P.M. Hearing a squeaking noise in the street, I
have just looked out, and observed a policeman [or a being of that kind]
on his beat. (The last three quotations from *Journal of a Tour in Russia
in 1867*.)

And so on, for pages.

1935

EZRA POUND

I

TA HIO

Thus, if her colour
Came against his gaze,
Tempered as if
It were through a perfect glaze

He made no immediate application
Of this to the relation of the state
To the individual, the month was more temperate
Because this beauty had been.
      'The Age Demanded,' *Hugh Selwyn Mauberly*

This classifying of values shows Pound sufficiently moral.

For a quarter of a century he has been engaged in 'the expression of an idea of beauty (or order)' and his results are one aspect of a further personal comprehension.

          out of key with his time
    He strove to resuscitate the dead art
    Of poetry; to maintain 'the sublime'
    In the old sense.

—intent upon 'language not petrifying on his hands, preparing for new advances along the lines of true metaphor, that is, interpretative metaphor, or image, as opposed to the ornamental.' 'Artists are the antennae of the race,' words to him are principals of a line of action, a store, a purpose, a retaining of speech and manner, a constant reinterpreting of processes becoming in himself one continuous process, essentially simplification.

He has treated the arts as a science so that their morality and immorality become a matter of accuracy and inaccuracy.

The arts give us a great percentage of the lasting and unassailable data regarding the nature of man, of immaterial man, of man considered as a thinking and sentient creature. They begin where the science of medicine leaves off or rather they overlap that science. The borders of the two arts overcross.

From medicine we learn that man thrives best when duly washed, aired and sunned. From the arts we learn that man is whimsical, that one man differs from another.

As there are in medicine the art of diagnosis and the art of cure, so in the arts, so in the particular arts of poetry and of literature, there is the art of diagnosis and there is the art of cure. They call one the cult of ugliness and the other the cult of beauty. Villon, . . .Corbière, . . . Flaubert, . . . diagnosis. Satire, if we are to ride this metaphor to staggers, satire is surgery, insertions and amputations.

In the beginning simple words were enough : Food; water; fire. Both prose and poetry are but an extension of language. Man desires an ever increasingly complicated communication. Gesture serves up to a point. Symbols may serve. When you desire something not present to the eye or when you desire to communicate ideas, you must have recourse to speech. Gradually you wish to communicate something less bare and ambiguous than ideas. You wish to communicate an idea and its modifications, an idea and a crowd of its effects, atmospheres, contradictions. You wish to question whether a certain formula works in every case, or in what percent of cases, etc., etc., etc., you get the Henry James novel.

So that Pound's poetry of music, image and logopoeia, his humanity always the sieve through which the three commute to organic perception, is the same as his personal morality which harbors the clarity of words as well as all beautiful objects, and the peoples who have caused them. And while it harbors their permanence steers through, and around, and is aware of, their temporal situations.

The literary make-up which notices :

> The old swimming hole
> And the boys flopping off the planks
> Or sitting in the underbrush playing mandolins
>
> Canto 13

is inwrapped with the philosophy of Kung, who said :

> Without character you will
>   be unable to play on that instrument
> Or to execute the music fit for the Odes.
> The blossoms of the apricot
>   blow from the east to the west,
> And I have tried to keep them from falling.
>
> Canto 13

'Character' implies enough order to be radiated outward. Order allows that Kung may permit himself to raise his cane against Yuan Jang,

> Yuan Jang being his elder,
> For Yuan Jang sat by the roadside pretending to
>   be receiving wisdom.
>
> Canto 13

And Kung may also note :

> Wang ruled with moderation,
>   In his day the State was well kept,
> And even I can remember
> A day when historians left blanks in their writings,
> I mean for things they didn't know,
> But that time seems to be passing.
>
> Canto 13

Concern with 'the bright principle of our reason,' with the use of Ta Hio or The Great Learning as a gauge of action, involves : recognition of the beauty of everytime in which alone we have being; interest in the present, so that life, as Pound has said, may not make mock of motion and humans not move as ossifications.

It follows that Pound has been both the isolated creator and the worldly pamphleteer. To put the defences of his own being in order, he has drafted himself into the defence of innovation clarifying and making sincere the intelligence. Contrasted with the leavings of transcendentalism and belated scholasticism around him, he has said that 'Lenin invented . . . a new medium, something between speech and action which is worth . . . study'; (*Exile* 4, 1928)

That the Soviet Idea is as old as the Ta Hio's 'Private gain is not prosperity';

That 'a new language is always said to be obscure . . . After a few years the difficult passage appears to be a simple lucidity';

That 'perhaps art is healthiest when anonymous . . . in the Gros-stadt Symphony we have at last a film that will take serious aesthetic criticism : one that is in the movement, and that should flatten out the opposition (to Joyce, to [Pound], to Rodker's *Adolphe*) with steam-rolling ease and commodity, not of course that the authors intended it';

And has implied that Sovkino's *The End of St Petersburg* had an inertia of mass power behind it impossible of attainment in a single Chekov.

Pound anticipated *The End of St Petersburg* as poetry some years before the production of the film :

> There was a man there talking,
> To a thousand, just a short speech, and
> Then move 'em on. And he said :
> Yes, these people, they are all right, they
> Can do everything, everything except act;
> And go an' hear 'em, but when they are through
> Come to the bolsheviki . . .
>
> And when it broke, there was the crowd there,
> And the cossacks, just as always before,
> But one thing, the cossacks said :
>   'Pojalouista.'
> And that got round in the crowd,
> And then a lieutenant of infantry
> Ordered 'em to fire into the crowd,
>   in the square at the end of the Nevsky,
> In front of the Moscow station,
> And they wouldn't,
> And he pulled his sword on a student for laughing,
> And killed him,
> And a cossack rode out of his squad
> On the other side of the square,
> And cut down the lieutenant of infantry
> And that was the revolution . . .
>   as soon as they named it.
> And you can't make 'em,

Nobody knew it was coming. They were all
      ready, the old gang,
Guns on the top of the post-office and the palace,
But none of the leaders knew it was coming.

And there were some killed at the barracks,
But that was between the troops.

                                                    Canto 16

That Pound, previous to this presentation, chose to benefit by the
clarity and intelligence of Chinese written character and Confucius is
an indication of the scale he has constructed to measure his values.

Good humor has a great deal to do with this measure. The *Cantos*
say 'nothing of the life after death.'

                        Anyone can run to excesses.

                                                    Canto 13

Good humor, which is not ashamed to set down fact, has also to
do with Pound's transcriptions of the spoken tongue—his colloquial
spelling, and with exploring music.

II. TRANSLATION

Pound's comparative standard of literature turned him to translation in the beginning. 'The translations,' Pound wrote of his versions
of Arnaut Daniel (*Instigations*), 'are a make-shift; it is not to be expected that I can do in ten years what it took two hundred troubadours
a century and a half to accomplish.' What, then, is his contribution?
Briefly, the distinction of rendering into English unexplored poetic
forms, and of translating himself through personae.

'Poetry,' he wrote in the essay on James—as contrasted with prose—
intellectual analysis—and there is a qualification about 'the highly untechnical, unimpressionist, in fact almost theological manner of statement—is the assertion of a positive, i.e. of desire. . . . Poetic satire is
only an assertion of this positive, inversely, i.e. of an opposite hatred. . . .
Most good poetry asserts something to be worthwhile, or damns a contrary; at any rate asserts emotional value . . . Poetry=Emotional Synthesis.'

In Pound's poetic work other than the *Cantos*, two assertions appear constantly : vivid translation of the work of certain poets who invented technique; and homage, though this appears mostly between the lines, to the poets themselves—whose characters Pound has translated, not merely dramatized, for the duration of a poem, himself to become but their reflection. There are thus : the form of the ballade and Villon; the song to Audiart and Bertran of Born; the sestina and Bertran at Altaforte; the· canzoni and Arnaut Daniel; the sonnets, ballate, and Guido Cavalcanti; the albas, songs, etc., of the langue d'oc and Girart Bornello, etc.; the alliteration of 'The Seafarer' and the seafarer (loquitur); the English equivalent of the Chinese ideograph and Rihaku; the Latin elegiac meter and Sextus Propertius.

In contrast, Pound's sketches in *Lustra*, the 'Millwins,' 'Bellaires,' 'Moeurs Contemporaines,' 'Mauberley,' group themselves in Pound's second division of poetry, poetic satire, as assertion of a positive, but assertions of an opposite hatred. In these poems, renditions of social, rather than individual, personae, his concern is with the classical as well as with his own running unaccentuated form of the Epigram, and with the development of the quatrain (vide the opening of this article) given over to the precision of rendering an idea and all its sensual, musical definitions. That is, Pound is not confined entirely to the 'opposite assertion' of satire. *Lustra* and *Mauberley* redound frequently to complete expressions of a positive—as in 'Ortus,' and the 'Envoi (1919).' The perfect retardation of the end of the 'Envoi'

> Till change hath broken down
> All things save Beauty alone.

holds out only the more perfectly when considered with the lines of a poem preceding it :

> Charm, smiling at the good mouth,
> Quick eyes gone under earth's lid,

> For two gross of broken statues,
> For a few thousand battered books.

Translation and reliving of personae summarize the subject matter of Pound's shorter poems. The possibility that the personae are weightless dramatizations, or archaistic renditions of original people, is one which he has apprehended in 'Near Périgord' : What after all does Ezra Pound know about En Bertrans to attempt a persona? What did even En Bertrans' contemporaries, Daniel and Coeur de Lion know of the truth of his story? What can one say of it, after reading Dante, *Inferno*, XXVIII? In short, what construction can be considered truth about the past?

En Bertrans, as Pound's measure reflects him, and as he reflects Pound, can bear but the relation of a veracious actor to his historic original, and act him, mask penetrated, per sonum—through sound. Only speech transforms whatever skeleton remains of the past and conveys judgment of it to the intelligence. Try as a poet may for objectivity, for the past to relive itself, not for his living the historical data, he can do only one of two things : get up a most brief catalog of antiquities (people become dates, epitaphs), or use this catalog and breathe upon it, so that it lives as his music. This latter action need not falsify the catalog.

III CANTOS 1–27

The *Cantos* are an aggrandisement over the shorter poems in that, beyond a few personae, 'they have invented a whole world of persons' (said W. C. Williams) and given this world oneness, notwithstanding a multiplicity of speech. Yet the *Cantos* retain the direction and locus of the shorter poems—a cognizance of poetry as assertion of a positive and of poetic satire as assertion of this positive by way of an opposite hatred : the narrator as contrasted with the obstructors of knowledge and distribution (Canto 14); T. E. H. who read Kant in a war hospital, and the hospital staff who didn't like it (Canto 16); Jim X's tale of the Honest Sailor, and the hard luck stories of his banker friends (Canto 12); 'and the fabians crying for petrification of putrefaction,' as against 'bathed myself with acid to free myself of the hell ticks' (Cantos 15 and 16), etc., etc.

Pound's speech, however, as it appears in the *Cantos'* work with monolinear rhythm is a departure from the poetic invention of his shorter poems. He no longer 'cracks his wit' on rhymed renditions into English of 'delicate canzoni' ('Three Cantos' in *Lustra*). The *Cantos* (though some antedate Pound's 'early' work) cannot be understood through the forms of the shorter poems. The latter are obviously more simple, in the sense that they include less. But none of them are simpler than the *Cantos* in the sense that the content is the poetry, or that the words are bare and stripped of ornament. Reading Pound's shorter poems, or for that matter the reading of whatever poetry has been written, should help towards an understanding of the 'novelty' of the *Cantos*, but it is questionable whether their organic quality can be grasped by proceeding merely from the simple to the 'complex.'

For an exegesis of the *Cantos*, a run while you read commentary on the unfamiliar in them, nothing will serve better than Pound's prose. Several implicit comparisons between the prose and the *Cantos* have already been suggested in Part I of this essay. A number of other parallels out of many may be cited :

1. Canto 1 —a translation of Andreas Divus' Latin version of *The Odyssey* and Pound's 'Translators of the Greek' (*Instigations*).

2. Canto 2 —'Hang it all, Robert Browning,
          there can be but the one "Sordello" ' :
          and the prose comment 'Browning . . . his sometimes excellent top-knot' (again from 'Translators of the Greek').

3. Canto 3 —'My Cid rode up to Burgos' etc. and the chapter 'Geste and Romance' in *The Spirit of Romance* (an attempt to define somewhat the charm of Pre-Renaissance Literature of Latin Europe, London, 1910).

4. Canto 25—'notes as facets of air
          and the mind there, before them, moving,
          so that notes needed not move'
          and all Pound has to say about 'horizontal' music in *Antheil*.

5. Canto 21—'Keep the peace, Borso !' where are we?
          'Keep on with the business,
                    That's made me
          'And the res publica didn't'
          and the article 'Peace' (*Exile* 4); also a letter to *Poetry*, June 1929.

6. Canto 16—'Sigismundo and Malatesta Novello, and founders, gazing at the mounts of their cities.'
    Canto 25—'The dead concepts, never the solid, the blood rite,
          The vanity of Ferrara'

and

> Our envy must be for a period when the individual
> city (Italian mostly) tried to outdo its neighbor in the
> degree and intensity of its civilization, to be the vortex
> for the most living individuals—(*The Dial*, Jan. 1922).

7. Canto 27—'J'ai obtenu,' said M Curie, or some other scientist
   'A burn that cost me six months in curing'
   And continued his experiments.
   England off there in black darkness,

and

> You understand that I am continuing the attempt to
> disentangle our national qualities—(*The Dial*, Nov.
> 1922).

8. Canto 27—'And rose, and talked folly on folly'
   and

> A sense of style would protect the public from a num-
> ber of troubles, if they could ever be persuaded to ob-
> tain it.

In addition to the prose, the discarded 'Three Cantos of a Poem of Some Length' (*Lustra*, 1917) serve to explain how the *Cantos* as they now stand developed stylistically. The flavor of Faust's 'Habe nun, ach ! Philosophie'—'phantastikon,' 'filmy shell that circumscribes,' 'actual sun,'—is now absent. The revised version is not only removed from *Faust*—and all meditative, egocentric poetic-drama and dramatic monologue evolved in the nineteenth century—but closely related in method to the ideation of Dante's *Divine Comedy*, which referred to Virgil who referred to Homer. It is an ideation directed towards inclusiveness, setting down one's extant world and other existing worlds, interrelated in a general scheme of people speaking in accord with the musical measure, or spoken about in song; people, of their own weight determining, or already determined.

The poet and his personae in the *Cantos* are not present in sharp, mediaeval outline. Dante wore robes and had a theology to accompany him on his journey. The lack of argumentative piety in Pound's contemporary world does not permit his continual explicit appearance on the scene nor a simple passage from inferno to purgatorio to paradiso. These three loci in Pound's world—which are present as hate, comprehension and worship rather than as religious geometry—may be found often, next to each other, or continually intersecting, but Pound, in relation to them, becomes instead of a Dantesque persona, his own lines which are all his other people.

At intervals his presence occurs in the manner of a judgment : yet one naturally identifies the revenge of his choros nympharum with the intricacy of the renewal of matter, rather than with the determinism of the theologian's geometry :

> 'The air burst into leaf'
> 'Hung there flowered acanthus
> Can you tell the down from the up?'
>
> Canto 27

The skepticism and the music of a line like the last quoted make for the reality of those walls in time and judgment which even in calligraphy, not merely in history, exist between Odysseus and Myo Cid, Myo Cid and Tovarisch.

Whatever else might be said about the *Cantos* would seem but pro-tracted treatise, enumeration of personae; observation, for instance, that if the following passage had been written by Dante, the judge would be in hell, the girl in purgatory—who may say—even in paradise :

> And the judge says : That veil is too long.
> And the girl takes off the veil
> That she has stuck on to her hat with a pin,
> 'Not a veil,' she says, ' 'at's a scarf,'
> And the judge says
>   Don't you know you aren't allowed all those buttons?
> And she says : Those ain't buttons, them's bobbles.
> Can't you see there ain't any button-holes?
> And the Judge says : Well, anyway, you're not allowed ermine.
> 'Ermine?' the girl says, 'Not ermine, that ain't,
> At's lattittzo.'
> And the judge says : And just what is a lattittzo?
> And the girl says :
>   'It'z a animal'
>
> Signori, *you* go and enforce it.
>
> Canto 22

This is the classic matter of the epic as new poetic creation, and a phase of the present known by nervous and glandular operations.

Pound may pass safely and at once from Odysseus to Sordello (end of the first Canto and beginning of the second), from Proteus to the Dogano's steps (end of the second Canto and beginning of the third), from the subject matter of one canto to that of another comprehended in instant entirety because all new subject matter is ineluctably simultaneous with 'what has gone before.' Postulate beings and there is breathing between them and yet maybe no closer relation than the common air which irresistibly includes them. Movements of bodies, peoples through history, differences between their ideas, their connections, are often thus no closer knit, no further away than 'So that' and an 'and' which binds them (end of Cantos 1 and 2 respectively). The immediacy of Pound's epic matter, the form of the *Cantos*, the complete passage through, in and around objects, historical events, the living them at once and not merely as approximation of their statistical historical points of contact is as much a fact as those facts which historians have labelled and disassociated.

'Neither prose nor drama,' Pound has written, 'can attain poetic intensity save by construction, almost by scenario; by so arranging the circumstances that some perfectly simple speech, perception, dogmatic statement appears in abnormal vigor.' With *however's* and *it follows that* omitted, the presentation of the *Cantos* resembles the flash on the screen of century after century. Distrust of this method is like the distrust of building construction nowadays : there must be something weak in the materials or they couldn't come up so fast.

To the contrary effect, emotion such as the *Cantos* is of an order like Kung's (Canto 13) :

> They have all answered correctly,
> That is to say, each in his nature—

Comprehension of this aim will be, in the last analysis, a matter of each reader's own emotion meeting that of the poem : the matter of the epic, people, their actions, implied thoughts about them, held simultaneously in the music—charming distance, or strenuous coursing, travelling intelligence. Or : audition, following the game by sight, and the intellect scenting : *poetry* in a word—Pound's 'theological, untechnical opinions,' expressed elsewhere, aside from the matter :

'It is possible to divide poetry into three sorts (1) melopoeia, to wit, poetry which moves by its music, whether it be a music in words or an aptitude for, or suggestion of, accompanying music; (2) imagism, or poetry wherein the feelings of painting and sculpture are predominant (certain men move in phantasmagoria; the images of their gods, whole countrysides, stretches of hill land and forest, travel with them); and there is, thirdly, logopoeia, or poetry that is akin to nothing but language which is a dance of the intelligence among words and ideas and modifications of ideas and characters. Pope and eighteenth century writers had in this medium a certain limited range. The intelligence of Laforgue ran through the whole gamut of his time.' (*Instigations*)

(I.) The music of the *Cantos* is of three kinds, (a) the music of the words themselves, their sound effects, (b) the music caused by the juxtaposition of word and word, line and line, strophe and changing strophe, entire canto against canto, and the time-pauses between each of these, (c) the suggested music of all the *Cantos* at once: that is, as there is the entire developing and concluding music of the sonnet, not only the pairing or quadruplicating of its rhymes, there is the entire music of a single poem of length such as the *Cantos*. Pound's achievement is that despite the successive process of writing, unavoidable in a poem of length, the music is always an immediacy of the entire structure.

All the *Cantos* together are needed to prove (c), but the sounds of the words themselves and their interrelated music are well illustrated in the Ityn passage of the fourth Canto :

> Ityn !
> Et ter flebiliter, Ityn, Ityn !
> And she went toward the window and cast her down
>
> .   .   .
>
> Ityn !
>
> .   .   .
>
> 'Tis—'Tis—Ytis !
> Actaeon . . .

There are pages and pages of music in the *Cantos*. Talk about it resolves into an analysis of metric. Pound indicates his intention in *Pavannes* : 'I think progress lies rather in an attempt to approximate classical quantitative metres (NOT to copy them) than in a carelessness regarding such things.' Also in 'Donna Mi Prega,' *The Dial*, July 1928 :

Those writers to whom vers libre was a mere 'runnin' dahn th' road' videlicet escape, and who were impelled thereto by no inner need of, or curiosity concerning, the quantitative element in metre; having come to the end of that lurch, lurch back not into experiment with the Canzone or any other unexplored form, but into the stock and trade sonnet.

There are further hints to an understanding of this metric : in the essay on Arnaut Daniel—

And if the art . . . of saying a song . . . is like the art of En Arnaut, it has no such care for the words, nor such ear for hearing their consonance . . . of clear sound and opaque sound . . . a clear sound with staccato, and of heavy beats and of running and light beats.

And in the essay on vers libre and Arnold Dolmetch in which Pound quotes Mace, 'Musick's Monument' (1613) :

You must know, that, although in our First Undertaking, we ought to *strive*, for the most Exact Habit of *Time-keeping* that possibly we can attain unto (and for several good Reasons) yet, when we come to be Masters, so that we *can command all manner* of Time, at our own Pleasures; we then *take Liberty* (and very often, for Humour, and good Adornment-sake, in certain Places) to *Break Time*; sometimes Faster, and sometimes Slower, as we perceive the *Nature of the Thing* Requires, which often adds, much grace, and luster, to the Performance.

'Take Liberty' and 'Humour' would explain Pound's remark: 'How can you have "PROSE" in a country where the chambermaid comes into your room and exclaims: "Schön ist das Hemd!" ' ; and his breaking up and inclusion of letters in the *Cantos*:

Messire Malatesta is well and asks for you every day. He is so much pleased with his pony, it would take me a month to write you all the fun he gets out of that pony. I want to again remind you to write to Georgio Rambottom Etc.

Canto 9

and

To the supreme pig, the archbishop of Salzburg :
Lasting filth and perdition.
Since your exalted pustulence is too stingy

To give me a decent income
And has already assured me that here I have nothing to hope
And had better seek fortune elsewhere;
And since thereafter you have
Three times impeded my father and self intending departure
I ask you for the fourth time
To behave with more decency, and this time
Permit my departure.
                    Wolfgang Amadeus, August 1777

                                        Canto 26

One notes the perfect epistolary sequence of lines 5 and 6, and turns to more local subject matter :

'Could you,' wrote Mr Jefferson,
'Find me a gardener
Who can play the French horn?
The bounds of American fortune
Will not admit the indulgence of a domestic band of
Musicians, yet I have thought that a passion for music
Might be reconciled with that economy which we are
Obliged to observe.'

                                        Canto 21

Other aspects of Pound's music may be illuminated by further quotation from Mace : 'the thing to be done, is but only to make a kind of *Cessation*, or *standing still* . . . in due place an excellent grace.' This might refer to pauses in the *Cantos*.

These lines from Canto 27 describe much of the music of the *Cantos* :

And the perfect measure took form
        .   .   .
Or they rose as the tops subsided
        .   .   .
And three forms became in the air
        .   .   .
And the waves like a forest
Where the wind is weightless in the leaves
But moving,
                    So that the sound runs upon sound.

And these (quoted previously) from Canto 25 :

>   notes as facets of air,
>   and the mind there, before them, moving,
>   so that notes needed not move.

(II.) 'Imagism, or poetry wherein the feelings of painting and sculpture are predominant——'

Imagism and music direct the composition of the *Cantos*. The cadence carries the picture, and properly, for as Pound has said : 'The proportion or quality of the music may, and does, vary; but poetry withers and "dries out" when it leaves music, or at least an imagined music, too far behind it.' (*Pavannes*)

The result is that the imagism of the *Cantos* is not a static brittleness, a fragility of bits. The feelings of painting and sculpture travel with the movement; the body of what is seen is in the music :

>   And she went toward the window and cast her down
>   Canto 4

>   The students getting off for the summer,
>   Freiburg im Breisgau,
>   And everything clean, seeming clean, after Italy.

>   And I went to old Lévy, and it was by then 6 :30
>   in the evening, and he trailed half way across Freiburg
>   before dinner, to see the two strips of copy,
>   Arnaut's settant 'uno R. superiore (Ambrosiana)
>   Not that I could sing him the music
>   Canto 20

>   Leaf over leaf, dawn-branch in the sky
>   And the sea dark, under wind
>   Canto 23

The style in these passages and everywhere in the *Cantos* is so free from complications, frequently taken for literature, that the workmanship expended on the imagism, its clean-cut outline and suggestion of visual vibration in the music, tend to pass unnoticed. For moments, the imagism-in-music of the *Cantos* would seem bare statement without further connotation. There is no excuse for this feeling but an unfortunate lack of acuteness to music and a verbal training founded on characteristic sentimentalisms : redundant simile and personification, and 'messing up the perception of one sense by trying to define it in terms of another.' (*Pavannes*)

Pound has never had to make use of these sentimentalisms to prove his originality. Instead, he has contented himself with a parsimony of adjective (about four adjectives to a folio page is almost an exaggerated estimate); with the common speech meanings of nouns, their bareness their entire attraction; and, primarily (thanks to his study of the Chinese ideograph) with implicit metaphor present in simple verbs and their modifiers : (vide the examples quoted)—

'went toward,' 'cast her down'

'seeming clean'
'6 :30,' 'he trailed' 'sing'

Leaf *over* leaf
And the sea dark, *under* wind

In short, Pound has not wrapped mannerisms around his subject matter but made the subject matter his style. His archaisms vary with his subjects. Pound's objectivity and range are, therefore, his only identifications. He has not obtruded personally, never found it worth his while to discover an interesting subjective self to please people. One does not generally deplore sincere attempts at self-discovery but notes that Pound's objectivity in the *Cantos* is an excellent way of doing it. As philosopher in them he has avoided the merely playful appurtenances of thinking, that is, a pseudo-logical, argumentative ability in a kind of idiom which is not much more than mannerism.

(III.) Logopoeia

'The dance of the intelligence among words and ideas and modifications of ideas and characters.'

This aspect of poetry in the *Cantos* has already been discussed in the earlier part of this chapter under 'Dantesque ideation.' Without further divagation, it might be well merely to cite the remarkable example of the dramatic play on

Peace ! Keep the peace, Borso

                .   .   .

Peace !
                    Borso, . . . Borso !

                .   .   .

Keep the peace, Borso !

                                        Cantos 20 and 21

and the pages of modifications of ideas and character connected with this theme of keeping the peace.

                                        1929

HIM

Only Him and Me are real—Him, since he believes in himself and when he is told the audience is pretending his reality says in the coil of his tragedy, 'I wish I could believe this,' and Me, because she becomes next to the protagonist of the play solely through her relation with Him. And everything else is real:—the three Weirds—fiercely projectile, miasmic oppressions, animosities social and individual, of a fate-cluttered mind—the chameleonic Doctor so much the image of our times, the circus folk, the American language as she is spoke (oreye mush blige), the ballad of Frankie and Johnnie, the poem 'Look at Johnnie was a man,' to mention a few, real in so far as they are springing verve in the being of Him's instant Now. Not Pirandello, nor right you are if you think you are, is the question begged in this play, but rather what are you if you are. If you are—'nothing but the cordial revelation of the fatal reflexive' is Him's answer, and in the event of the last good for nothing but that. Somewhere else in the play Him says—'And nothing is death.'

Mr Cummings is, of course, Him, 'the hero of the play who is writing a play about a man who is writing a sort of play.' And Mr Cummings, like Him, is going somewhere. In the *Enormous Room* he gave us the hint where by titling one of his chapters 'The Delectable Mountains' (the delectable mountains of Bunyan's Pilgrim). He repeats the hint with the quotation on his title page: 'looking forward into the past or looking backward into the future I walk on the highest hills and I laugh about it all the way.' Mr Cummings, it appears, wishes to be saved from the Slough of Despond. He is not content to be the Marquis de la Poussière. Few writers since John Donne have been bitten as much as Mr Cummings by dust and epicene angleworms and the awake which must dissolve before the asleep, indeed because he desires to walk on the highest hills and laugh all about it. To entirely laugh (as Mr Cummings himself might write it) he has not succeeded. Says the Gentleman, 'are you one of those God damned artists?' And Him answers, 'No. That is, not exactly; I earn money by taming jellyfish.' As in *Is 5*, so in *Him,* Mr Cummings is not merely the perfect acrobat or the genius carefully, yet easily and very skillfully inhabiting everything which we really are and everything which we never quite live. His intention is not not to be serious, but to be very serious and to get away with it. In *Him,* Mr Cummings while aware that an artist, a man, a failure must proceed is also aware of himself and his struggle in the social milieu. When his age (give it twenty-five years or give it a hundred) is finally gone down escorted by its darkness or light or both, Mr Cummings' play should remain not only a fitting record of it but a conscious criticism.

This, for example, is not nonsense : 'If you wore your garters around your neck you'd change them oftener.' The words hit at the very heart of the social dungheap. And as a social critic Mr Cummings excels. Besides the conscience of Cummings' Gentleman, taking off his clothes in the snow because, having discovered what hunger is, he has just been born and will wear only what little babies wear, Ernst Toller's masses are theatrical strong stuff.

This, then, is the way Mr Cummings is, has been, going ever since *Tulips and Chimneys*, if one remembers his little lame balloon man whistling far and wee. And his art runs parallel. His is not (or at least very rarely and then unfortunately) the dreampistol of philosophy which goes off bang—into flowers and candy. In speech always exactly human because it is more human than we speak it, he manages one impossibility after another :—a play in the making which is a play; a stage which is black depth, yet which is filled with action; a room which has only three walls before which people move as though there were four; scenes which seem accidents yet carry out the plot existing as interior structure in the mind of Him; amorphousness which is really structural; nonsense which is morality, morality which is reductio ad absurdam; and disillusionment which is vision.

That Mr Cummings will himself walk the Delectable Mountains depends perhaps more on the times than on Mr Cummings. But the artist in him writes with all his five senses. 'Where I am I think it must be getting dark : I feel that everything is moving and mixing, with everything else.'

1927

HENRY ADAMS

A Criticism in Autobiography

PREFACE

These chapters on the writings of Henry Adams illustrate two actuating forces of his nature: poetic intellect is its continual undertow, and detached mind the strong surface current in the contrary direction. As this seems the developing action of a lifetime, a complete and chronologically arranged edition of Adams' works can be of great value for its description. No such edition exists; works that he published in the seventies and eighties, and even the *Life of George Cabot Lodge*, which appeared as late as 1911, are now out of print and forgotten.

Scholarship, in the present instance, could not prompt an unnecessary officiousness. The unpublished papers of Henry Adams, of which there must be enough to interest the sensitive and the intelligent, have not been sought out. Not so those once published anonymously and under a pseudonym.

The editor of the *North American*, asked if any of the unsigned reviews in the old numbers of his magazine had been written by Adams, cordially submitted a list of about twenty-five, all considerable in length.

The librarian of Harvard also sent photostats of a suppressed review of Taylor's *Faust* bearing this note in Adams' handwriting:

This notice, written originally by a strong admirer of Mr Taylor, but much changed by me in tone, led to a protest from the author, and a request from Mr Osgood that the notice should be suppressed. Which was done.

Henry Adams

One might have gone further and asked for photostats of Henry Adams' Class Oration of 1858, of his efforts in old Harvard College magazines, of his articles for the press. Adams, who was reserved, knew how to warn people. In 1908 he wrote to one of his 'nieces' :

You must not read what you call your book [The Education], because the Chartres is good enough for you, and me too, and the pigs all about.

Yet Adams' development as a writer reflects the process of education as he saw it in his autobiography. The autobiographical matter of *The Education* has, therefore, been quoted throughout this essay to offset the works as situations in 'the process.'

For the rest, these quotations assume that his attainment or non-attainment to power (clarity as to the futility of education and as to the meaning of 'something else') matters a great deal in relation to the treatment, which, as a writer, he gave these things.

I

Twenty (1860–65)

Henry Adams lived long and wrote well. He began, when he was ten, by reading proof of his great-grandfather's *Works*. Whether the boy, plying his task at the biddance of his father, was led astray by the anti-slavery politics of four mature gentlemen busy with him in the same room can perhaps never be known. The merit of the boy's literary venture was an exception to the approaching rule. 'In after years his father sometimes complained that, as a reader of Novanglus and Massachusettensis, Henry had shown very little consciousness of punctuation.'

'His brothers were the type; he was the variation.' The boy felt this instinctively. Detachment and the poet's receptivity for torment were part of him from the beginning. If Henry Adams had looked back and seen each incident in his life a parable of the Son forsaking the Mother to go about his Father's business, as in his 'Prayer to the Virgin,' he might have dwelt with less detachment than he did on his grandfather's act of leading the boy to school in spite of his desires.

The boy's body was a matter of sensitivity as all bodies are; his mind showed a lineage of worthies. It slaved over the works of John Adams because an Adams was his father and he, too, was an Adams. The tragedy was, here was a child possessing the moral sensitivity of his fathers; yet a child, whose clearness was not always in the possession of his moral sense, but in his enjoyments, his antics, his curiosity, his love of Scott, peaches and pears.

The tragedy may be exaggerated. The boy's mind may have been led to school in tears, but the tears may have dried while the boy considered how funny the mind of his grandfather was. 'On the whole,' wrote Adams, 'he learnt most then.' The early life was happy. Any prosaic soul, like the boy's father, could have declaimed with tremulous voice Wordsworth's 'Thou little Child' over Henry, who might have heard and not felt profound melancholy or pride, or even Henry Adams.

The boy went to Harvard when he was sixteen. 'He took to the pen. He wrote. The College Magazine printed his work, and the College Societies listened to his addresses. Lavish of praise, the readers were not; the audiences, too, listened in silence; but this was all the encouragement any Harvard collegian had a reasonable hope to receive; grave silence was a form of patience that meant possible future acceptance; and Henry Adams went on writing.'

No one cared enough to criticize, except himself who soon began to suffer from reaching his own limits. He found that he could not be this— or that—or the other; always precisely the things he wanted to be. He had not wit or scope or force. Judges always ranked him beneath a rival, if he had any; and he believed the judges were right. His work seemed to him thin, commonplace, feeble. At times he felt his own weakness so fatally that he could not go on; when he had nothing to say, he could not say it, and he found that he had very little to say at best. Much that he then wrote must be still in existence in print or manuscript, though he never cared to see it again; for he felt no doubt that it was in reality just what he thought it. At best it showed only a feeling for form; an instinct of exclusion. Nothing shocked—not even its weakness.

Adams was timid, and timidity often breaks into astonishing temerity. His Class Oration of 1858 was delivered with perfect self-possession. Whatever detachment Adams then possessed must have appeared in his speech and in his delivery; whatever poetry he had must have been plain in his features to those who cared to see it, if any did. A photograph taken at this time remains. The face is too young for lines. But the boy is, twenty, revealed in the lips and eyes.

Henry had a high, straight forehead, as well, though education had not begun. He was human and wanted to go to Europe. In Germany, Lowell had taught him, there was scholarship; in Germany, Adams believed, young men learned Civil Law. In Thüringen,

his three companions—John Bancroft, James J. Higginson, and B. W. Crowninshield, all Boston and Harvard College like himself, were satisfied with what they had seen, and when they sat down to rest on the spot where Goethe had written—

> 'Warte nur! balde
> —Ruhest du auch!'—

the profoundness of the thought and the wisdom of the advice affected them so strongly that they hired a wagon and drove to Weimar the same night.

In Germany foreign students took notes. Adams left for Rome.

Perhaps the most useful purpose he set himself to serve was that of his pen, for he wrote long letters, during the next three months, to his brother Charles, which his brother caused to be printed in the *Boston Courier*; and the exercise was good for him. He had little to say, and said it not very well, but that mattered less. The habit of expression leads to the search for something to express. Something remains as a residuum of the commonplace itself, if one strikes out every commonplace in the expression.

He went on to Naples, and there, in the hot June, heard rumors that Garibaldi and his thousand were about to attack Palermo. Calling on the American Minister, Chandler of Pennsylvania, he was kindly treated, not for his merit, but for his name, and Mr Chandler amiably consented to send him to the seat of war as bearer of despatches to Captain Palmer of the American sloop of war *Iroquois*. Young Adams seized the chance, and went to Palermo in a government transport filled with fleas, commanded by a charming Prince Caracciolo.

He told all about it to the *Boston Courier*, where the narrative probably exists to this day, unless the files of the *Courier* have wholly perished.

The files of the *Courier* are few. Of the seven letters of Adams to his brother Charles, the *American Historical Review* for January 1920 reprinted those of July 10 and July 13, 1860. They show that Henry had no difficulty as a writer. He could be picturesque when he desired, and he desired to be frequently :

I took a boat and landed. Numbers of men and boys, nearly all armed and looking very disreputable, were lounging and talking on the quay and round the Porta Felica. Here and there a red shirt showed itself. They make a very good uniform—rowdy but pugnacious; and now that Garibaldi has made them immortal, all young Sicily is putting them on, and swelling about in them almost as vulgarly, though more excusably, than New York firemen.

. . . we had a grand flea-hunt, for the beasts were all over us by dozens, and they were the biggest and hungriest specimens yet discovered. The *Illustrated News* correspondent, who was one of the party, is to make a sketch representing us dancing about and diving at each other's pantaloons. The officers' white duck showed the game beautifully, but our woolen ones only gave them shelter, and the consequence is that I am never free nor quiet, for my clothes bagged the most and concealed them the best.

He could express feeling that carried accents of restraint :

It was curious to see that night, how people can sleep. At about midnight, after finishing supper and smoking, and while every one was looking up their berths, I went forward to see how the soldiers managed to get along. They were lying all over the deck, tumbled down anywhere, and all snoring like hogs. They lay so thick and it was so dark that I trod on three or four who were in the way, but they did not mind it, and when the engineer, who was passing, kicked them out of the passage, they dragged themselves a few inches on one side, with a groan, but never woke up.

He reflected on the humors of human nature, as a Fielding writing another *Journal of a Voyage* might have done.

The next morning all was still, bright and clear. The poor soldiers' wives on deck looked very unhappy, and some, who had fine dark eyes, and pretty olive complexioned faces, looked so pale and patiently sad that they might have made beautiful studies for Magdalens and Madonnas. Certainly sea-sickness is one of the trials of life which bring us all down soonest to our common humanity; these women seemed absolutely refined by it, and their husbands and friends were as careful and gentle toward them as if they were all a set of refined and educated heroes and lovers.

Adams questioned early, in the manner of *The Education* :

And yet Heaven knows why he, of all men, has been selected for immortality. I, for one think that Cavour is much the greater man of the two; but practically the future Italy will probably adore Garibaldi's memory, and only respect Cavour's.

As he [Garibaldi] sat there laughing and chattering and wagging his red gray beard, and puffing away at his cigar, it seemed to me that one might feel for him all the respect and admiration that his best friends ask, and yet at the same time enter a protest against fate.

Not many months passed before Henry Adams again wrote letters to his brother, Charles. As private secretary to his father, to whom he referred as the 'chief,' and who was then ambassador to England, he observed British diplomacy, as he had observed Italian rebellion. The times were troubled ones for America; and news of the Union army in the States was not always assuring. Henry worried over the Declaration of Paris, and one thing or another, and London society was so monotonous at first that he longed for a commission and a chance to join Charles in the army. With time, however, he grew accustomed to his position, and, when opportunity offered, he wrote to Charles of other things than failure, British diplomacy and campaigns. He had really won his place in English society and seen Browning plain :

Browning went on to get into a very unorthodox humor, and developed a spiritual election that would shock the Pope, I fear. According to him, the minds or the souls that really did develop themselves and educate themselves in life, could alone expect to enter a future career for which this life was a preparatory course. The rest were rejected, turned back, God knows what becomes of them, these myriads of savages and brutalized and degraded Christians. Only those that could pass the examination were allowed to commence the new career. This is Calvin's theory, modified; and really it seems not unlikely to me. Thus this earth may serve as a sort of feeder to the next world, as the lower and middle classes here do to the aristocracy, here and there furnishing a member to fill the gaps. The corollaries of this proposition are amusing to work out. (from *A Cycle of Adams' Letters*, vol. 2, as the letters that follow)

Adams tried to work out many things. In the same year, 1863, he wrote:

I write and read, and read and write. Two years ago I began on history, our own time, I labored at financial theories, and branched out upon Political Economy and J. G. Mill. Mr Mill's works, thoroughly studied, led me to the examination of philosophy and the great French thinkers of our own time; they in their turn passed me over to others whose very names are now known only as terms of reproach by the vulgar; the monarchist Hobbes, the atheist Spinoza and so on. Where I shall end, dass weiss der liebe Gott! Probably my career will be brought up at the treadmill of the bar some day, for which, believe me, philosophy is as little adapted as war. Who will lead us back to the pleasant pastures and show us again the rich grain of the lawyer's office! Verily I say unto you, the time cometh and even now is when neither in these mountains nor in Jerusalem ye shall worship the idols of your childhood.

Did you ever read Arthur Clough's Poems? The man that wrote that pastoral with the unpronounceable name, the Bothie of Tober-na-Vuolich. If you have not, I would like to send them to you. Young England, young Europe, of which I am by tastes and education a part; the young world, I believe, in every live country, are reflected in Clough's poems very clearly.

Youth had not yet broken with the child and was best reflected in his own words:

The weeks dance away as merrily as ever they did in that dimly distant period when we were boys and you used to box my ears because your kite wouldn't fly and were the means of getting them boxed by disseminating at the tea-table truthless stories that I was painting myself a moustache with pear-juice—incidents of an early youth which you no doubt have forgotten, as I was the injured party, but which have remained deeply rooted in my associations with an ancient green-room called the dining room in a certain house on a hill. At the present day, life is a pretty dull affair, but it passes quick enough. Still, before I die I would like to have one more good time such as I knew in former areas of the earth's history . . .

II

The North American Review (1857–1876)

Henry Adams dearly loved to show facts bottoms up. This might be the key to all the essays which he published in the *North American*. His first contribution was made when Lowell was editor—an article which showed that John Smith was an excellent story-teller, but that Pocahontas never saved his head. Adams' researches no doubt stirred up a little revolution in history, but no school-teacher of his time ever heard of it, nor, judging from fact, has any guide of the young become edified since his time. The articles, 'British Finance in 1816' and 'The Bank of England,' which followed 'Captain John Smith,' made the point that England as financier in the past was by no means infallible, and suggested that the States during their straitened period of Reconstruction might take a hint from history.

Adams had in fact begun as antiquary. With his review of Lyell's *Principles of Geology* in 1868 he implied, to his friends around him, that he was ready to follow the current of his own time. Sir Charles gave Adams his field compass in token of his admiration. But Henry's mind was already admitting to himself that what attracted it was not evolution, but change. Still Lyell's appreciation was not in vain : Adams had presented the geologist's views in orderly fashion, at great length, and with gusto surprising for a study in uniformity.

Sir Charles wanders among the monotonous and flowerless forests of the coal-measures without saddening our spirits, and describes the enormous reptiles of the lias in language as calm and little sensational as though ichthyosauri were still gambolling in shoals along the banks of the Thames.

These articles enrolled him on the permanent staff of the *North American Review*. Precisely what this rank was worth, no one could say; but, for fifty years the *North American Review* had been the stage coach which carried literary Bostonians to such distinction as they had achieved. Few writers had ideas which warranted thirty pages of development, but for such as thought they had, the *Review* alone offered space. An article was a small volume which required at least three months' work, and was paid, at best, five dollars a page. Not many men even in England or France could write a good thirty-page article, and practically no one in America read them; but a few score of people mostly in search of items to steal, ran over the pages to extract an idea or a fact, which was a sort of wild game —a blue fish or a teal—worth anything from fifty cents to five dollars. Newspaper writers had their eye on quarterly pickings. The circulation of the *Review* had never exceeded three or four hundred copies, and the *Review* had never paid its reasonable expenses. Yet it stood at the head of American literary periodicals; it was a source of suggestion to cheaper workers; it reached far into societies that never knew its existence; it was an organ worth playing on; and in the fancy of Henry Adams, it led, in some indistinct future, to playing on a New York daily newspaper.

The *North American* led to nothing of the kind. Adams wrote his reviews of Grant's administration—several articles which ran under the name of 'The Session,' his 'Civil Service Reform,' all full of facts, which were never popular, and brilliant with the spirit of reform. He criticized the administration so successfully that one of the 'Session's' was reprinted by the Democratic National Committee and circulated as a campaign document by the hundred thousand copies. Not even a Senator's insult of likening Adams to a begonia stopped Adams' political pyrotechnics. He criticized the legal tender act, and revealed the New York gold conspiracy of Jay Gould and James Fisk to the *Westminster Review*. The facts of the matter no longer interest anyone, except historians, but Adams' picture of the American Aladdin in his palace was a *tour de force* :

The atmosphere of the Erie offices was not supposed to be disturbed with moral prejudices; and as the opera itself supplied Mr Fisk's mind with amusement, so the opera *troupe* supplied him with a permanent harem. Whatever Mr Fisk did was done on an extraordinary scale. (*Chapters of Erie*)

Henry might have continued in this gay manner, but his family interposed and decided that Harvard needed him in its folds again. 'His function was not to be that of teacher, but that of editing the *Review* which was to be coupled with the professorship. Adams did not see much reason in changing his course of action; yet he joined Lowell as co-editor of the *Review* in October, 1870.

The editor had barely time to edit; he had none to write. If copy fell short, he was obliged to scribble a book-review on the virtues of the Anglo-Saxons or the vices of the Popes; . . . for seven years he wrote nothing.

Adams was far from kind to himself in *The Education*. The editorship of the *Review* was by no means a holiday, though it must have been a literary one. Without signing his name to his articles he reviewed every historian that came in the form of a book to his desk—Freeman, Stubbs, Kitchen, Parkman, Van Holst, Bancroft, Green; every work on early law and custom, whether Maine's, Sohm's or Coulange's. In the case of a work like Sohm's *Procédure de la lex Salica,* a foreign product, Adams translated liberally, to explain the author's position.

Occasionally Adams went out of his historical field to comment shortly on the *Saturday Review*. Or Clarke's *Building of a Brain* interested him enough to make him express an opinion which he made much of in his *Education* :

In order that the family should exist at all, two individuals were necessary to it. And unless children are to be afterwards reared and educated like chickens in an Egyptian oven upon Phalansterian principles, it is impossible to escape division of labor as an inevitable sequence in their care and education. Female education must be moulded to meet this inevitable contingency, and in point of view, our female education, mental as well as physical, is often a lamentable failure.

Adams' literary holiday especially deserved its epithet when he reviewed Howells' *Wedding Journey*, Palgrave's *Poems* and Tennyson's *Queen Mary*. Noticing that Palgrave in his 'Alcestis' subdued passion to rhetorical form, Adams ventured a comment which American 'Classicists,' past and present, must find disturbing :

Neither Euripides nor Sophocles would have cared to throw the treatment of 'Alcestis' into a mould which was difficult for their countrymen to appreciate, and if they had done so, the sense of effort would have taught them and their audience that they were following an unnatural process. And so with Mr Palgrave and with all the other poets, great and small, who have imitated the Greeks; as studies, their work is no doubt not only valuable but necessary to high excellence; as poems one might almost say that the greater the success the greater is the failure : the closer the copy the more obvious is the *tour de force*.

On Tennyson, he was fifty years ahead of the sanest criticism of fifty years later.

If Queen Mary is, as has been said, not a subject for high tragical interest, it was for Mr Tennyson to overcome that difficulty or abandon the subject. It must be acknowledged that the difficulty is not overcome. The drama embodies no profoundly tragical human interest or passion. The Queen Mary of this play is the Queen Mary of history, essentially prosaic even in her most exalted or depressed moments. Mr Tennyson has added nothing to the thought, such as it was, that history furnished to him. He has not elevated it, he has not intensified it, he has not even suppressed the pettiness of it.

Adams summed up his argument and found Tennyson not the master of thought the age cherished, but a singer of delicacies:

> Shame upon you, Robin
> Shame upon you now!
> Kiss me would you? with my hands
> Milking the cow?

Adams stopped writing for the *Review* in 1876. The October number of that year contained an interesting publisher's notice:

The editors of the *North American Review* having retired from its management on account of a difference of opinion with the proprietors as to the political character of this number, the proprietors, rather than cause an indefinite delay in publication have allowed the number to retain the form which had been given to it, without, however, committing the *Review* to the opinions expressed therein.

The editors who had resigned were Henry Adams and Henry Cabot Lodge.

III

Cambridge (1870–1877)

Adams found six years sufficient time to spend on the *North American*, and he left Harvard at the end of seven. A professor has literary duties, besides his boys, to take care of. Adams prepared himself for his definitive work on American history; he began with the remote past and delivered a lecture titled 'Primitive Rights of Women,' which he later revised and printed in a book of historical essays. The paper denied that early woman under early institutions had been a slave. As Adams revealed her she held a high place in primitive society; her attractive force and strength had made the family an institution.

As early as 1876 he had found a theme which was to become a passion with him in after years.

On the whole, Harvard left little time for writing. Adams included one essay of his own in a volume on Anglo-Saxon Law which he edited. His essay effected a compact manual of English Law from the earliest times to Edward the Confessor. Adams amused himself with the discovery that his ancestors were sensible enough in legal procedure to accept 'the informal decision of their friends.'

He cited the names of German professors, intentionally, or unintentionally, but so graciously that they immediately became humorous: 'Nevertheless, it must be conceded that, even here, Dr Schmidt is, at least technically, correct.' The essay gave the impression of precise phraseology and order of thought—two prerequisites not the least important for a poet; and of hidden paradox not in the least to be dispensed with by a wit.

Documents Relating to New-England Federalism, 1800–1815 was Adams' final work at Harvard. Though the volume had no apparent controversial purpose—it was a work of pure editing, with a very limited number of notes—it did much to appraise the importance in American history of John Quincy Adams' 'Reply to the Appeal of the Massachusetts Federalists' by publishing it.

There Adams' task at Harvard ended. He did not need to teach and edit to live; and since he had married in 1872 and the society of Washington was more alluring than that of either Boston or Cambridge, he wrote an epitaph for the professor:

HIC JACET
HOMUNCULUS SCRIPTOR
DOCTOR BARBARICUS
HENRICUS ADAMS
ADAE FILIUS ET EVAE
PRIMO EXPLICUIT
SOCNAM

IV

An American Plutarch (1879–1884)

In Washington, with his work on American history during the times of Jefferson and Madison still in view, Adams pursued his researches diligently and invented prolifically. He edited three large volumes of Albert Gallatin's writings, and wrote a voluminous life of him; he also wrote a life of John Randolph; and, finally, an article, in French, which he later translated and reprinted, on Napoleon I at St Domingo. Adams' French was perfectly clear as might have been expected; the article said nothing of Napoleon and Toussaint l'Ouverture that he was not to repeat in a chapter of his *History*.

The contrast in styles between the *Albert Gallatin* and the *John Randolph* volumes was striking. The *Life of Gallatin* was more than half quotation; Adams' contributions to the study of the life were the barest facts, though these were many; there was no ornament; emotion was reticent; a very sedate man seemed to be back of all. The *Life of Randolph* quoted less; the facts were there, but fewer, and arranged for effect; emotion was more candid and often gave itself to rigorous judgment; a brilliant satire seemed to be the main intention.

In the *Gallatin* humor was often achieved by quotation, as from Voltaire's note to Gallatin's mother : 'Vos figues, madame, sont un présent d'autant plus beau que nous pouvons dire comme l'autre : car ce n'était pas le temps des figues.' In the *Randolph* humor served a direct purpose; the joke had to be on John Randolph; the effect was often wrenched through a juxtaposition of words—'Henceforward the little Randolphs ran wild at Bizarre.' A different approach to each life was immediately apparent, though Adams may have had no contrast in mind.

It has been said that Adams shared a family prejudice toward John Randolph; and it was true that Henry Adams could not have been very sympathetic towards a professed *ami des noirs*, who kept slaves all his life. This does not entirely account for the captious tone of the volume. For that matter, Federalism was also rooted in Adams' nature. He might have been as captious about Gallatin—secretary of the treasury under Jefferson.

Adams had a rare type of mind. To it a poet's religion remained apart from the expression of that religion, and the poet was criticized for the expression; a statesman's personal character was judged by the historian only as it affected his statesmanship. In private, John Randolph might have been the Bacchus of Virginia; the historian gave no serious thought to this side of the man. But when John Randolph showed the statesmanship of a man on a drunken carousal, on the floor of the House, the historian had a serious reason for judgment. Like the

Hellenes, Adams looked upon virtue not as goodness, but as virtuosity, the mastery of an art. Historians for the most part agree that Albert Gallatin's well-considered ideas on finance, his foreign predilection for saying things clearly, were politically superior to John Randolph's oratory. Adams' method and aim were especially clear in the last lines of each biography. He concludes the portrait of Gallatin :

his life had left no traces to be erased, and his death would create no confusion and required no long or laborious forethought. He had felt a certain pride in his modest means; his avowed principle had been that a Secretary of the Treasury should not acquire wealth. He had no enemies to forgive.

The last lines on Randolph follow in contrast :

Neither sickness nor suffering, however, is an excuse for habitual want of self-restraint. Myriads of other men have suffered as much without showing it in brutality or bitterness, and he himself never in his candid moments pretended to defend his errors : 'Time misspent, and faculties misemployed, and senses jaded by labor or impaired by excess, cannot be recalled.'

As a historian Henry Adams was unbiased. That in private life he may have felt whoever thought in French to be clear, and, on the contrary, whoever walked in high boots and was lank to be grotesque, was a personal matter.

v

'The Five of Hearts' (1880–1884)

'The Five of Hearts' lived in Washington, and they were Clarence King, Hay and his wife, and the Adamses. In 1884 Adams joined Hay in employing H. R. Richardson to build them adjoining houses on La Fayette Square.

Nowhere in the United States was there then, or has there since been, such a *salon* as theirs [the Adamses']. Sooner or later, everybody who possessed real quality crossed the threshold of 1603 H Street. Host and hostess were fastidious, and only the select came to them. Mr Adams sought nobody out; he regarded himself as solitary, and knew very well that official Washington cared nothing for him, and little enough for the intellectual sphere in which he lived . . . To his intimates—and these included women of wit and charm and distinction—the hours spent in his study or at his table were the best that Washington could give. (Thayer, *Life and Letters of John Hay*, vol. 2)

Out of this society came the novels, the anonymous *Democracy* in 1880, and *Esther* in 1884, which was published under the pseudonym of Frances Snow Compton.

In his novels Adams began with a theme. Like many English writers—Pope, Blake, Wordsworth, Shaw—Adams risked the inclusion of contemporary material which might become musty with time. *Democracy*, like his articles, the 'Session' and 'Civil Service Reform,' exposed the meager substance of the democratic ideal; *Esther* revealed the superficialities of fashionable religion.

The theme of *Democracy* took up the first chapter :
For reasons which many persons thought ridiculous, Mrs Lightfoot Lee decided to pass the winter in Washington . . . She wanted to see with her own eyes the action of primary forces; to touch with her own hand the massive machinery of society; to measure with her own mind the capacity of the motive power. She was bent upon getting to the heart of the great American mystery of democracy and government.

Esther, as well, immediately considered its problem :

The new Church of St John's, on Fifth Avenue, was thronged the morning of the last Sunday of October, in the year 1880. Sitting in the gallery, beneath the unfinished frescoes, and looking down the nave, one caught an effect of autumn gardens, a suggestion of chrysanthemums and geraniums, or of October woods, dashed with scarlet oaks and yellow maples. As a display of austerity the show was a failure, but if cheerful content and innocent adornment please the Author of the lilies and roses, there was reason to hope that this first service at St John's found favor in His sight, even though it showed no victory over the world or the flesh in this part of the United States. The sun came through the figure of St John in his crimson and green garments of glass, and scattered more color where colors already rivaled the flowers of a prize show; while huge prophets and evangelists in flowing robes looked down from the red walls on a display of

human vanities that would have called out a vehement Lamentation of
Jeremiah or Song of Solomon had these poets been present in flesh as
they were in figure.

Solomon was a brilliant but not an accurate observer; he looked at
the world from the narrow stand-point of his own temple. Here in New
York he could not have truthfully said that all was vanity, for even a
more ill-natured satirist than he must have confessed that there was in
this new temple today a perceptible interest in religion. One might almost
have said that religion seemed to be a matter of concern. The audience
wore a look of interest, and even after their first gaze of admiration and
whispered criticism at the splendors of their new church, when at length
the clergyman entered to begin the service, a ripple of excitement swept
across the field of bonnets until there was almost a murmur as of rustling
cornfields within the many colored walls of St John's.

The Clergyman, Mr Hazard,

took possession of his flock with a general advertisement that he owned
every sheep in it, white or black, and to show that there could be no doubt
on the matter he added a general claim to the right of property in all
mankind and the universe . . . After sweeping all human thought and will
into his strongbox, he shut down the lid with a sharp click, and bade his
audience kneel . . . 'And how did it suit you, Esther?'
  'I am charmed,' replied his daughter, 'only it certainly does come
just a little near being an opera-house. Mr Hazard looks horribly like
Meyerbeer's Prophet.'

The plots follow out the settings. In *Democracy*, Mrs Lee comes
near being a sacrifice to the corruption of representative government in
the form of Senator Ratcliffe; in *Esther*, Miss Dudley is almost an
Iphigenia offered to the religious knife of Reverend Hazard. The action
centers on the women.
  'Adams owed more to the American woman than to all the
American men he ever heard of.' Yet sometimes, at dinner, he

might wait till talk flagged, and then, as mildly as possible, ask one's
liveliest neighbor whether she could explain why the American woman
was a failure . . . The cleverer the woman, the less she denied the failure.
She was bitter at heart about it. She had failed even to hold the family to-

gether, and her children ran away like chickens with their first feathers; the family was extinct like chivalry. The American woman at her best— like most other women—exerted great charm on the man, but not the charm of a primitive type. She appeared as the result of a long series of discards, and her chief interest lay in what she had discarded.

In any previous age, sex was strength. Neither art nor beauty was needed. Every one, even among Puritans, knew that neither Diana of the Ephesians nor any of the oriental goddesses was worshipped for her beauty. She was goddess because of her force; she was the animated dynamo; she was reproduction—the greatest and most mysterious of all energies; all she needed was to be fecund.

Mrs Lightfoot Lee and Esther Dudley were American women and failures. To Adams they were almost as great failures as himself. The worthwhile women in America Adams suggested in the young, buoyant types of Sybil Ross in *Democracy* and Catherine Brooke in *Esther*. They had, at least, something of Laura, St Cecilia, something of the luxurious-ness of 'L'Aube, Mois du Juin.' Madeline Lee, on the other hand,

cared little where her pursuit might lead her, for she put no extravagant value upon life, having already, as she said, exhausted at least two lives, and being fairly hardened to insensibility in the process. 'To lose a hus-band and a baby,' said she, 'and keep one's courage and reason, one must become very hard or very soft. I am now pure steel. You may beat my heart with a trip-hammer and it will beat the trip-hammer back again.'

And Esther for an American Virgin is quite hopeless. While she combs her hair she looks out through a window upon Niagara : Force and an understanding of immortality strike her with great suddenness —'immortality is a sort of great reservoir of truth, and what is true in us just pours into it like raindrops.' Adams himself could not have expressed it any better in the scientific deviousness of his *Education*. His women characters are brilliant, profound, but they escape marriage.

The novels were disillusioned. Disillusion often gave free reign to most sensitive expression :

Esther was now twenty-five years old, and for fifteen years had been absolute mistress of her father's house.

So she went to her bed, in the cold, gray dawn of a winter's day, with the tears still running down her face. When she awoke again the day was already waning, a dripping wasting thaw, where smoking and soot-defiled snow added sadness to the sad sky.

After her father's death, Esther, to forget, goes to the children's hospital; the children request stories: 'She took her old seat and looked through the yellow eyes of the fire-dogs for inspiration.'

She felt quite sure, by a sudden flash of feminine inspiration, that the curious look of patient endurance on his face was the work of a single night when he had held his brother in his arms, and knew that the blood was draining drop by drop from his side, in the dense, tangled woods, be-yond the reach of help, hour after hour, till the voice failed and the limbs grew stiff and cold. When he had finished his story, she was afraid to speak.

In February the weather became warmer and summerlike. In Vir-ginia there comes often at this season a deceptive gleam of summer, slip-ping in between heavy storm-clouds of sleet and snow; days and some-times weeks when the earliest plants begin to show their hardy flowers, and when the bare branches of the forest trees alone protest against the conduct of the seasons.

On the whole, however, the novels meant to be charmingly gay. Adams was no Dostoyevsky, seeking character under guise on guise of passionate attitude. Neither did he, like Henry James, make an aesthetic of manners and character. His people were by all means the choicest, but he did not trouble to explain why each one of them spoke in his own way. Adams just had them speak as he had heard them. Count Popoff:

'Mees Ross,' said Count Popoff, leading in a handsome young foreigner, 'I have your permission to present to you my friend, Count Orsini, Sec-retary of the Italian Legation. Are you at home this afternoon? Count Orsini sings also.'

Adams suggested parables in a name: Mr Hartbeest Schneide-koupon, Senator Nathan Gore from Massachusetts, Senator Silas P. Ratcliffe from Illinois, Miss Virginia Dare, Lord Skye, George Hazard. *Democracy*, in its description of the fête given by the society of Washington to the Grand-Duke and Duchess of Saxe-Baden-Hombourg, rivals the lightning grace of a Max Beerbohm.

The 'Five of Hearts' must have gloried in Adams' wit—especially in the success he attained in Sybil's letter to Carrington :

I read Mr Browning's 'Last Ride Together,' as you told me; I think it's beautiful and perfectly easy, all but a little. I never could understand a word of him before—so I never tried. Who do you think is engaged? Victoria Dare, to a coronet and peatbog, with Lord Dunbeg attached. Victoria says she is happier than she ever was before in any of her other engagements, and she is sure this is the real one. She says she has thirty thousand a year derived from the poor of America, which may just as well go to relieve the poor of Ireland. You know her father was a claim agent, or some such thing, and is said to have made his money by cheating his clients out of their claims. She is perfectly wild to be a countess, and means to make Castle Dunbeg lovely by-and-by and entertain us all there. Madeleine says she is just the kind to be a great success in London. Madeleine is very well, and sends her regards. I believe she is going to add a postscript. I have promised to let her read this, but I don't think a chaperoned letter is much fun to write or receive. Hoping to hear from you soon,

Sincerely yours,
Sybil Ross.

Henry Adams was happy then. The nieces remember him and their aunt and the summer house in the Beverly woods.

Often in the afternoons, the nieces would watch—almost enviously—the two figures on horseback vanishing into the flickering sunlight of the woods. An impression of oneness of life and mind, of perfect companionship, left an ideal never to be effaced.

VI

The History (1880–1891)

Mabel La Farge pursues the story of the happiest days :

At that time he was writing his *History*; hours of concentration were passed in his den and sheets on sheets of beautifully written pages lay beside him. One could not forget that handwriting. Each letter seemed to be carved rather than written, and the effect of the whole page was that of an interlacing Byzantine design, but perfectly clear to read. The nieces remember him as he sat at his desk, in cool white summer clothes—his fine head and thoughtful forehead dominated a small frame; his movements were deliberate—only the scratch of his pen would break the silence of the room, until the delicious moment came when he would stop, and turn to them with an irresistibly droll remark. (*Letters to a Niece*)

Adams, also, reconsidered the *History* in his *Education* :

Adams had given ten or a dozen years to Jefferson and Madison, with expenses which, in any mercantile business, could hardly have been reckoned at less than a hundred thousand dollars, on a salary of five thousand a year; and when he asked what return he got from this expenditure, rather more extravagant in proportion to his means than a racing-stable, he could see none whatever.

The History of the United States during the Administrations of Jefferson and Madison, in nine volumes of over four thousand pages, easily placed Henry Adams among such American historians of rank as Prescott and Parkman. For impartial judgment, for literary power that can turn documentary research to useful reflection and absorbing story, authorities, like Worthington Chauncey Ford, Carl Becker, Henry Osborn Taylor, think it unrivaled. John Hay informally averred that the volumes on the first administration of Madison (5 and 6) 'took the cake. The style is perfect, if perfect is a proper word applied to anything so vivid, so flexible and so powerful. I never expected to read anything which would give me so much pleasure.' Hay never expected Adams to get the Loubat Prize, and wondered 'that Columbia College could have done so evidently sensible a thing.'

The general reader will perhaps give 'the cake' to the introduction —(volume I—chapters 1–6) which consists of the chapters, Physical and Economical Conditions, Popular Characteristics, Intellect of New England, Intellect of the Middle States, Intellect of the Southern States, and American Ideals. The preliminary is at once broadly descriptive and specific, and throughout once a picture is presented it stays in mind :

Nature was rather man's master than his servant, and the five million Americans struggling with the untamed continent seemed hardly more

competent to their task than the beavers and buffalo which had for countless generations made bridges and roads of their own.

A traveller on the levee at Natchez, in 1808, overheard a quarrel in a
flatboat near by : 'I am a man; I am a horse; I am a team,' cried one
voice; 'I can whip any man in all Kentucky, by God !' 'I am an alligator,'
cried the other, 'half man, half horse; can whip any man on the Mississippi, by God !' 'I am a man,' shouted the first; 'I have the best horse, best
dog, best gun, and handsomest wife in all Kentucky, by God !' 'I am a
Mississippi snapping-turtle,' joined the second, 'I have bear's claws, alligator's teeth, and the devil's tail; can whip *any* man, by God !'

Moore was but an echo of fashionable England in his day. He seldom
affected moral sublimity; and had he in his wanderings met a race of
embodied angels, he would have sung of them or to them in the slightly
erotic notes which were so well received in the society he loved to frequent
and flatter.

Most picturesque of all figures in modern history, Napoleon Bona-
parte, like Milton's Satan on his throne of state, although surrounded by
a group of figures little less striking than himself, sat unapproachable on
his bad eminence; or, when he moved, the dusky air felt an unusual
weight. His conduct was often mysterious, and sometimes so arbitrary
as to seem insane; but later years have thrown on it a lurid illumination.
(vol. 1)

Passage after passage must be quoted to give an adequate idea of the
sentence rhythm, which always meets the subject with a master's grace.
Poetry, in the simple direct phrasing, is concentrate :

The poor came, and from them were seldom heard complaints of decep-
tion or delusion. . . . A week afterward Jefferson quitted Washington
forever. On horseback, over roads impassable to wheels, through snow
and storm, he hurried back to Monticello to recover in the quiet of home
the peace of mind he had lost in disappointments of statesmanship. He
arrived at Monticello March 15 and never passed beyond the bounds of
a few adjacent counties. (vols. 1, 4)

Humor is abundant, especially in portraiture. Jefferson, who was
sensitive, affectionate, heroic, in his own eyes, and more refined than

many women in the delicacy of his private relations, again sits on one hip. John Marshall's calm is Rhadamanthine. Napoleon in his bath overrules his brothers on the Louisiana treaty. When the British fleet steamed up the Potomac, 'the House of Representatives ordered a fast and went into secret session to consider modes of defence.' As Adams said of Irving's *History of New York*: it is hard to burlesque without vulgarizing, and to satirize without malignity. Adams succeeded in doing both.

The direction of the entire work is not only American; it is international. It is not only a progression of great narratives that embraces the Napoleonic Wars, the growth of America from the backwoods to the beginning of industrialism, but it is specific in many branches of knowledge—law, finance, sociology, American literature in the early eighteen hundreds. Yet, after all this mass of detail, the ninth volume ends on a number of questions:

The traits of American character were fixed; the rate of physical and economic growth was established; and history, certain that at a given distance of time the Union would contain so many millions of people, with wealth valued at so many millions of dollars, became thenceforward chiefly concerned to know what kind of people these millions were to be. They were intelligent, but what paths would their intelligence select? They were quick, but what solution of insoluble problems would quickness hurry? They were scientific, and what control would their science exercise over their destiny? They were mild, but what corruptions would their relaxations bring? They were peaceful, but by what machinery were their corruptions to be purged? What interests were to vivify a society so vast and uniform? What ideals were to ennoble it? What object besides physical content must a democratic continent aspire to attain?

Adams wrote the *History* during the happy years, suggesting desirable answers in his questions. The *History* is a presentation of facts. No philosophy controls them; no science that indicates a 'decline and fall.' The last was perhaps not in the nature of Adams' subject.

'Art,' says Delacroix, 'is exaggeration in the right place.' In his *History*, Adams did not exaggerate. But by the time he came to publish it, the happy years were gone. The *History* seemed a worthless labor.

Always, to Adams, education, brought face to face with friendship, as when he met Clarence King, was no longer possible. And before Nature—

the human mind felt itself stripped naked, vibrating in a void of shape-less energies, with resistless mass, colliding, crushing, wasting, and des-troying what these same energies had created and labored from eternity to perfect . . . Flung suddenly in his face, with the harsh brutality of chance, the terror of the blow stayed by him thenceforth for life, until repetition made it more than the will could struggle with; more than he could call on himself to bear.

VII

December 6, 1885

When John Hay heard that his friend's wife had died, he wrote to him:

You and your wife were more to me than any other two. I came to Wash-ington because you were there. And now this goodly fellowship is broken up forever. I cannot force on a man like you the commonplaces of con-dolence . . . You have a great sorrow, but no man should bear sorrow bet-ter than you.

Adams lived it all through, but ever so silently. He might imply that his life had been a broken arch, but he felt repose and self-restraint as nothing else. Leaving art to make the best of death in a monument at Rock Creek, Adams went on submissive. To the heart, at least, infinite peace meant something.

Adams' world lay all before him. His best works were yet to be written. Still, to the sensitive with whom great contacts were few, and these a very quiet matter, the greatest was never to be recorded.

VIII

Wanderings (1890–1904)

Sorrow set Henry Adams wandering—to the South Seas—to Aus-tralia, Ceylon, Egypt. He sent back letters to his niece, full of humor through his tears, as it were. The letters of themselves often made little tender stories moving with the simple narrative genius of a Tolstoy:

The canoe is a dug-out; the trunk of a tree, chopped out with an adze, and held steady by a rough outrigger which rests on the water. With me alone in it, the boat is very steady, and rides easily on any breaker that is not so high as to flop over the edge. When two persons are in it, especially when they are large, the canoe is not so steady, as I found out yesterday when I took La Farge out for the first time. Then I could do nothing with it. The wind and current were strong and the wretched canoe would not head any way but broadside to the current. Still we drifted down to the harbor point, to see the sunset and then paddled back. Suddenly, without apparent cause, the canoe slowly leaned over, and tipped us both into the water. The water was not a foot deep, and I might just as well have stepped out, for I always go barefoot on the water, with linen trousers rolled to my knees; but the thing did it so gently that I was too late, and I am still wondering why it should have chosen that instant, rather than any other, to play us such a trick. Anyway, both La Farge and I were soused in the water, and we were just opposite the British Consulate, on a Sunday afternoon. Some little girls, about Molly's age or size, who were playing on the beach, laughed uproariously at us, and then ran out, crying in Samoan, 'Wait, Akamu'—that's my name, Akamu, Atamu, Adam, out of their Bible—and very soon swashed the water out of the canoe and set us going again, shoving us along through the water. (*Letters to a Niece*)

The year 1892 found Adams again in London, this time in a hospital. After his recovery he sailed for home.

His first step, on returning to Washington, took him out to the cemetery known as Rock Creek, to see the bronze figure which St Gaudens had made for him in his absence . . . He supposed its meaning to be the one commonplace about it—the oldest idea known to human thought . . . The interest of the figure was not in its meaning, but in the response of the observer. As Adams sat there, numbers of people came, for the figure seemed to have become a tourist fashion, and all wanted to know its meaning. Most took it for a portrait-statue, and the remnant were vacant-minded in the absence of a personal guide. None felt what would have been a nursery-instinct to a Hindu baby or a Japanese jinricksha-runner. The only exceptions were the clergy, who taught a lesson even deeper. One after another brought companions there, and, apparently fascinated by their own reflection, broke out passionately against the expression they felt in the figure of despair, of atheism, of denial. Like the others, the priest saw only what he brought. Like all great artists, St Gaudens held up the mirror and no more. The American laymen had lost sight of ideals; the American priest had lost sight of faith. Both were more American than the old, half-witted soldiers who denounced the wasting, on a mere grave, of money which should have been given for drink.

The East still drew Adams and he would rather have gone back, if 'only to sleep forever in the trade-winds under the southern stars, wandering over the dark purple ocean, with its purple sense of solitude and void.' But he went on to Chicago, to study the Exposition. '. . . possibly, if relations enough could be observed, this point might be fixed.'

From Guada'-C-Jara, on December 12, 1894, he sent a tentative communication, to the American Historical Society, now known as 'The Tendency of History.' 'Evidently I am fitted only to be an absent president,' he wrote, 'and you will pardon a defect which is clearly not official, but a condition of the man.'

And, some months later, he wrote to John Hay :

Once La Farge and I, on our rambles, stopped for an hour to meditate under the sacred Bo-tree of Buddha in the ruined and deserted city of Amuradjapura in the jungle of Ceylon; and, then, resuming our course, we presently found ourselves on the quiet bosom of the Indian Ocean. Perhaps I was a little bored by the calm of the tropical sea, or perhaps it was the greater calm of Buddha that bored me. At all events I amused a tedious day or two by jotting down in a notebook the lines which you profess to want. They are yours. Do not let them go further.

Adams had resorted to verse—presumably not his métier :

> The Buddha, known to men by many names—
> Siddartha, Sakya Muni, Blessed One—
> Sat in the forest, as had been his wont
> These many years since he attained perfection;
> In silent thought, abstraction, purity,
> His eyes fixed on the Lotus in his hand,
> He meditated on the perfect Life,
> While his disciples, sitting round him, waited
> His words of teaching, every syllable
> More and more precious as the Master gently
> Warned them how near was come his day of parting.
> In silence, as the Master gave example,
> They meditated on the Path and Law,
> Till one, Malunka, looking up and speaking,
> Said to Buddha : 'O Omniscient One,
> Teach us, if such be in the Perfect Way,
> Whether the World exists eternally.'

Buddhas take long in answering and in the end they merely bend their eyes to fix them upon the Lotus. Ironically, to Adams who contemplated all his life, a young man found himself in the far more practical Brahman, whose entire wisdom lay in three words : Think not ! Strike ! The young Henry Adams had learned this was education; the practical life was to remain part of him until the end. After all—according to the Veda—the beginning contained the end; the universal had no limit. In the end, all Thought was identical; travelling through constant contradictions it returned upon itself in silence. The fates of Buddha and the Brahman were not essentially different :

> Your master, you, and I, all wise men,
> Have one sole purpose which we never lose :
> Through different paths we each seek to attain,
> Sooner or later, as our paths allow,
> A perfect union with the single Spirit.
> Gautama's way is best, but all are good.
> He breaks a path at once to what he seeks.
> By silence and absorption he unites
> His soul with the great soul from which it started.
> But we, who cannot fly the world, must seek
> To live two separate lives; one, in the world
> Which we must ever seem to treat as real;
> The other in ourselves, behind a veil
> Not to be raised without disturbing both.

Adams accepted the concept of necessity, so as not to perish among the follies of his own reflection. When he returned to the world he needed, as he wrote, no noble way to teach him freedom amid slaves; no Lotus to love purity.

In Paris, in 1901, he lingered over memories of his recent experiences. He had been adopted in Tahiti into the principal clan by the old chiefess, and given the native name of Taura Atua. The old queen had been kind to him and in a letter Adams remembered her as pure native who spoke no foreign language.

She is sixty-eight years old and refuses to sit at table with us but sits on the floor in the old native way, and is a very great person indeed. In the evenings we lay down on the mats about her, and she told us of the old Tahiti people, who were much more interesting than now. She told us, too, long native legends about wonderful princesses and princes, who did astonishing things in astonishing ways, like Polynesian Arabian nights. (*Letters to a Niece*)

Adams wrote down these legends, and printed them, in a private publication called *Tahiti*, as the memoirs of Arii Taimai, afterwards Mrs Salmon. The style of the book was purposely ingenuous, but the work was more than translation. It was a romantic history, written perhaps at Hay's suggestion of 1890: 'I have just read Daudet's "Port Tarascon." It is his definite Waterloo—everything is manqué. Now is your chance. Do a South Sea book, comme il n'y en a pas. It is a felt want.'

Adams' mind revelled in a society where women, under 'primitive' institutions, shared equal sovereignty with men; where they not only caused wars but directed them. In Harvard, and as editor of the *North American*, he had read widely in works of anthropology; but he had perhaps never dreamt of studying, at close range, a society as old as India; a people, subject to the intoxication of Kava, moving in canoes through shallow waters, quarreling over its women, white of skin and round of figure. Adams mastered poems and legends, and rendered each with the proper sentiment of phrase and cadence :

'Teva the rain, Teva the wind
Teva the roe, the roe dear to Ahurei.'

I suppose it means that Teva is strong and swift like the rain and wind, and numerous like the roe of fish; but I do not know why Ahurei loved fish-roe.

This visitor, our first ancestor, was what Europeans call a demi-god; he was only half human; the other half was fish, or shark-god; and he swam from the ocean, through the reef, into the Vaihiria river, where he came ashore, and introduced himself as Vari Mataauhoe. The chiefess received him with the hospitality which was common to the legends of most oriental races, and Vari Mataauhoe took up his residence with Hototu; but after their intimacy had lasted some time, one day, when they were together, Hototu's dog came into the house and showed his affection for his mistress by licking her face, or, as we should say, kissing her, although in those days the word was unknown, for Polynesians never kissed each other, but only touched noses as an affectionate greeting. At this, the man-shark fell into a mood of reflection, and after turning the subject in his mind, decided that the fault was so grave as to require him, as a person of refinement, to abandon Hototu : 'You have been untrue to your husband with me,' he told her, 'you may be untrue to me with the dog.'

A boy was born, and, as foretold, in rain and wind.

The husband's pride of generosity overcomes his desire for vengeance, and he gives his wife away to her lover : 'Take, then, your wife! Taurua, my friend! We are separated, she and I! Taurua, the morning star to me. For her beauty I would die. You were mine, but now—take, then, Taurua! my friend! we are separated! She and I!'

Adams also rendered Aromaiterai's *Lament*, which recalls the Anglo-Saxon *Wanderer* :

'From Matoe I look toward my land Tetianina, the mount Tearatapu, the valley Temaite, my drove of pigs on Mouurahi, the great mountain. Mist hides the mountain. My cloak is spread. Oh that the rain clear away, that I may see the great mountain. Aue! Alas! the wall of Mapuhi, dear land of mine!

'The drums that sound above Fareura draw to me the winds of the South for a fan to the Chief Aromaiterai. [I long for] the sight of my home.'

Nothing could well be simpler, [wrote Adams] and if perfect simplicity is a beauty or homesickness is poetic, even a foreigner who never has seen or heard of Papara can understand that the Tevas, who are not in the least introspective and who never analyze their sensations or read Browning or Wordsworth, should ask no more. 'There is my field!' Aromaiterai laments; 'There is my hill! there is my mountain-grove, my drove of pigs! How I wish I were there!' Aromaiterai used no more words; but each word calls up a picture to the singer, and what more can any poet do.

Europeans, who are puzzled to understand what the early races mean by poetry look for rhythm as likely to explain a secret which they cannot guess from the sense of words; but Polynesian rhythm is, if anything, rather more unintelligible to European ears than the images which are presented by the words. Tahitian poetry has rhythm, but it is chiefly caused by closing each strophe or stanza by an artificial, long drawn e-e-e-e. The song is sung with such rapidity of articulation that no European can approach or even represent it in musical notation.

His *Tahiti* completed, Henry Adams lived quietly.

IX

Palladium (1904–1909)

Between repeated voyages from Paris to Washington, and back again, Adams continued to live in silence. The tendency of history still weighed on his mind, when at the Great Exposition of 1900 the dynamo became to him a symbol of infinity.

As he grew accustomed to the great gallery of machines, he began to feel the forty-foot dynamos as a moral force, much as the early Christians felt the cross. The planet itself seemed less impressive in its old-fashioned deliberate, annual or daily revolution, than this huge wheel, revolving within arm's length at some vertiginous speed; and barely murmuring—scarcely humming an audible warning to stand a hair's breadth further for respect of power—while it would not wake the baby lying close against its frame. Before the end, one began to pray to it; inherited instinct taught the natural expression of man before silent and infinite force. . . . And thus it happened that, after ten years' pursuit, he found himself lying in the gallery of machines, at the Great Exposition of 1900, his historical neck broken by the sudden eruption of forces totally new.

[Man] was an acrobat, with a dwarf on his back, crossing a chasm on a slack-rope, and commonly breaking his neck. By the path of the newest science, one saw no unity ahead—nothing but a dissolving mind—and the historian felt himself driven back on thought as one continuous Force, without Race, Sex, School, Country or Church . . . Any schoolboy could see that man as a force must be measured by motion, from a fixed point. Psychology helped here by suggesting a unit—the point of history when man held the highest idea of himself as a unit in a unified universe. Eight or ten years of study had led Adams to think he might use the century 1150–1250 expressed in Amiens Cathedral and the works of Thomas Aquinas, as the unit from which he might measure motion down to his own time, without assuming anything as true or untrue, except relation. The movement might be studied at once in philosophy and mechanics. Setting himself to the task, he began a volume which he mentally knew as *Mont-Saint-Michel and Chartres: A Study of Thirteenth-Century Unity*. From that point he proposed to fix a position for himself, which he could label : *The Education of Henry Adams: A Study of Twentieth-Century Multiplicity*. With the help of these two points of relation, he hoped to project his lines forward and backward indefinitely, subject to correction from anyone who should know better. Thereupon, he sailed for home.

Henceforward, the historian was to reflect on man's education from the palladium of culture.

For years past, incited by John La Farge, Adams had devoted his summer schooling to the study of the [Virgin's] Glass at Chartres and elsewhere, and if the automobile had one *vitesse* more useful than another, it was that of a century a minute; that of passing from one century to another without break. The centuries dropped like autumn in one's road, and one was not fined for running over them too fast. When the thirteenth lost breath, the fourteenth caught on, and the sixteenth ran close ahead . . . the ocean of religion, which had flooded France, broke into Shelley's light dissolved in star-showers thrown, which had left every remote village strewn with fragments that flashed like jewels, and were tossed into hidden clefts of peace and forgetfulness . . . he went on wooing, happy in the thought that at last he had found a mistress who could see no difference in the age of her lovers. Her own age had no time measure.

He went straight to the Virgin at Chartres,

and asked her to show him God, face to face, as she did for St Bernard. She replied, kindly as ever, as though she were still the young mother of today, with a sort of patient pity for masculine dullness : 'My dear outcast, what is it you seek? This is the Church of Christ! If you seek him through me, you are welcome, sinner or saint; but he and I are one. We are Love! We have little or nothing to do with God's other energies which are infinite, and concern us the less because our interest is only in man, and the infinite is not knowable to man. Yet if you are troubled by your ignorance, you see how I am surrounded by the masters of the schools! Ask them!

In his *Mont-Saint-Michel and Chartres*, Adams studied St Thomas Aquinas, as well as twelfth and thirteenth century glass and poetry and, to him, this was all :

Of all the elaborate symbolism which has been suggested for the Gothic cathedral, the most vital and most perfect may be that the slender nervure, the springing motion of the broken arch, the leap downwards of the flying buttress—the visible effort to throw off a visible strain—never let us forget that Faith only supports it, and that, if Faith fails, Heaven is lost. The equilibrium is visibly delicate beyond the line of safety; danger lurks in every stone. The peril of the heavy tower, of the restless vault, of the vagrant buttress; the uncertainty of logic, the inequalities of the syllogism, the irregularities of the mental mirror—all these haunting nightmares of the Church are expressed as strongly by the Gothic cathedral as though it had been the cry of human suffering, and as no emotion had ever been expressed before or is likely to find expression again. The delight of its aspiration is flung up to the sky. The pathos of its self-distrust and anguish of doubt is buried in the earth as its last secret.

Another quotation must suffice for the 'delight' and the 'pathos'— a translation of a lyric from *Aucassin and Nicolette* :

Estoilete, je te voi	I can see you, little star,
Que la lune trait a soi.	That the moon draws through the air.
Nicolete est aveuc toi,	Nicolette is where you are,
M'amiete o le blond poil.	My own love with the blond hair.
Je quid que dix le veut avoir	I think God must want her near
Por la lumière de soir	To shine down upon us here
Que par li plus cler soit.	That the evening be more clear.
Vien, amie, je to proie !	Come down, dearest, to my prayer
Ou monter voiuroie droit.	Or I climb up where you are !
Que que fust au recaoir.	Though I fell, I would not care
Que fuisse lassus a toi	If I once were with you there
Ja te baiseroi estroit	I would kiss you closely, dear !
Se j'estoie fix a roi	If a monarch's son I were
S'afferies vos bien a moi	You should all my kingdom share,
Suer douce amie !	Sweet friend, sister !

In the song of a gentle creature, with eyes of vair, whose muscular Christianity is ready to do for any heathen who has it in his head that he is pregnant, whose *courtoisie* is ready to scale heaven, Henry Adams expressed his aspiration and his anguish.

In the *Mont-Saint-Michel*, whatever Adams translated, either the poetry of the court, or the chanson de geste, or the cathedral arch, or the miracles of Our Lady, he rendered not only the spirit of an age, but his own portrait. It may be grotesque to imagine him, like his tombeor, capering naked before the image of the Virgin in the shadow of the monastery of Clairvaux. But he was there exposed before the image.

Adams had not the faith which makes of its thoughts a system to be put forward as a text. He even feared that his interpretation of the Middle Ages was not always true, and whether he was right or wrong would make a fool dispute. But the human significance, the poetry of its life and society, he felt deeply, perhaps too sensibly for the world to see that he did.

Singularly enough, not one of Adams' many schools of education had ever drawn his attention to the opening lines of Lucretius, though they were perhaps the finest in all Latin literature, where the poet invoked Venus exactly as Dante invoked the Virgin:

'Quae quoniam rerum naturam sola gubernas.'

After Henry Adams' death some verses were found in a little wallet of special papers—entitled 'Prayer to the Virgin of Chartres.' In life he had shown the poem only to one friend, 'a sister in the twelfth century.' This is the end of the prayer :

A curious prayer, dear lady ! is it not?
    Strangely unlike the prayers I prayed to you !
Stranger because you find me at this spot,
    Here, at your feet, asking your help anew ...

When your Byzantine portal still was young,
    I came here with my master Abailard;
When Ave Maria Stella was first sung,
    I joined to sing it here with Saint Bernard.

When Blanche set up your glorious Rose of France,
    In scholar's robes I waited on the Queen;
When good Saint Louis did his penitence,
    My prayer was deep like his : my faith was keen.

What loftier prize seven hundred years shall bring,
    What deadlier struggles for a larger air,
What immortality our strength shall wring
    From Time and Space, we may—or may not—care;

But years, or ages, or eternity,
   Will find me still before your throne,
Pondering the mystery of Maternity,
   Soul within Soul—Mother and Child in One !

Help me to see ! not with my mimic sight—
   With yours ! which carried radiance, like the sun,
Giving the rays you saw with—light in light—
   Tying all suns and stars and worlds in one.

Help me to know ! not with my mocking art—
   With you, who knew yourself unbound by laws;
Gave God your strength, your life, your sight, your heart,
   And took from him the Thought that Is—the Cause.

Help me to feel ! not with my insect sense—
   With yours that felt all life alive in you;
Infinite heart beating at your expense;
   Infinite passion breathing the breath you drew !

Help me to bear ! not my own baby load,
   But yours; who bore the failure of the light,
The strength, the knowledge and the thought of God—
   The futile folly of the Infinite !

The Education of Henry Adams said no more, though it said things at greater length, in its dynamic theory of history and law of acceleration, with the same unusual emotion ordered by more than usual mind. If the *Mont-Saint-Michel and Chartres* expressed his feeling, *The Education* displayed his humor that was at once the comic verging on the tragic. St Gaudens once wrote to Adams: 'You dear old Porcupinus Poeticus, you old Poeticus under a Bushelibus.' And when the sculptor in a caricature bas-relief represented a head of Adams flying by means of celestial wings feathered with porcupine quills, and sent it to him, Adams, then in Paris, answered:

My dear St Gaudens : Your winged and pennated child arrived yesterday by the grace of God and his vicar the Secretary of State, or his satellites Adee and Vignaud. As this is the only way in which the secretary will ever fulfill his promise of making me cardinal and Pope I can see why he thinks to satisfy me by giving me medallic rank through you. Docile as

I always am to suggestion, I agree that the medal is probably worth more than the hat . . . Work! and make a lot of new porcupuses. I'm sorry you can't give Hay wings too, he needs them more than I who live in holes. Adieu!

In his *Education* the 'porcupinus' flew on wings; he pictured character and situation as could only a seventeenth century dean or an eighteenth century novelist. It might be remembered also that before Lytton Strachey came Henry Adams. And this touch is cause enough for remembering the book:

Next to smell came taste, and the children knew the taste of everything they saw or touched, from pennyroyal and flagroot to the shell of a pig-nut and the letters of a spelling-book—the taste of A–B, A B suddenly revived on the boy's tongue sixty years afterwards.

x

Phase (1909–1910)

The year 1908 made Henry Adams a septuagenarian. *The Education* had not yet been given to the public; Adams no longer dreamt of doing it.

A seal [as he put it] dislikes to be worried to death in age by creatures that have not the strength or the teeth to kill him outright : . . . silence, next to good temper, was the mark of sense.

Adams was old, but the world was at no loss for students; and for them he explained history as science.

Susceptibility to the highest forces is the highest genius; selection between them is the highest science; their mass is the highest educator . . . Unable to define Force as a unity, man symbolized it and pursued it, both in himself, and in the infinite, as philosophy and theology; the mind is itself the subtlest of all known forces, and its self-introspection necessarily created a science which had the singular value of lifting his education, at the start, to the finest, subtlest, and broadest training both in analysis and synthesis, so that, if language is a test, he must have reached his highest powers early in his history; while the mere motive remained as simple an appetite for power as the tribal greed which led him to trap an elephant . . .

Only a historian of very exceptional knowledge would venture to say at what date between 3000 B.C. and 1000 A.D., the momentum of Europe was greatest; but such progress as the world made consisted in economies of energy rather than in its development; it was proved in mathematics, measured by names like Archimedes, Aristarchus, Ptolemy, and Euclid; or in Civil Law, measured by a number of names which Adams had begun life by failing to learn; or in coinage, which was most beautiful near its beginning, and most barbarous at its close; or it was shown in roads, or the size of ships, or harbors; or by the use of metals, instruments, and writing; all of them economies of force, sometimes more forceful than the forces they helped; but the roads were still travelled by the horse, the ass, the camel, or the slave; the ships were still propelled by sails or oars; the lever, the spring, and the screw bounded the region of applied mechanics. Even the metals were old . . .

In the year 305 the empire had solved the problems of Europe more completely than they have ever been solved since. The Pax Romana, the Civil Law, and Free Trade should, in four hundred years, have put Europe far in advance of the point reached by modern society in the four hundred years since 1500, when conditions were less simple.

The efforts to explain, or explain away, this scandal had been incessant, but none suited Adams unless it were the economic theory of adverse exchanges and exhaustion of minerals; but nations are not ruined beyond a certain point by adverse exchanges, and Rome had by no means exhausted her resources . . . in northwestern Europe alone the empire had developed three energies—France, England, and Germany—competent to master the world . . . If the student means to try the experiment of framing a dynamic law, he must assign values to the forces of attraction that caused the trouble; and in this case he has them in plain evidence. With the relentless logic that stamped Roman thought, the empire, which had established unity on earth, could not help establishing unity in heaven. It was induced by its dynamic necessities to economize the gods . . .

No doubt the Church did all it could to purify the process, but society was almost wholly pagan in its point of view, and was drawn to the Cross because, in its system of physics, the Cross had absorbed all the old occult or fetish-power . . . The emperors used it like gunpowder in politics; the physicians used it like rays in medicine; the dying clung to it as the quintessence of force, to protect them from the forces of evil on their road to the next life . . . Fetish-power was cheap and satisfactory, down to a certain point . . . Great numbers of educated people—perhaps a majority—

cling to the method still, and practise it more or less strictly; but, until quite recently, no other was known . . .

Outside of occult or fetish-power, the Roman world was incredibly poor. It knew but one productive energy resembling a modern machine— the slave. No artificial force of serious value was applied to production or transportation, and when society developed itself so rapidly in political and social lines, it had no other means of keeping its economy on the same level than to extend its slave-system and its fetish-system to the utmost . . . The economic needs of a violently centralizing society forced the empire to enlarge its slave-system until the slave-system consumed itself and the empire too, leaving society no resource but further enlarge-ment of its religious system in order to compensate for the losses and horrors of the failure. For a vicious circle, its mathematical completeness approached perfection. The dynamic law of attraction and reaction needed only a Newton to fix it in algebraic form.

. . . the Western mind reacted in many forms, on many sides, express-ing its motives in modes, such as Romanesque and Gothic architecture, glass windows and mosaic walls, sculpture and poetry, war and love, which still affect some people as the noblest work of man, so that, even today, great masses of idle and ignorant tourists travel from far countries to look at Ravenna and San Marco, Palermo and Pisa, Assisi, Cordova, Chartres, with vague notions about the force that created them, but with a certain surprise that a social mind of such singular energy and unity should still lurk in their shadows . . .

The dynamic scheme began by asserting rather recklessly that between the Pyramids (B.C. 3000), and the Cross (A.D. 300), no new force affected Western progress, and antiquarians may easily dispute the fact; but in any case the motive influence, old or new, which raised both Pyramids and Cross was the same attraction of power in a future life that raised the dome of Sancta Sofia and the Cathedral at Amiens.

. . . two forces seemed to drop from the sky at the precise moment when the Cross on one side and the Crescent on the other, proclaimed the com-plete triumph of the *Civitas Dei* . . .

The fiction that society educated itself, or aimed at a conscious pur-pose, was upset by the compass and gunpowder which dragged and drove Europe at will through frightful bogs of learning. At first, the apparent lag for want of volume in the new energies lasted one or two centuries, which closed the great epochs of emotion by the Gothic cathedrals and scholastic theology . . . and for another century or two, Western society seemed to float in space without apparent motion . . . Society began to resist, but the individual showed greater and greater insistence, without realizing what he was doing . . .

Except as reflected in himself, man has no reason for assuming unity in the universe, or an ultimate substance, or a prime-motor. The *a priori* insistence on this unity ended by fatiguing the more active—or reactive —minds . . . As Galileo reversed the action of earth and sun, Bacon reversed the relation of thought to force. The mind was thenceforth to follow the movement of matter, and unity must be left to shift for itself.

The revolution in attitude seemed voluntary, but in fact was as mechanical as the fall of a feather . . . After 1500, the speed of progress so rapidly surpassed man's gait as to alarm every one, as though it were the acceleration of a falling body which the dynamic theory takes it to be. Lord Bacon was as much astonished by it as the Church was, and with reason. Suddenly society felt itself dragged into situations altogether new and anarchic—situations which it could not affect, but which painfully affected it. Instinct taught it that the universe in its thought must be in danger when its reflection lost itself in space. The danger was all the greater because men of science covered it with 'larger synthesis,' and poets called the undevout astronomer mad. Society knew better. Yet the telescope held it rigidly standing on its head; the miscroscope revealed a universe that defied the senses; gunpowder killed whole races that lagged behind; the compass coerced the most imbruted mariner to act on the impossible idea that the earth was round; the press drenched Europe with anarchism . . .

Very slowly the accretion of these new forces, chemical and mechanical, grew in volume until they acquired sufficient mass to take the place of the old religious science, substituting their attraction for the attractions of the *Civitas Dei,* but the process remained the same. Nature, not mind, did the work that the sun does on the planets. Man depended more and more absolutely on forces other than his own, and on instruments which superseded his senses.

'A Letter to American Teachers of History,' written some years after the foregoing thoughts, seems to have been intended for the student who would never have access to any one of the hundred privately printed copies of *The Education,* and ranged from the following paragraph in the earlier 'Tendency' :

Any science assumes a necessary sequence of cause and effect, a force resulting in motion which cannot be other than what it is. Any science of history must be absolute, like other sciences, and must fix with mathematical certainty the path which human society has got to follow. That path can hardly lead toward the interests of all the great social organizations. We cannot conceive that it should help at the same time the church and state, property and communism, capital and poverty, science and religion, trade and art. Whatever may be its orbit, it must, at least for a time, point away from some of these forces toward others which are re-garded as hostile. Conceivably, it might lead off in eccentric lines away from them all, but by no power of our imagination can we conceive that it should lead toward them all. (Both letters are included in Brooks Adams' *The Degradation of the Democratic Dogma*.)

In 'A Letter,' Adams—who left the processes of evolution to evolu-tionists and, as historian, found his interest in the reaction between mind and nature—anticipated the moral difficulties of teaching history as science, if degradation of energy in man and nature was accepted law. Where *The Education* reenforced perplexities and disillusion chapter by chapter, the 'Letter' did similarly, paragraph by paragraph, quotation by quotation. Adams' amazing knowledge summoned to his aid the science of the twentieth century in all its phases, so that Thought appeared but the false name for truncated Will, until Will itself was rendered ineffectual by Adams' variations on the macabre theme.

As mathematically insistent, and more daring than 'A Letter,' was the posthumous 'Rule of Phase Applied to History.' Drawing a parallel between the physics of Willard Gibbs and History, Adams suggested that Thought in time—like water or gas subject to certain forces—passes through a variety of phases, or changes, or states of equilibrium; that a law of acceleration may be applied to these changes or directions of thought—a formula which describes force increasing in the direct ratio of its squares. If the human mind might be compared to a meteo-roid—*The Education* had said—as 'it approached the sun or center of attractive force, the attraction of one century squared itself to give the measure of attraction on the next.'

Supposing the Mechanical Phase to have lasted 300 years from 1600 to 1900, the next or Electric Phase would have a life equal to $\sqrt{300}$, or about seventeen years and a half, when—that is, in 1917—it would pass into another or Ethereal Phase, which, for half a century, science has been promising, and which would last only $\sqrt{17.5}$, or about four years, and bring Thought to the limit of its possibilities in the year 1921. It may well be! Nothing whatever is beyond the range of possibility; but even if the life of the previous phase, 1600–1900, were extended another hundred years, the difference to the last term of the series would be negligible. In that case, the Ethereal Phase would last till about 2025.

The mere fact that society should think in terms of Ether or the higher mathematics might mean little or much. According to the Phase Rule, it lived from remote ages in terms of fetish force, and passed from that into terms of mechanical force, which again led to terms of electric force, without fairly realizing what had happened except in slow social and political revolutions. Thought in terms of Ether means only Thought in terms of itself, or, in other words, pure Mathematics and Metaphysics, a stage often reached by individuals. At the utmost it could mean only the subsidence of the current into an ocean of potential thought, or mere consciousness, which is also possible, like static electricity. The only consequence might be an indefinitely long stationary period, such as John Stuart Mill foresaw. In that case, the current would merely cease to flow.

Prophecies nearly always come true; they depend on interpretation of facts, and human beings are persistent interpreters. They notice, in unison with Adams' prediction, that the year 1917 was a turning point in history, and that the year 1923 brought Einstein to America. Truth is not the standard for judging Adams' essay. 'Phase' is at least a true picture of Adams' mind, if not of 'the facts.' And those who look around them and see the product of the age—the child, as Adams called him, of incalculable forces yet undetermined—seeking with his own disillusion to avoid repetition—can sense the desires behind Adams' 'ocean of potential thought, mere consciousness, like static electricity.'

Written today Adams' thought would probably stress what *The Education* said of Russia, and pore over more recent science.

Adams found his formula for Russian inertia exasperatingly correct . . . the great Atlantic powers . . . a working system . . . even Russia seemed about to be dragged into a combine of intelligent equilibrium based on an intelligent allotment of activities.

As for science, Adams heralded all its difficulties of mathematical philosophy in 'Phase' :

If the physicist-historian is satisfied with neither of the known laws of mass,—astronomical or electric,—and cannot arrange his variables in any combination that will conform with a phase-sequence, no resource seems to remain but that of waiting until his physical problems shall be solved, and he. shall be able to explain what Force is. As yet he knows almost as little of material as of immaterial substance. He is perplexed before the phenomena of Heat, Light, Magnetism, Electricity, Gravitation, Attraction, Repulsion, Pressure, and the whole schedule of names used to indicate unknown elements, as before the common infinitely familiar fluctuations of his own Thought whose action is so astounding on the direction of his energies. Probably the solution of any one of the problems will give the solution for them all (1909).

XI

'There It Ended' (1910–1914)

Henry Adams was candid with himself : when Clarence King left him, 'he could only blunder back alone, helplessly, wearily, his eyes rather dim with tears; and when Hay died, it was time to go. The three friends had begun life together; and the last of the three had no motive —no attraction—to carry it on after the others had gone.'

Yet a new generation had appeared overnight and Henry Adams found himself part of it. There was no difficulty in keeping up with his time, or the poet-son of a Massachusetts senator. It was the fortune of Henry Adams to stand near, while a plant blossomed and, still frail in fulfillment, declined with the morning. [In Paris, in 1901, Adams had tottered about with]

Joe Stickney, talking Greek philosophy or recent poetry, or studying *Louise* at the Opéra Comique, or discussing the charm of youth and the Seine with Bay (George Cabot) Lodge and his exquisite young wife.

Bay Lodge and Joe Stickney had given birth to the wholly new and original party of Conservative Christian Anarchists, to restore true poetry under the inspiration of the *Götterdämmerung*. [One] wing of the anarchistic party consisted rigorously of but two members, Adams and Bay Lodge. The conservative Christian anarchist, as a party, drew life from Hegel and Schopenhauer rightly understood. By the necessity of their philosophical descent, each member of the fraternity denounced the other as unequal to his lofty task and inadequate to grasp it. Of course, no third member could be so much as considered, since the great principle of contradiction could be expressed only by opposites; and no agreement could be conceived because anarchy, by definition, must be chaos and collision, as in the kinetic theory of a perfect gas. Doubtless this law of contradiction was itself agreement, a restriction of personal liberty inconsistent with freedom; but the 'larger synthesis' admitted a limited agreement provided it were strictly confined to the end of larger contradiction. Thus the great end of all philosophy—the 'larger synthesis'—was attained, but the process was arduous, and while Adams, as the older member, assumed to declare the principle, Bay Lodge necessarily denied both the assumption and the principle in order to assure its truth.

Bay Lodge was also amused, but not so much as Adams: he was young, and wrote long poetic dramas about it. There it ended: the poet died in 1909. Adams, who had been a father to this boy was seventy-one.

In such labyrinths, the staff is a force almost more necessary than the legs; the pen becomes a sort of blindman's dog, to keep him from falling into the gutters. The pen works for itself, and acts like a hand, modelling the plastic material over and over again to the form that suits it best. The form is never arbitrary, but is a sort of growth like crystallization, as any artist knows too well; for often the pencil or pen runs into side-paths and shapelessness, loses its relations, stops or is bogged. Then it has to return on its trail, and recover, if it can, its line of force. The result of a year's work depends more on what is struck out than on what is left in; on the sequence of the main lines of thought, than on their play or variety.

Adams had stopped thinking about his education in 1905; in the life of his young friend, George Cabot Lodge, he saw education play its game all over again. The older man could well be quizzical through tears. 'Consider the life of Bay,' he might have reflected, 'so very like the song of the wave he sung about, falling on still shores as I have fallen, of a certain duration, it receded with the tide, and the tide is neap. Dear Lodge, like Blake's sunflower, he sought after a sweet golden clime. And he learned—not much—that the sun was not as round as the shield of his fathers. If I write down his brief life, I should be writing my *Education* all over again.'

The Life of George Cabot Lodge was Henry Adams' last book. It implied more than it stated; between the lines, it wrote about Henry Adams:

Boys are naturally sensitive and shy. Even as men, a certain proportion of society, showed, from the time of the Puritans a marked reserve, so
that one could never be quite sure in State Street, more than in Concord,
that the lawyer or banker whom one consulted about drawing a deed or
negotiating a loan, might not be consciously immersed in introspection,
as his ancestors, two centuries before, had been absorbed in their chances
of salvation. The latent contrasts of character were full of interest, and
so well understood that any old Bostonian, familiar with family histories,
could recall by scores the comedies and tragedies which had been due to
a conscious or unconscious revolt against the suppression of instinct and
imagination.

Poetry was a suppressed instinct; and except where, as in Longfellow,
it kept the old character of ornament, it became a reaction against society,
as in Emerson and the Concord School, or further away and more
roughly, in Walt Whitman. Less and less it appeared, as in earlier ages,
the natural favorite expression of society itself. In the last half of the
nineteenth century, the poet became everywhere a rebel against his sur-
roundings. What had been begun by Wordsworth, Byron and Shelley,
was carried on by Algernon Swinburne in London or Paul Verlaine in
Paris or Walt Whitman in Washington, by a common instinct of revolt.
Even the atmosphere of Beacon Street was at times faintly redolent of
Schopenhauer.

This was the setting, and the biographer followed his subject
through experiences which he himself had shared as a young man:
Boston, Harvard, Paris, Berlin, war, singular friendships with women
as well as men. If Adams had prayed to the Virgin as redeemer, Lodge
had seen in Eve the redeemer of Cain, and had expressed it in a drama.
'All the men appeal to Eve,' wrote Adams describing Lodge's *Cain*,
'and then refuse to listen to her.' Writing these words he must have
thought of his own lines to the Virgin :

> If then I left you, it was not my crime
> Or if a crime, it was not mine alone.

And writing what follows of Lodge, he might have thought it true of
himself : 'From first to last he identified himself with the energies of
nature . . .; he did not invent images for amusement, but described
himself in describing the energy.'

In inventing images for *The Life of Lodge* Adams described his finest thoughts:

From the earliest forms of mammal life, the mothers of fauns have been more in love with their offspring than with all else in existence; and when the mother has had the genius of love and sympathy, the passion of altruism, the instinct of taste and high-breeding, besides the commoner resources of intelligence and education, the faun returns the love, and is moulded by it into shape.

The little book of two hundred pages also contained some excellent literary criticism, such as the analysis of Lodge's *Herakles*.

Old men stop writing books, though they often continue their studies and write letters. Adams, who was an excellent letter writer from the time he was twenty, kept on writing letters successfully; whether on various matters to Whitelaw Reid, or on John La Farge to Royal Cortissoz, or on his studies in the Chansons—the Guillaume and others—to Bliss Luquiens and Stanburrough Cook.

When Reid, in the position of ambassador to England, delivered an address on Byron at University College, in Nottingham, in the winter of 1910, Adams wrote to him:

Byron I envy you. One can hardly keep one's hands off him. His is one of the few really amusing figures in the British Pantheon. One can praise or criticize, admire or detract, as one likes, in perfect safety. One is sure to be more or less right. One need not even treat him seriously. He did not treat himself seriously, and would have jibed us for it. He is the only complex figure, except perhaps Sheridan, in the whole galaxy. You saved yourself some ugly risks by keeping Shelley and Keats out of sight, who had nothing at all, that I can see in common with Byron, whose parallel is Chateaubriand or Voltaire. Curiously enough, the closest English parallel is certainly Disraeli. I wonder whether there was any Jew in Byron. There is certainly some Heine in him.

One of the last letters, from 1603 H Street, Washington, was written on December 29, 1914, to Luquiens:

My dear Sir
    Yesterday, my brother Charles sent me down your notice of the Chartres in your July (Yale) *Review*. Owing perhaps to the troubles of

last summer, I had not seen or heard of it and was much touched by its kindness and sympathy. Let me, at once, thank you for it, and express my regret for having failed to do so long ago. Of course we have had much else to think about, but we have still had time to push our studies of the Chansons until I think we are acquainted with them all—the music, I mean, for that is my attraction. We have sung them all, or all the best, and have copied or photographed all that we liked. The charm of the pursuit has almost obliterated that of the other studies, for indeed, I am quite serious in considering the Chatelain, Conon, the Vidame, etc. etc. as artistically the equals or superiors of the architects and glass workers. Doubtless the Chatelain, the Roi de Navarre, Conon etc. are the best; but what troubles me is that Gasse, who was placed almost first by his own age, should seem to us invariably dull and commonplace.

Throughout all the terrors and roars of German howitzers we have lived on 'Seigneurs sachez' and 'A vous amants,' in France and England as here, and they alone have given us repose. Reims fell, but Thibaut rose.

Ever yrs
Henry Adams

Life had done its worst; nature, as he once said, had educated herself to a singular sympathy for death. It was an easy matter to die like the Crusader with 'Seigneurs sachez' and 'A vous amants' on his lips.

XII

March 27, 1918

Henry Adams lies buried in Rock Creek Cemetery, in Washington. The casual visitor might perhaps notice, on a slight elevation, a group of shrubs and small trees making a circular enclosure. If he should step up into this concealed spot, he would see on the opposite side a polished marble seat; and placing himself there he would find himself facing a seated figure, done in bronze, loosely wrapped in a mantle, which, covering the body and the head, throws into strong relief a face of singular fascination. Whether man or woman, it would puzzle the observer to say. The eyes are half closed, in reverie rather than in sleep. The figure seems not to convey the sense either of life or death, of joy or sorrow, of hope or despair. It has lived but life is done; it has experienced all things, but is now oblivious of all; it has questioned, but questions no more. The casual visitor will perhaps approach the figure, looking for a symbol, a name, a date—some revelation. There is none. The level ground, carpeted with dead leaves, gives no indication of a grave beneath. It may be that the puzzled visitor will step outside, walk around the enclosure, examine the marble shaft against which the figure is placed; and, finding nothing there, return to the seat and look long at the strange face. What does he make of it—this level spot, these shrubs, this figure that speaks and yet is silent? Nothing—or what he will. Such was life to Henry Adams, who lived long, and questioned seriously, and would not be content with the dishonest or the facile answer.—Carl Becker.

Henry Adams himself once quoted Heine :

> Also fragen wir beständig,
> Bis man uns mit einer Handvoll
> Erde endlich stopft die Maüler,
> Aber ist das eine Antwort?

'Life has become almost intolerable,' he said the day before his death, when the vandalism of war was diverting society. But in death, remembered one of his friends, he was found asleep, in the morning, with a look of thoughtful interest—almost of curiosity—upon his face.

Dear Infant, [he wrote in the spring, two years before] Yesterday I walked in the spring woods, and met a fly. To that fly I said : 'Fly, do you want me to tell you the truth about yourself?' And that fly winked at me —carefully—and said, 'You be damned.'—They have told me that just seventy-eight times. They are not tired, but I am.

[Adams] had no complaint to make against man or woman. They had all treated him kindly; he had never met with ill-will, ill-temper, or even ill-manners, or known a quarrel. He had never seen serious dishonesty or ingratitude. He had found readiness in the young to respond to suggestion that seemed to him far beyond all he had reason to expect.

1924
a few brief additions 1928/9

WITH *LITTLE*
For Careenagers

The subtitle of this novel implies ships leaning on their sides, sometimes in drydock for repairs. The epigraph, which introduces the story beginning with the hero's birth into universal society— only about 6000 years old—poses a question:

> Where coincidence
> intends no harm
> who will sue the
> first stone in
> celebrating?

This rhetorical question is answered in this reading from Chapters 4, 8, 13 and 18.

My introduction to a reading from *Little*, "The Spoken Word Program," Radio Station WNYC FM, November 19, 1970. —L.Z.

About

INFLUENCE

The matter of an influence acting in common upon individual temperaments results in differences which have variegated it and been variegated by it in accordance with : 1. its presence in the air : sometimes the proximity of a poet's edified literary acquaintances, however conscious or unconscious a poet may be of the almost literal drafts around him; 2. coincidence of the temperament affected and the temperament only apparently, not actually affecting; since the modality of events of a period of fifty or seventy-five years may show, at any time of their calendar, two similar individuals, different as to locale, and contemporary or anachronistic as to their birth and mortuary dates; 3. conscious choice or rejection of a literary tradition.

1930

POETIC VALUES

Naturally the values poets deal with are alike for all of them. 'Bare ruined choirs where late the sweet birds sang' : omit the word 'sweet' and read : 'Bare ruined choirs where late the birds sang'—and the line's poetic substance is not very different from Rimbaud. Not that Shakespeare's line has not more tonal value—and certainly more value of cadence—than the 'the twitter of birds' or some other expression; but omitting 'sweet,' one thinks of the English line as it might possibly sound in French: i.e. 'Moi, l'autre hiver, plus sourd que les cerveaux d'enfants.'

1930

AMERICAN POETRY 1920–1930

I

The brain and conscience of Joyce are that of his literary generation. After him : his visible influence on Cummings (of course, Cummings might have existed of himself)—'mil(lions of aflickf) litter ing brightmillion of S hurl; edindodg : ing'; on what is fairly readable in Hart Crane—*smithereens*; on the newest generation of *Blues* (edited by C. H. Ford, Columbus, Miss., 1929), mainly via Cummings.

Cummings' Elizabethan *in american* became Chaucerian *in american* in Ernest Walsh's Poems (*This Quarter*, No. 3) : at times curious amoretti, at times poetry. The influence of Joyce is again evident, but Walsh too was Irish. Joyce's sense of simultaneity carries over in Williams, whose work shows also a kinship with the work of Gertrude Stein, in its analytical aspects Joyce's opposite. New writers had perhaps better be given a chance to find their own forbears. Varying from possibly evolutionary implications of statement one may study the progress of individual work rather than its use in an 'evolution' of poetry.

'No man ever writes much poetry that matters.' Yet if a man once does, one likes to see him continue for at least twenty years.

The first generation developed, after 1920 or shortly before, as did Joyce, literary mechanisms for expressing the movements of individual brains. An accurate consideration of the matter of influence may have to deal with the relation of Pound's *First Canto*, opening with the voyage of Ulysses, and the process of immediately shifting from one fact to the next in the other *Cantos*, to Joyce. Pound's first three *Cantos* preceded Joyce's *Ulysses* by some years.

Pound, Williams, Eliot, Marianne Moore, H. D. (when she does not suffer from an Anglicized dilution of metric and speech, defeating her double effort towards emotional expanse and condensation) did not stop with the monolinear image; they extended it to include 'a greater accessibility to experience' (Marianne Moore, 'N. Y.'). For that matter, they never started merely with the image (1913). They are thus not a gang-plank for a younger generation to step onto. Or if they are, their individual rungs matter, and Cummings is maybe on shore or sometimes certainly on board.

Robert McAlmon in *Unfinished Poem* has recalled in the inclusiveness of his American mock-historical, geographical scene, the scope of Marianne Moore's 'An Octopus,' retained an isolate individualism similar to hers while communizing quotation, hardly ever reached her incisiveness—the definite hardness of Whitman when he writes of a stallion 'Head high in the forehead, wide between the ears'—and added the indigenous cynicism of American song blues. Ezra Pound's conversation of American personae in the *Cantos* is much better than the conversation of similar personae in McAlmon's *Portrait of a Generation* (1926) and *Unfinished Poem* (1929).

The principle of varying the stress of a regular meter and counting the same number of syllables to the line was transferred from 'traditional' to cadenced verse in Williams' *Spring and All*. Not that he made each line of a stanza or printed division carry absolutely the same number of syllables, but there seems to have been a decided awareness of the printed as well as quantitative looseness of vers libre. Obviously, what counts is quantity; print only emphasizes—yet printing correctly a poet shows his salutary gift of quantity.

New work by Wallace Stevens, with the exception of *Academic Discourse at Havana* (1929), has not appeared since 1924. He returns with the same resonant elegance of precision—at least with 'Jehovah and the great sea-worm,' 'a peanut parody for peanut people,' 'the thickest man on thickest stallion-back,' and 'How full of exhalations of the sea.' His return, however, is marked by an attenuated 'accessibility to experience' characteristic of the latest Eliot (*Animula, A Song for Simeon, Ash Wednesday*), perhaps because, like Eliot, he has purposely led his rather submerged intellectual excellences (as contrasted with Pound's rebelliousness) to a versification clambering the stiles of English influence. Stevens'

> Speak and the sleepers in their sleep shall move,
> Waken, and watch the moonlight on their floors . . .

is good, but is too obviously Milton :

> That sing, and singing in their glory move
> And wipe the tears forever from his eyes.

The work of other 'formalists' seems also to droop from the stem of English influence; perhaps via Eliot. In any case, their linear and stanzaic impalings do not possess Eliot's spark of craftsman's accomplishment. Their steadiness is that of truncated emotions. Their poems are not *metaphysical*, as they intend perhaps, in the seventeenth century sense of emotional constructions mentally alive, precise, ramified and sub-ramified in their meaning. The poetic emotion is lacking, and the product is 'intellectual' rhetoric : blurred disjointed tangibilities.

The work of Hart Crane (including *The Bridge*), whose technical regularities tend to place him in a class with this last 'group,' is emotionally preferable. He has energy. Yet it is an energy too often pseudo-musical and amorphous in its conflation of sense values. His single words are hardly ever alone, they are rarely absolute symbols for the things they represent, e.g.

> The incunabula of the divine grotesque.

The result is an aura—a doubtful, subtle exhalation—a haze. All of which is more to the bad than the good, unless a kind of 'heat proper' gets across :

> Take this sea, whose diapason knolls
> On scrolls of silver snowy sentences
>
> .   .   .
>
> Mark how her turning shoulders wind the hours,
> And hasten while her penniless rich palms
> Pass superscription of bent foam and wave.

'*Snowy* sentences' are not 'knolled.' Ezra Pound with reference to the Wagnerian ideal might be quoted : 'You confuse the spectator by smacking as many of his senses as possible at every possible moment, this prevents his noting anything with unusual lucidity, but you may fluster or excite him to the point of making him receptive.' The lines have interesting anthropomorphic feelings, but for this reason they are not the latest word in 'modern' writing, and they are too much of a metrical rocker to be 'primitive.'

To what extent Crane's music which is often Elizabethan in drive— iambic in the grand manner—helps an indefinite language and pro- longs verbal indecision past the useful necessity of meaning is indicated by the poverty of his unrhymed work in recent numbers of *transition*. In these poems his words are obviously ineffectual. Their spirals of conceit are difficult to no good purpose, and the musical twisters of his metrical form are not present to carry them.

These strictures do not apply to Crane's 'O Carib Isle' which, but for a minimum of haze and a melody drummed by a kind of linguistic pedal, leaves the sensationally 'classic' and is, with distinction, of the senses. His other poems are mystical, filmy. If fish were a dead meta- phor, the sea-film they wear is the logic surrounding these poems: the result is rhetoric—'noon's tyranny,' 'sulphur dreams.'

Crane errs on the side of mysticism—to a recurrent shifting from one feeling-tone (one kind of ecstasy) to another. That there is a pseudo-substratum of idea contrasting with the feeling-tone is unfor- tunate in the first place. In Donne, the idea was also his feeling-tone and was also a particular metaphysical concept of his time—emotion propelling the crowding on of metaphysical things:

> For, nor in nothing, nor in things
> Extreme, and scatt'ring bright, can love inhere;
> Then as an Angell, face, and wings
> Of aire, not pure as it, yet pure doth weare,
> So thy love may be my love's spheare;

Strangely enough, the criticism of dialecticians inclined to think of Wm Carlos Williams as a mountain goat butting among crags, has never stopped to analyse the metaphysical concept behind his improvisa- tions. But it is a definite metaphysical concept: the thought is the thing which, in turn, produces the thought. Williams' feeling-tone, as Donne's, groups an order of tangible objects:

> Say it! No ideas but in things. Mr.
> Paterson has gone away
> to rest and write. Inside the bus one sees
> his thoughts sitting and standing. His thoughts
> alight and scatter—

who are these people (how complex
their mathematic) among whom I see myself
in the regular ordered plateglass of
his thoughts, glimmering before shoes and bicycles—?
They walk incommunicado, the
equation is beyond solution, yet
its sense is clear—that they may live
his thought is listed in the Telephone
Directory—

(Paterson)

Of its time, but definitely the rare inheritance of metaphysical poetry. It is obvious why Williams should prefer the intellectual specifications, even dryness, of Mina Loy (*Contact Anthology*) to the pseudo-ecstatic work of a half dozen accepted lyricists or as many anthologized lyrics.

II

It is in the nature of things that poets should want to live; and ethically living cannot be a Wordsworthian dilution.

For exactness one goes back to Herrick's 'Divination' :

When a Daffadill I see
Hanging down his head t'wards me
Guess I may, what I must be :
First, I shall decline my head;
Secondly, I shall be dead;
Lastly, safely buryed.

This is not death, or if it is 'we do not sell and buy things so necessary' (Cummings).

Ultimately, poetry is a question of natures, of constitutions, of mental colorings. But it is understood that if the author of 'Canto XXX' were incapable of the distinction of an ethical commonplace by Spinoza, it is not likely that he would have written the composite of internal rhyme, repetition of word, repetition of line with one word altered, delayed and rapidly extended cadence, and tendency towards wrenching of accent :

Now if no fayre creature followeth me
It is on account of Pity,
It is on account that Pity forbideth them slaye.
All things are made foul in this season,
This is the reason, none may seek purity
Having for foulnesse pity
And things growne awry;
No more do my shaftes fly
To slay. Nothing is now clean slayne
But rotteth away.

For bearings this essay returns to the several poets it started with.
Its portmanteau bibliography of poetry after 1920 is brief: Pound's
Cantos; Eliot's *The Waste Land*; Marianne Moore's *Observations*;
Williams' *Spring and All*, 'Primavera' (the edition in the new *Imagist
Anthology* is incomplete, yet anything but the fiasco which the rest of
this anthology is); Cummings' *Is 5*; references to earlier volumes by
Cummings, Stevens' *Harmonium*; *Exile* 3 and 4. Traditions and influences of one upon the other aside, it is to be noted that these poets
come out of a country which after a great deal of versified mess produced Emily Dickinson and the raw Whitman who giving 'the soul of
literature' the cold shoulder 'descended upon things to arrest them all'
and 'arrested' them 'all faithful solids and fluids.'

One proceeds with useful principle (Ezra Pound's *Pavannes and
Divisions*, or *Instigations*, or *How to Read*, or all three). 'Emotion is an
organizer of forms.' The image is at the basis of poetic form. In the last
ten years Pound has not concerned himself merely with isolation of the
image—a cross-breeding between single words which are absolute symbols for things and textures—

> The sand that night like a seal's back
> Glossy

—but with the poetic locus produced by the passage from one image to
another. His *Cantos* are, in this sense, one extended image. One cannot
pick from them a solitary poetic idea or a dozen variations of it, as out
of Eliot's *Waste Land*, and say this is the substance out of which this
single atmosphere emanates. The *Cantos* cannot be described as a
sequence. A synopsis may no more be given of them than of a box, a

leaf, a chair, a picture : they are an image of his world, 'an intellectual and emotional complex in an instant of time.'

In Williams, the advance in the use of image has been from a word structure paralleling French painting (Cézanne) to the same structure in movement—'Della Primavera Transportata Al Morale.'

Marianne Moore has allowed the 'neatness of finish' of her 'octopus of ice' to clarify ubiquitously the texture of at least a hundred images with a capacity for fact. Cummings is more sensuously evocative, sometimes fanciful ('after all white horses are in bed') but continually interested in something like capillaries, 'everything which we really are and never quite live,' the sources where images begin—

> if scarcely the somewhat city
> ...... in considerable twilight

and are known perhaps only negatively—

> touch (now) with a suddenly unsaid
> gesture lightly my eyes?

His typography, illustrated by the use of the parenthesis around 'now' also suggests the image, by doubting it.

*

'A new cadence means a new idea' (Pound).

Naturally in a poem image, cadence, and idea are inseparable. The passage from Pound on Pity, quoted above, is effective because the cadence of the word 'pity' itself is never perfectly expected. The versification is not a matter of each syllable finding its usual place in an iambic pentameter, as in Frost's

> One bird begins to close a faded eye

whose drawback is submission to accent. Pound's contribution is quantity, and stock and trade sonnets and iambs have never taken up his challenge. It is time someone resurrected the sonnet from a form that has become an exercise. Cummings has partly done so in those attempts in which he is not palpably Shakespearean—with lines like

> moon's bright third tumbling slowly
> (sonnet IV—Is 5)

Occasionally his music has recalled Pound's with a difference in print and somewhat loosely :

> Cats which move smoothly from neck to neck of bottles, cats
> smoothly willowing out and in
> (Three—III—Is 5)

But for the most part, excepting a quatrain now and then in the manner of Eliot, he has been himself, the cadence approximating the actuality :

> the very swift and
> invisibly living
> rhythm of your Heart possibly
> (Four—XVII—Is 5)

and—

> bring on your fireworks, which are a mixed
> splendor of piston and of pistil; very well
> provided an instant may be fixed
> so that it will not rub, like any other pastel
> (One—XXXIX—Is 5)

Eliot has always been more interesting in his effects with quantity than in his effects with accent :

> Lord, the Roman hyacinths are blooming in bowls and

as against

> Kept faith and fast, provided for the poor

—both lines from *A Song for Simeon*.

The music of Marianne Moore's *Observations* varies from the quantitative couplets in 'An Egyptian Pulled Glass Bottle in the Shape of a Fish' to the complex stanza of 'Those Various Scalpels' (compared to which Donne's 'A Valediction of Weeping' seems easy), to the energy of her longer poems :

> in which action perpetuates action and angle is at variance
>   with angle
> till submerged by the general action;
> obscured by 'fathomless suggestions of color,'
>
>   .   .   .
>   ocean of hurrying
> consonants
>
>   .   .   .
> crashing itself out in one long hiss of spray.
>   ('Novices')

The resonance of her 'Fear is Hope,' the length of its rhetorical periods carried over despite the fall of the rhymes, are worthy of Donne :

>   ... round glasses spun
> To flame as hemispheres of one
>   Great hourglass dwindling to a stem.

Williams' extremely important revisions and condensations of vers libre, his contribution to an emphasis of word and stress in *Spring and All* and 'Primavera,' have already been discussed. 'Primavera' contains this perfect lyric :

>   as love
>   newborn
>   each day upon the twig
>   which may die
>   springs your love
>   fresh up
>   lusty for the sun
>   the bird's companion

also this original stanzaic pattern with effective stress variations :

Trundled from
the strangeness of the sea—
a kind of
heaven—

Ladies and Gentlemen !
the greatest
sea monster ever exhibited
alive

the gigantic
sea-elephant—O wallow
of flesh where
are

there fish enough for
that
appetite stupidity
cannot lessen?

Music of word in a poem is to a great extent a matter of diction. The sedate will likely reject the last quotation from Williams and will admire the uncertain Elizabethan virtues of Cummings' 'my very lady,' or an extension of it, 'your crisp eyes actually,' rather than his 'why are these pipples taking their hets off?' (One—XVIII—*Is 5*), or the straightforward diction of

And send life out of me and the night
absolutely into me
(Five—I—*Is 5*)

Whatever one's preferences, the diction of these poets remains their fully varied material, which includes quotations from sources apparently useful to an interest in preserving poetry wherever it is found. Pound's 'Canto XXVIII' contains :

Joe hittin' the gob at 25 feet
Every time, ping on the metal
(Az ole man Comley wd. say : Boys ! . . .
Never cherr terbakker ! Hrwwkke tth !
Never cherr terbakker !

also—

> If thou wilt go to Chiaso wilt find that indestructible female
> As if waiting for the train to Topeka

'Canto XXIX':

> .   .   .
> narrow thighs,
> The cut cool of the air.

The diction which is dead today is that of poets who, as someone said of Matthew Arnold, have put on singing robes to lose themselves in the universal. Anent this matter, a paragraph from Roger Kaigh's *Paper* (still unpublished) is not inappropriate:

The bias of paper, to this day, most radically affects logicians and philosophers. Logicians will admit that a word may have more than one meaning, but each must be definite and thus distinct. Infinite shades of meaning cannot be recognized, for the instrument of formal logic depends upon static or categorical meanings, that is, definitions, for its operation. Otherwise the logician detects the fallacy of four terms. But categories which appear distinct upon paper derive an infinity of variations in speech. 'Yes' and 'No' are categorically distinct upon paper, but either may mean anything from emphatic 'Yes' to emphatic 'No' when spoken. For the context, gesture, intonation and pronunciation give words a stamp of meaning which a written form will lack.

The diction employed by Pound, Eliot, Williams, Marianne Moore and Cummings has always tended towards precise intension and to varied play of connotation. The devices of emphasizing cadence by arrangement of line and typography have been those which clarify and render the meaning of the spoken word specific. The things these poets deal with are of their world and time, but they are 'modern' only because their words are energies which make for meaning.

III

The Work of William Carlos Williams

He is of rare importance in the last decade (1920–1930), for whatever he has written the direction of it has been poetry—and, in a special sense, history. History, or the attractions of living recorded—the words a shining transcript.

On the oak-leaves the light snow lay encrusted till the wind turned a leaf over.

No use, no use. The banality wins, is rather increased by the attempt to reduce it. Better to learn to write and to make a smooth page no matter what the incoherence of the day, no matter what erasures must be sacrificed to improve a lying appearance to keep ordered the disorder of the pageless actual.

A Novelette (1929)

He has looked around—the dimensions of writing like those of music continually audible to him (somehow in a discussion of writing today, after his discussions, the word 'dimension' gets in) : 'I think these days when there is so little to believe in—when the old loyalties—god, country, and the hope of Heaven—aren't very real, we are more dependent than we should be on our friends.' Isolation. Yet he has imagined 'each step enlarged to a plain'—known, in fact, 'his intimate, his musician, his servant.'

The aesthetics of his material is a living one, a continual beginning, a vision amid pressure; *The Great American Novel* (1923), the only one because it is the product of the scene given its parallel in words. America, the shifting, as one hurriedly thinks of it or sees it perhaps as one changes from street car to street car, resulted in this book in the swift hold of art on things seen, in the sudden completeness of the words envisioning them. 'He could see the red tail-light still burning brightly with the electricity that came from the battery under the floor boards. No one had stolen the spare tire.' (Chapter II). 'Corners of rooms sacred to so many deeds. Here he had said so and so, done so and so.' (Chapter XIII). Such things are seen and recorded not as notes, but as finished, swiftly trained deliberations of the mind between leaps to other work or the multiplicity of living scenes.

Therefore, his exclusion of sentimentalisms, extraneous comparisons, similes, overweening autobiographies of the heart, of all which permits factitious 'reflection about,' of sequence, of all but the full sight of the immediate, in *Spring and All* (1923). A collection of his works should contain only *the facts of his words*, even those which jar as they brighten in the composition—for these, too, illuminate, as against the personally lyric padding, the idly discursive depressing stages of writing not the product swift out of the material. In this he is almost unrelated : in a kind of morality which is his visioned impact against the environment; in a complete awareness of values in the living broken down for others by sentimentalisms.

In *The Tempers* (1913), *Al Que Quiere* (1917) and *Sour Grapes* (1922) there are poems that will stay though many lines are invalidated by his subsequent criticism. It is salutary that these lines may be omitted and still leave a number of structures. The process of rehabilitating the good to its rightful structure is always possible with writing in which something was seen, a quantity heard, an emotion apprehended to begin with.

One is faced with the same difficulties in the *Improvisations* (1920), and the same outlet : what he learned later to exclude may be omitted in the reading. The element is often not seen from the emanation, or as he has said, the paper is not felt from the glaze. But at best the writing in the *Improvisations* attains a Shakespearean verbalism :

When beldams dig clams their fat hams (it's always beldams) balanced near Tellus' hide, this rhinoceros pelt, these lumped stones—buffoonery of midges on a bull's thigh—invoke, what you will : birth's glut, awe at God's craft, youth's poverty, evolution of a child's caper, man's poor inconsequence. Eclipse of all things; sun's self turned hen's rump. (XI, 2).

At best, there is a continual friskiness, the writing is a fugue, comparable to the scene in *Twelfth Night* in which the Clown proves Olivia a fool. (In 'The Descent of Winter' (1928) and in a few other scattered notes, he has written about the best Shakespearean criticism there is— at least, it is no more nor less serious than the incidental.)

Porpoises risen in a green sea, the wind at nightfall bending the rose-red grasses and you—in your apron running to catch—say it seems to you to be your son. How ridiculous ! You will pass up into a cloud and look back at me, not count the scribbling foolish that put wings to your heels,

at your knees.' (1920). [To prove :] there is no thing that with a twist of
the imagination cannot be something else. (*Improvisations, XXVII,* 2)

He has, since 1923, printed his poems differently—used print as a
guide to the voice and the eye. His line sense is not only a music heard,
but seen, printed as bars, printed (or cut as it were) for the reading—
the sentimentalisms which might possibly have encroached brushed off
like flies as at those clear times when the dynamic feeling of a person is
not disturbed. One does not think of line-ends in him but of essential
rhythm, each cadence emphasized, the rhythm breaking and beginning
again, an action, each action deserving a line :

> the harried
> earth is swept.
>   The trees
> the tulip's bright
>   tips
>   sidle and
> toss

nouns : acts as much as verbs.

He has apparently broken with his own stylistic standards when
the power behind the words demanded it. Thus, the conceit of his
'Botticellian Trees' : but one feels 'the alphabet of the trees' identified
with roots and growths which make the alphabet of his actual writing.
The conceit does not stick out of the verse, but builds it : his kinship
with Donne, with Shakespearean metaphor.

For these attainments, he has no need to make concessions to the
'obstinate rationalists.' Yet he has come across, and retained, more
learning than he himself may be satisfied to allow he has : *In the
American Grain* (1925) and *A Voyage to Pagany* (1929).

History is in these pages and in the poems—history defined as the
facts about us, their chronological enlivening for the present set down as
art, and so good for the next age and the next. *The pure products of
America go crazy* is the poem it is through its realization of aesthetic,
living values, social determinism of American suburbs in the first thirty
years of the twentieth century. The poem could perhaps be realised only
by one who has vicariously written, rather than painted as he has always wished to do, but in any event it has been realized by one vitally
of his time.

No outside program has influenced his social awareness. It is the product of the singular creature living in society and expressing in spite of the numb terror around him the awareness which after a while cannot help be but general. It is the living creature becoming conscious of his own needs through the destruction of the various isolated around him, and till his day comes continuing unwitnessed to work, no one but himself to drive the car through the suburbs, till they too become conscious of demands unsatisfied by the routine senseless repetition of events.

1930

DOMETER GUCZUL

The painting of Dometer Guczul at his Art Gallery overlooking Lake George comprises eighteen oils. Four Adirondack Mountain landscapes, in the vicinity of Lake George, form detailed backgrounds in 'The Chair Caner,' 'The Wanderer,' 'The Hunter,' and 'Children in a Blueberry Patch.' An interior of a cottage in the Adirondacks sets off the wrinkled woman in 'The Old Spinning Wheel.' Florida landscapes set off 'The Modern Girl,' the poor white family in 'The Jungle Life,' the Negro vendor in 'The Peanut Man,' and the little Negro girl in 'The Pickaninny.' The other paintings are genre landscapes and miniatures.

The original quality of all this work is in the candid and vividly accurate portrayal of characters and things. Guczul invites comparison with anonymous American *primitive* painters and other *primitives*. He has lived close to the life he paints, seen every detail of terrain and action rendered, and is fascinated by things growing, made and used.

But he is not a painter of nature or habitat for the mere record. As he says, his prime interest is in portraits. He 'paints the truth.' It is the unsophisticated truth of a man who thinks of himself as an artist and knows there are—or rather that there have been—other artists, but who does not remember their names, he is so wrapped up in his own works. Literally uninformed, his talent saves him from ignorance. And there is no absence of concept—of a simple philosophical approach—back of the 'truth' he presents as color, both in the way it has been applied and as finished surface.

Speaking of painters, he has mentioned only one by name—Rembrandt. But there is not a shadow of imitating the lights and shadows of the master, in Guczul's work. If his painting of leaves, grass, etc., brings to mind Rousseau it is also good in itself. In any case, he may escape, as he has to a great extent, repeating a method already known, and then not having heard of Le Douanier may not mean an ultimate loss of time—to him. To an intellectual, Guczul's evident thinking in 'Modern Girl' may recall an impression or two of the one-man show of Picabia in New York a few years ago. Picabia living in the same world might have thought that way. At that, the execution is different from —the net result of thinking along the same lines less technically compelling than—the total interest achieved by Picabia.

When Guczul is not doing the thing that has been done, he paints things, in his own way, as sincerely as Harnett. His people live with the same realism as characters.

His finest work—'The Chair Caner,' 'The Peanut Man' and 'The Pickaninny'—makes one feel that he would admire Chardin.

He does not trust his memory and always paints with people, objects and landscapes before him. Each of his large canvasses, he says, required fifty hours of posing and at least an additional hundred hours to complete the background. He inveighs against quick painters. Mixing his colors with half oil, half turpentine, he allows his surfaces to dry for six months before varnishing them to bring out the 'glows.' The result is a high finish, smooth to the touch. Except in the case of 'The Peanut Man,' which was painted over another finished portrait, the paint has not cracked.

He is 'against the imagination.' But his work and his comment on it qualify this statement. The veins around the eye, the use of white, ivory black, green and deep brown, in 'The Chair Caner' are luminous without the least trace of violence. In 'Children in a Blueberry Patch' the eye is very near to the colorful youngsters though exhilaration is lacking except for the painting of the legs. In the ascending intricate background, however, the eye creates a multiplicity of detail in depth, properly submerging perspective, through use of color and the brush. Though Guczul may not have been conscious of the necessity to create distance, it has taken him away from the literal heaviness of representation felt by the merely opaque painter. The cows in the underbrush, among the many things in the background visualized as parts of distance, have become color and creative sight. A variety of space is achieved by paint applied to find its own order or process.

Guczul speaks with animation of the many still and live objects in 'The Old Spinning Wheel' : 'I wanted to put in everything.' The naive, obviously *primitive* detail of the little girl with doll on the bed strikes him now as 'too small and out of place in this picture.' Neither of these statements denies the artist's imagination. Nor does his criticism of the woman's face, from the point of view of his intention, in 'The Jungle Life': 'The sun was in her eyes, so I couldn't get her too well.' The effective painting in this picture is in the eyes of the man and in the palms, clouds and sky of the upper left background.

He has not picked flaws in 'The Peanut Man,' 'The Pickaninny' and 'The Chair Caner'—rightly letting the intense force of character of both artist and subject in these paintings speak for itself. As he says of the tiny 'Orange and Grapefruit,' they are 'on the live tree.'

Dreams, he admits, have often made him see things better the next morning while his subject poses. A recent dream he had might add to the short biography given here:

He finds himself in a Chinese city, and sees one Chinese walking down the street, reading a paper and laughing to himself. Suddenly he is surrounded by four or five Chinese, all gesticulating and laughing over the paper—saying 'Germany is a great country.' Guczul wonders to himself in the dream, saying 'They like Germany!'

As he tells this story he gesticulates like all the four or five Chinese at once, and shows surprise over the fact that 'They like Germany!'

He was born in 1886, at Temetes Kubin, Hungary, near the Roumanian and Serbian border, of Serbian extraction. After serving in the Hungarian army, he escaped to New York City, in 1913, where on the East Side he worked as a baker, his occupation in the homeland. He attended classes at the Art Students League from 1924 to 1926; motorcycled to the West Coast and back in 1924. He came to one of the islands in Lake George, in 1926, starting, he says, his original work in 1927 and staying to do the backgrounds of his large paintings. He has since terraced, landscaped, and planted most of a five-acre wooded mountain all by himself. His 'Gallery' of one small room in a temporary wood cottage in which he lives, is on one of the lower terraces. In the late winter and spring for the last several years, he has pitched tent in the Florida everglades.

He remembers drawing and painting as a child and as a baker on cardboard and cigar boxes, and carrying a sketchbook in New York's subways. Copies of Old Masters he did some years ago have been discarded. He has never exhibited outside of his 'Gallery.' What he has there, he says, is 'the very beginning. My next work will be 100 per cent.'

1942

BASIC

I

The letters of the word BASIC—first used by its sponsors Charles Kay Ogden and Ivor Armstrong Richards about 1920 with reference to an available easy English that might be made into a second language for all peoples—stand for: *British, American, Scientific, International, Commercial.* This expanded trademark gives the aim of BASIC or BASIC ENGLISH at a glance.

To grow, BASIC has fed chiefly on the Basic English Word List. It includes, printed on one side of a sheet of paper, 850 words arranged as follows: 100 words for *operations* (comprising 16 verbs, 2 auxiliary verbs, about 20 prepositions or 'directives,' an assortment of pronouns, conjunctions and expletives); 400 names for *general things*; 200 names for *picturable things*; and 150 adjectives (100 of these describing *general qualities*, and the remaining 50 the familiar *opposites* of half of these qualities). On the same sheet of paper there is also this *Summary of Rules*: Plurals in 's'; Derivatives in 'ER', 'ING', 'ED' from 300 nouns; Adverbs in 'LY' from qualifiers; Degree with 'more' and 'most'; Questions by inversion and 'do'; Operators and pronouns conjugate in full; Measurement, numerals, currency, calendar, and international terms in English form.

A writer may approach the use of BASIC in two ways: 1. As one looking for a vocabulary which will best present his special field—radio, or whatever it may be. 2. As writer. 1 and 2 are interdependent, or probably the same.

With this in mind, this running comment is offered along with extracts from C. K. Ogden's *Basic English: Introduction and Rules* (London, 1938).

Chapter I of his book is scarcely readable because of terms like

Panoptic. Ogden's wise sentence, 'Humor is out of place in a book on language'—used by the way to put over some detail of grammar—is true of part I of the book, which is not written in BASIC. Part II is, and to advantage. Perhaps the dice were loaded—that is, part I was written badly on purpose to show off part II.

From part I :

Basic English, as may be seen from the vocabulary, in which 600 out of 850 words are noun-forms, is a system in which the noun plays a predominant part. Much space has been wasted on the barren controversy between noun and verb advocates, with their claims that one or the other of these forms was historically the first speech-unit to appear. Both sides seem to have supposed that by stressing such a claim the adjective 'natural' could receive additional justification if applied to their system.

One important advantage, however, of any system which features the noun is the assistance to be derived from the pictorial method, and particularly from the pictorial dictionary to which the various Larousse compilations are already pointing the way.

Ogden's acute observation of the presumptuous use of 'natural' is good analysis of *mores*. As for the pictures in Larousse, there are also Walt Disney's and they *move*. Animated every split second they can perhaps never be absorbed as any stationary picture. They do not *tend* to confine thought like a name. We are told that the Chinese ideograph acts with the same degree of multiple suggestion. The Chinese written characters are names and acts at one and the same time. There are a good many Chinese, and perhaps after they have made BASIC their second language, they can turn around to BASIC's sponsors and say with a great deal of resignation : 'You were right, BASIC is after all a second language.'

This thought might be backed up by a story. 'It was a cold winter afternoon toward sunset. The Chinese laundryman had brought back the week's wash and left. When the package was opened, none of his patron's handkerchiefs were in it. The patron walked back in the cold to tell the laundryman. Without looking up the Chinese laundryman said merely : "Go home, you find." "Maybe you come, you find," the patron answered. "All light," the laundryman said gaily. He went out into the cold without bothering to put on a coat and this move troubled the patron.' (Patron, by the way, is not a BASIC word.)

In any case, in the house of the man who gives him a week's wash the first act of the Chinese was to go over to the mantelpiece, look at the lot of books and ask : 'How much?' 'It doesn't much matter,' he was told. The laundryman was not interested in looking at the man's linen. 'You read English?' the man queried. 'No, no savvy.'

The man had another kind of book on his desk shelf, one of the pages opened to a few Chinese ideographs—the characters resembling men standing with legs apart. The English under the Chinese writing read : 'Knowledge is to know men; Humanity is to love them.' The man thrust the book onto the laundryman, who responded gaily : 'Heh, heh, yeh, handkerchiefs tomorrow !'

Evidently the Chinese was not interested in handkerchiefs that day. And the other man was not a little impressed by the effect on the Chinese of a force that might be sensed as active in the Chinese characters. At any rate, something more active than the man could find that day in a list of 400 *general things* and 200 *picturable*.

In addition to these names [of 200 picturable things] there are a number of nouns (for example, *harmony, quality*) which do not stand for anything concrete, though all languages by a convenient make-believe have treated them as though they did. These are names of Fictions. (See Jeremy Bentham, *Theory of Fictions*). They present no special problem from a grammatical point of view, but the distinction is important if we are to understand what language is communicating . . .The nature of linguistic fictions is perhaps made clearer if they are recognized as a branch of metaphor. Metaphor as commonly understood is the analogical use of a word : a fiction may be loosely described as the analogical use of a word-function (noun) . . . *force of circumstance* is an analogy borrowed from the world of the physicist, but *force* itself, even as the physicist uses it, is a name for which no corresponding object can be found in the universe.

This quotation is not uninteresting rhetoric, but suffers from a stuffiness of extra words that flaw the thought. Why need a fiction 'be loosely described' since the author knows all about it? 'Force, as the physicist uses it' etc.—but the physicist might well say that his mathematical formula of *force* which stands for a relation of things is a kind of object. For that matter is there any object that does not represent a relation, whether a *chair*, say, or a chemical element? Not that one need get away from simplicity : chairs, grass, copper etc., but if one goes in for philosophy, explaining for the maximum number of contingencies is desirable. Otherwise there is something immoral (or *unmoral* according to BASIC usage) about the explanation. The simple man or the moral Chinese will probably decide: 'Yes, no one has found a force, but for the purpose of talking together we rather know what the word means, or should if we use it.'

The danger of analysis such as Ogden's becomes more apparent in the next few paragraphs:

There are two main ways in which the scope of a noun, or of any other word in the [BASIC] vocabulary, may be expanded: extension and specialization.

Extension is the use of a symbol, devised for one thing or group of things, to refer to some related thing or group. The relation may be that of a part to whole, as in the derivation of *letter* (epistle) from *letter* (of the alphabet); of cause to effect, as in the use of *bite* for the act of biting and the thing bitten; (etc.)

Specialization is the differentiated use of an undifferentiated word. A man who 'sends in an account' is understood to have sent in a bill. When we read in the papers of 'the death of a famous Judge' we do not speculate as to whether he was a judge of horses, wine, or pictures; we know at once that he was a legal judge. Specialization is in one sense a limiting factor, but it enlarges the scope of a general vocabulary by enabling it to dispense with words having only a very particularized usage.

Ogden could probably have avoided one of these definitions, and called 'enlarging the scope of a general vocabulary' by both methods he describes *either* 'extension' *or* 'specialization.' But to go on:

From any Basic word it is legitimate to form one specialization, and as many recognized extensions as are simple and convenient . . .

Another means of extending the vocabulary is to use one word as more than one part of speech. The most important of these transferences are:

Back, as an adverb, having the sense of the opposite of forward;
Light as an adjective (to cover 'pale');
Round as directive (preposition);
The use of certain adjectives as nouns: acid, chief, chemical, cold, cut, etc., etc . . .

But this is how Standard English so-called has grown. What then becomes of the 850 BASIC words and Ogden's claim:

The small word-list of Basic has a special value at all stages of word-learning. The list is representative of every sort of word, and gives us all the material necessary for a more detailed knowledge of the behaviour of languages of unlimited range. It is a sort of instrument for testing the use of words in newspapers and the effects desired in verse. When we put a language such as Spanish or Russian into English there is a danger of going only from words to words, with the least possible adjustment. In Basic it is necessary to keep in mind all the time what is being said, so that we are never exchanging one fixed form for another at the same level.

He says further of the teaching of idioms, collocations and the like: 'The teacher is dependent on a book which gives no reasons for anything, but is full of tests by which the learner may be marked for memory-work and even more memory-work.'

Very nice. But by means of *extension* and *specialization*, the BASIC 850 words become many more. One who is neither for nor against BASIC need not object. Yet it is only fair to stress that in BASIC as in Standard English 'it is necessary to keep in mind all the time what is being said'; that in BASIC, too, there are 'idioms' because certain words are used as more than one part of speech; and that the learner will not always find it easy to remember how to use them. Thus the BASIC word list includes *cut* as a general quality (or adjective). As an example, *the cut diamond* does not sound so good. Perhaps the predicate is intended, e.g. 'The diamond is cut.' Obviously one has to think before using this word even if one is not *learning* to speak English. Now use *cut* as a noun. It is not listed under *Things* in the BASIC word list. Think of the foreign butcher's puzzled look if you ask him to give you 'a good cut.'

The complexity of the matter increases when one realizes that the use of the word *cut* as an operative or a verb is forbidden in BASIC. As Ogden says, 'Much space has been wasted on the barren controversy between noun and verb advocates.' If the use of *cut* can be extended from qualifier to noun, why not to verb? With all respect to BASIC's founder, *cut* as a verb does sound more 'natural' to the normal English ear than *cut* as qualifier.

Moreover, the word list under 600 THINGS General and Picturable includes about 200 words which, if the BASIC system allowed, could be used as verbs to the enrichment of BASIC. Nearly all of these 200 words are the recurring familiar verbs of Standard English: act, answer, attack, back, bite, blow, control, cry, design, dust, end, etc., etc. Many of them need only 'ed' to form the past tense. The objection that the learner of English finds the conjugation of its *strong* verbs difficult is therefore minimized.

A writer can find little reason for looking for a BASIC paraphrase of the verb *control* if he has occasion to use it, other than that in BASIC *control* as a verb is forbidden. The problem becomes all the more annoying when the writer is allowed only 50 additional words in his own field and 100 words in the general field of science.

Yet in the truncated list of *operators* or verbs in BASIC there is 'be,' the contention of philosophers from Aristotle on down. This is not a surprising inclusion on the part of the author of a book with the ominous title *The Meaning of Meaning*. Perhaps the Northwest Coast tribe of Indians who have a verb which may be translated as 'to-not' have done better along this line of thinking.

The first step to a simpler word list, then, is to take out all the more complex [sic !] sorts of 'verbs,' in which in addition to the *operation* of one body on another, the *direction* of the act is more or less clearly named. Sometimes the thing talked about, in addition to the operation, is covered by one word, as when we 'rise,' 'shave,' 'feed,' and 'grumble'— where bodies and beds, hair and faces, food and mouths, feelings and the weather may be part of the word picture.

Like Swift's Laputans, the founder of BASIC begins by building from the roof down. If the thing talked about, in addition to the operation, is already covered by one monosyllabic verb, why destroy a foundation which is already there? 'Rise,' 'shave,' 'feed,' etc., are not hard words, certainly not harder than BASIC's *destruction, distribution,* and *education*. The former have the advantage of conciseness as against *to get up, to take hair off the face,* and *to take food*. The *simple* English verbs, a full number of which BASIC includes as nouns, are a shorthand for *act* and *thing* that the Chinese sees perhaps in his ideograph. From the point of view of an international speech what seems to be arbitrary neglect of these verbs is a loss.

In any case, trying to conform to BASIC the writer of instruction books on radio by looking for a paraphrase runs the risk of losing time and conciseness. He may even end up with BASIC words which both BASIC's founder and Jeremy Bentham have called *fictions*. These make mental cowards of us all, in as much as *things* and relations of things that should be pretty close to words which stand for them become dim behind films of thought, which are so to speak fifth removed from things.

*

An alternative method of forming the possessive is to use the suffix *'s* instead of the possessive preposition *of.* This makes for a more concise style.

True. But if used too often, also for a crabbed style?

There are 50 qualifiers which may form negatives, coinciding in many cases with the opposites, by adding the prefix *un* : . . . automatic, beautiful, chemical, complex, sweet, probable, regular.

Aside from the departure here from Standard English, this innovation seems pointless especially if one's prime interest is in the 850 words of BASIC, which incidentally affords the use of *not* for forming the negative of all these words.

*

Getting back to verbs again:

The operators are ten in number, if *be, seem,* and *have* are treated for convenience with the two auxiliaries *may* and *will.* In addition to these there are three analogical extras, *say, see,* and *send*—included in the vocabulary because they lend facility to communication and provide a useful link between the operators and the verb-system proper.

The combination of the ten operators and the three operator-auxiliaries with the twenty directives immediately gives us the equivalents of roughly 200 simple English verbs. Thus, *put in* = 'insert.' But since the ordinary English vocabulary is chiefly composed of synonyms distinguished by subtleties which are not relevant in more than 10 per cent of their uses, *put in* is actually the equivalent of many other verbs in particular situations. Thus, *put* (a word) *in* = 'interject,' *put* (an account) *in* = 'render,' *put* (the tea) *in* = 'infuse,' *put* (the sheep) *in* = 'fold,' *put* (a request) *in* = 'file,' *put* (a seed) *in* (the earth) = 'plant,' *put* (the baby) *in* (the bath) = 'immerse,' *put* (things) *in* (a house) = 'install,' and so forth. Let us suppose that twenty of these be on the surface for the average translation, and we have in fact not 200 but 4,000 fresh 'words,' i.e. self-evident, bipartite analytic equivalents for what in ordinary English usually involves an extra word, all without adding a single 'idiom' proper, or increasing in any way the phonetic difficulty of the foreigner.

There is a great deal of sensitivity to language in the foregoing. But by whatever name Ogden may call an idiom—'proper' or improper— the foreigner will have no end of difficulty mastering the various shades of meaning of the words *put in* in all the contexts given.

Since the purpose of the BASIC word list is to be both short and complete, its total of 18 verbs might be cut down perhaps. It is not urged that this suggestion be taken up, but the verbs appearing in the following order in the BASIC list—*come, get, give, go, keep, let, make, put, seem, take, be, do, have, say, see, send, may, will*—offer these ideas:

1. *Go* can be used with certain directives (prepositions), in accordance with BASIC practice, to cover *come*.
2. Either *get* or *take* can be dispensed with, their shades of meaning are so close.
3. The same is true of *have* or *keep*.
4. Used with certain directives, *put* can probably achieve the meaning of *send* and *give*: e.g. 'Put it in my hand' instead of 'Give it to me'; 'Put a letter in the box' instead of 'Send a letter.'
5. *Make* and *do* are very close, and *make* can include the uses of *do*.
6. Some of the connotations of *let* are included in *may* and *do*: e.g. 'Let me' or 'May I'; 'Let me, please' or 'Do, please!'
7. 'Be' can probably be discarded entirely by substituting a descriptive phrase: Instead of 'The book is on the table': 'The book on the table.'
8. *Seem* and *say* do 'very little work' (as Humpty-Dumpty once said) as compared with *see*, and probably need not be used as often as they are in English.

In any case from the point of view of BASIC there is reason for re- ducing the number of BASIC verbs. And if the objection is that the re- duction will make BASIC harder to handle, perhaps other verbs that 'do more work' than those BASIC permits might be substituted.

Of, the preposition signifying possession or close connection, is de- rived from *off*. If x is *off* y, it must have been *on* it, that is to say, in close proximity or belonging to it.

Quite kittenish! If logicians continue this line, the end of formal logic is perhaps not far off.

It would be foolish to take exception to the placing of the preposition at the end of a sentence. This word-order is sanctioned by old-established English idiom.

Good, and it would be foolish to take exception to anything that makes sense.

The tendency to let our thoughts be controlled by words is very deeply rooted . . . When we have to do without a word, we frequently become conscious for the first time of what we are saying with it. And sometimes we see that we were saying nothing—or nothing for which a special word was needed. So here is the great value of Basic for those who come to it with a knowledge of normal English.

One great step forward would be news every hour of the day and night, in a common language, from one or another of 24 stations working with a common purpose through Basic.

Ogden is against 'Babel,' the confusion of many languages. But the refreshing differences to be got from different ways of handling facts in the sound and peculiar expressions of different tongues is not to be overlooked, precisely because they have *international* worth.

II

'To know your meaning, and to state it as simply as possible' sums up the best in BASIC. Good writing means a grasp of and a closeness to subject or object rather than an addiction to a small or large vocabulary. If writing is a thing in a world of other things which it constantly tells of it cannot depend on one person's or another's 'taste.' Popular exposition may slide over facts. But good writing never does.

The following examples are given along with possible restatements in BASIC. If the BASIC versions come close to the originals, the use of the BASIC word list has not much more to do with it than mulling over a good text and a desire to keep it simple.

From Henri Poincaré's *The Value of Science* :

. . . to change the language suffices to reveal a generalization not before suspected . . .

Science in other words is a system of relations, of bringing together facts which appearances separate.

The same in BASIC : . . . to give the language a different turn is enough to make it take up a train of thought that we had no idea of before . . . Science in other words is a system of relations, of putting together facts that at a look seem separate.

1943

WORK/SUNDOWN

I should prefer to say nothing now. But a preference for silence might be misinterpreted by even the closest friends.

When he was here in 1939, I told him that I did not doubt his integrity had decided his political action, but I pointed to his head, indicating something had gone wrong. When he asked me if it was possible to educate certain politicians, I retorted, Whatever you don't know, Ezra, you ought to know *voices*. This exchange of frankness was accepted tacitly by both of us as a dissociation of values above personal bickering.

He approached literature and music at that depth. His profound and intimate knowledge and practice of these things leave that part of his mind entire. The heavy-footed never see the truth of his essay 'Mediaevalism' or know the worth of Canto I or Canto XIII, or of—

> *Sun up; work*
> *Sundown; to rest*
> *dig well and drink of the water*
> *dig field; eat of the grain*
> *Imperial power is ? And to us what is it?*
> *The fourth; the dimension of stillness.*
> *And the power over wild beasts.*

Or the weight of 'Anyone can run to excesses,' or the fact of 'Who even dead, yet hath his mind entire.'

I never felt the least trace of anti-Semitism in his presence. Nothing he ever said to me made me feel the embarrassment I always have for the 'Goy' in whom a residue of antagonism to 'Jew' remains. If we had occasion to use the words 'Jew' and 'Goy' they were no more or less ethnological in their sense than 'Chinese' and 'Italian.'

I remember an animated cartoon which pointed up human brutishness over which both of us could still chuckle. He may be condemned or forgiven. Biographers of the future may find his character as charming a subject as that of Aaron Burr. It will matter very little against his finest work overshadowed in his lifetime by the hell of Belsen which he overlooked.

1948

BOTTOM, A WEAVER

To me *Bottom: on Shakespeare* is :

1. A long poem built on a theme for the variety of its recurrences. The theme is simply that Shakespeare's text throughout favors the clear physical eye against the erring brain, and that this theme has historical implications.

2. A valid skepticism that as 'philosophy of history' (taking in the arts and sciences) my book takes exception to all philosophies from Shakespeare's point of view ('Shakespeare's,' as expressed above and as excused by my preface to the book.)

3. A continuation of my work on prosody in my other writings. In this sense my wife's music saves me a lot of words.

4. A poet's autobiography, as involvement of twenty years in a work shows him up, or as in the case of Shakespeare his words show it, are his life.

1961

FOUND OBJECTS (1962–1926)

With the years the personal prescriptions for one's work recede, thankfully, before an interest that *nature as creator* had more of a hand in it than one was aware. The work then owns perhaps something of the look of *found objects* in late exhibits—which arrange themselves as it were, one object near another—roots that have become sculpture, wood that appears talisman, and so on : charms, amulets maybe, but never really such things since the struggles so to speak that made them do not seem to have been human trials and evils—they appear entirely *natural*. Their chronology is of interest only to those who analyse carbon fractions, etc., who love historicity—and since they too, considering *nature as creator*, are no doubt right in their curiosity—and one has never wished to offend anyone—the dates of composition of the poems in this book and their out-of-print provenance are for them, not for the poets.

1962

ABOUT THE GAS AGE

[*Question*:] For one who *thinks* so much in his poetry, it seems rather strange to, in fact, *hear* you speak only of its music.

[*L.Z.*:] Somewhere in the long poem "*A*" I say—this is sort of part of me—I never remember my stuff but—

> Thinking's the lowest rung
> No one'll believe I feel this.

I can't help thinking.

The man who taught me most about history—I was saying to Dr. Goodell the other day—was Henry Adams. Drawing an analogy between Willard Gibbs' *rule of phases*, the second law of thermodynamics, and history, he saw the attractions of events happening in the human mind—you know, the old business of action and reaction and looked at it thermodynamically. There are three states of existence: one is solid, another is liquid, and the other is gas. And all thru history: it's so simple, not like 22 societies, as per Toynbee. I don't know why Mr. Toynbee never mentions Henry Adams. I mean, if you're going to have a historian, a great historian, Henry Adams is one of them, I don't know of anybody really better—maybe Gibbon.

There is solid state, and there is liquid, and there is gas. It's the same with the materials of poetry, you make images—that's pretty solid—music, it's liquid; ultimately if something vaporizes, that's the intellect. They all exist; but to tell somebody about the

My answer to a question from the audience following my reading at the American Embassy, London, May 21, 1969. It was not intended for publication, but an unauthorized mangled transcription of what I said was published in Newcastle upon Tyne that year without my knowledge.   —L.Z.

composition of the atom, whether a certain particle is left-handed or right-handed like I forget which Marx it was who talked about left-handed moths—it wasn't Karl anyway tho he had that wit.

I'd like to keep solid because I can't help myself, I was born in a gas age, but I don't want to falsify my time so I get it down; it's an attraction, but the older I get, oh I'd like to look at a leaf occasionally, and in the polluted city of New York with all the fumes and so on I really go out hunting for a crocus in an areaway.

Does that answer your question? There *is* wonderful thinking, there are some thinkers as I imply at the end of the *partita* section of "*A*". Actually I love Spinoza, but he is the gas stage and it really started for our time about then. You see it best in Shakespeare. He is just at the turning point. I wrote 500 pages about Shakespeare just to say one thing, the natural human eye is OK, but it's that erring brain that's no good, and he says it all the time. Of course, everybody says he says the opposite, but I don't think they read him right: and he begins with *Venus and Adonis*. It pursued him as if it were a mania and goes thru to *The Tempest*, the last play. You remember Prospero,

all eyes! Be silent.

And with a man like Hamlet, who you know is the opposite, the best way out is silence. I always wish I could shut up but, there again, I don't know, they say I'm a thinker—clean, I hope.

The wonderful thing about Spinoza's philosophy to me is that out of 8 definitions and 7 axioms he builds the whole system. But that's late, that's very late in philosophy, and to me it's the end of philosophy. After that they're just finding other terms for it, which is alright, every generation ought to redefine, you know, use a different term, but it ought to be a better one.

When I was a kid I started the Objectivist movement in poetry. There were a few poets who felt sympathetic towards each other and Harriet Monroe at the time insisted, we'd better have a title for it, call it something. I said, I don't want to. She insisted; so, I said, alright, if I can define it in an essay, and I used two words, *sincerity* and *objectification*, and I was sorry immediately. But it's gone down into the history books; they forgot the founder, thank heavens, and kept the terms, and, of course, I said *objectivist*, and they said *objectivism* and that makes all the difference. Well that was pretty bad, so then I spent the next thirty years to make it simple.

You see what I am talking about—well, actually I'm talking about *sight*, and *sound*, and then the third word has always bothered me but I've ended up with *intellection*. That is, Dante's *Paradiso* is a great intellect at work, not only an intelligence which is more involved with the senses, but it's when the senses vaporize and, the head floats, but sometimes it floats beautifully. All these gases are very nice if you know what you're talking about. Like mathematical formulae, that's pure abstract state, but who's not to say that that is as beautiful as some botanical convolvulae or something like that.

It occurs to me, I have this with me, I didn't intend to read it, this is heavy—would you want to hear it? It's another answer. Sometimes you do a thing in verse, and sometimes you do it in prose. To me they're both poetry. This, again, is a passage from the *partita* of "*A*". It's a short bit—

> The human son fathered by man and the sun sleeps
> As with the sun sleeps nights, but the earth
> Not quite the defense of "Still it does move"
> Goes on in my heart. His mother—
> They go on in your heart. You sit
> By and here's the Korean King who
> In the first half century—the style is—'of our Era'
> Sailed his half-cylinder of bark from the mainland
> ('In Korean,' said the Methodist native, '*paulownia* wood')
> Skirted the rapids, landfall, and there turned it down
> To dry and again over to string and play it
> His harp in the isolation of his island;
> As the child's half-size violin
> Sounded thru the test in a wind tunnel.
> Or as you may judge my Shakespeare theme—'*Love sees?*'—

Now here's the same thing as we say in prose, meaning loosely speaking the same thought, but the structure is different. It's the words that interest me. From *Bottom: On Shakespeare*:

If a man spend all time furthering himself where will he be? The reed of the grass discloses the wind; the musical reed, moisture of breath and touch. The voice or the tune is never seen. Riffling flows away on the shape of the riffle. Vico fabled: man sung before he spoke. A man longs, how can he get back what he once sang into speech. Once an ancient Korean poet crossed water in the body of an instrument that was both shallop and harp he strung to play on the other shore. As for the *music of the spheres*, the master of music, Pericles, sometimes sleeps after Pythagoras as before him to the music of interplanetary stations. It is literally not sense*less* (that is, it goes with the power of the senses) to speak of the surest sense, or of a hierarchy of senses, and like Aristotle to say there are five. The apparent intransigence of thought in such distinctions devolves from words—at least here it has just been said—'bodily motions,' Spinoza said—that twine as some stems one around another, and the intervals at which they twine are of interest only mutually—considered 'perfect' or 'short of the perfect' as the case may be or as the consideration comes up. That is the interest of the arts—and even the convolvuli of mathematics (and why may they not be called so) partake of it—the feeling that even the most intellective of them are *tangible*. This is after all a thoughtful word which has perhaps no closer definition than the casual sense of *substantial* or of *objective* intending *a solid object*. So when Dante 'thinks' a metric foot in *De Vulgari Eloquentia* a human foot stalks him like Cressid's. So the visible reference persists 'tangibly' as print, and the air of the voice in handwriting as notes.

Under the aspect of eternity, where all things exist equally with the same force as when they began to exist, nothing of the mutual need of course be *said*; thought is only conflation of extension, and extension of thought, *until* the bass-string of humility is suddenly aware of the presumption of having said something about the holiness of the treble. And then without reference to an all's equal, external existence art exists in agitation and activity where no human sense is cut off from another and netted in whatever *Ethics* such an organism as Spinoza can produce, or be increased or diminished by, 'in so far as it is understood by his nature.'

Well, maybe that explains it—they'll tell me it's difficult.

September 23, 1970

Index to Definitions

Louis Zukofsky / Additional Prose

[An Addendum to *Prepositions: The Collected Critical Essays*]

Edited by Mark Scroggins

Introduction

By Mark Scroggins

Louis Zukofsky carefully edited his essays for the collection *Prepositions*, published by Rapp & Carroll (London) in 1967 and by the Horizon Press (New York) in 1968. In 1976, two years before his death, he prepared three further items (one for each of the collection's prepositionally titled sections—"For," "With," and "About"), as well as an "index of definitions," for an expanded edition of *Prepositions*, which was finally published in 1981 by the University of California Press. *Prepositions* is Zukofsky's last word on his short critical prose. It presents his essays in the order, arrangement, and form that he most preferred. Of course, *Prepositions* does not collect all of Zukofsky's short critical pieces. During his long career, he published a number of book reviews and miscellaneous notes that did not find their way into the collection. The wisdom of his selection, however, is clear: while all of the excluded pieces are recognizably Zukofsky's, none of them comes up to the exacting standards of conciseness and intellectual density he applied to the essays included in *Prepositions*.

The eight pieces reprinted in this addendum to Zukofsky's collected critical prose must be recognized as separate and apart from— no part of—*Prepositions* itself. While they have been gathered here because of their compelling interest to readers of Zukofsky, those readers need continually to bear in mind that this is material which, when he came to gather his critical essays into a definitive statement, Zukofsky himself chose either to severely edit or to not reprint at all.

Most significant of these additional pieces are the five essays published as 5 *Statements for Poetry*. In early 1958, in preparation for a summer stint as poet-in-residence at San Francisco State College, Zukofsky put together what he clearly considered his five most important critical essays. Lightly edited by Zukofsky, typed by his wife Celia, and mimeographed and stapled in an edition of 110 copies, 5 *Statements for Poetry* was intended as a course text for his San Francisco students. Its first three essays—"Program: 'Objectivists' 1931," "Sincerity and Objectification," and "'Recencies' in Poetry"—had been published in 1931 and

1932, when Zukofsky had been the prime mover and theorist behind the Objectivist "movement" in poetry. "Program: 'Objectivists' 1931" served as the editorial note to the February 1931 "Objectivists" issue of *Poetry: A Magazine of Verse*, which Zukofsky had edited; "Sincerity and Objectification" also appeared in that issue. "'Recencies' in Poetry," which had begun life as a talk Zukofsky delivered at New York's Gotham Book Mart in August 1931, was published as the preface to Zukofsky's *An "Objectivists" Anthology*. The remaining two essays were more recent: "Poetry/*For My Son When He Can Read,*" written in 1946, had been published in 1948; "A Statement for Poetry," written in 1950, had been published in 1952.

In *Prepositions*, Zukofsky reprinted "Poetry/*For My Son When He Can Read*" and "A Statement for Poetry" in texts very similar to the versions published in *5 Statements for Poetry*. The three "Objectivist" essays, however, were radically revised for *Prepositions*—mostly, as Zukofsky points out in his "Prefatory Note" to *Prepositions* and in his 1968 interview with L. S. Dembo, through omission. "Program: 'Objectivists' 1931," "Sincerity and Objectification," and "'Recencies' in Poetry," which occupy thirty-five typescript pages in *5 Statements for Poetry*, were boiled down to the eight printed pages of *Prepositions'* "An Objective." In reducing these three often quite discursive essays to a quarter of their original length, Zukofsky wanted to isolate and lay bare his most essential statements of poetics. In so doing, he quite consciously removed those statements from their contexts as passages in manifestos for an emerging movement in American poetry. In their earliest published forms, and as they were reprinted in *5 Statements* in 1958, these three essays are deeply involved—often in quite pugnacious ways —with the literary landscape of the early 1930s: "Sincerity and Objectification," for instance, bases its advocacy of the poetic principles of its title on a close reading of the works of Zukofsky's friend Charles Reznikoff, a painstaking literary craftsman entirely ignored by the literary establishment, while "'Recencies' in Poetry" is in large part an attack on the emerging critical establishment that bases its evaluative methods on the practices exemplified in T. S. Eliot's journal *The Criterion* (founded in 1922).

When he came to revise these essays for *Prepositions*, Zukofsky had little use for the term "Objectivist" as applied to a particular historical moment. "The objectivist," as he puts it to Dembo, "is one person, not a group, and as I define him he is interested in living with the things as they exist, and as a 'wordsman,' he is a craftsman who puts words together into an object." The trappings of the Objectivist "movement," then, only obscured the extent to which Zukofsky's statements of objectivist poetics described the operations of his own poetry and served as universal descriptions of poetry he admired. Zukofsky's excision of the bulk of these "Objectivist" essays is also congruent with the general trends of his thought: as he grew older, he increasingly rejected both the political—as manifested in the local involvements of specific poets in specific struggles—and the historical—at least in its most common form, the chronicling of names, dates, and named events. "History's best emptied of names' / impertinence met on the ways," he writes in "A"-22. (In the only substantive change Zukofsky made in "Poetry/*For My Son When He Can Read*" between its 1948 periodical publication and its appearance ten years later in 5 *Statements*, "Roosevelt" becomes "a President" [*Prepositions*, page 6].)

Some of the few excisions Zukofsky made in the three "Objectivist" essays for their publication in 5 *Statements for Poetry* reflect his own turn away from the political (a turn also evident between the two halves of "A"-9). His radical condensing of the three essays into "An Objective" for *Prepositions* goes much further. By cutting these essays back to their most significant statements, Zukofsky in essence *generalizes* his doctrines of poetics, cutting them loose from their entanglements with the readings of specific texts and with the local struggles of literary politics. Once they are freed from such contingencies, the statements of "An Objective" can be seen, not as descriptions of "Objectivist" poetry, but as descriptions of poetry in general. "An Objective," then, becomes of a piece with "Poetry/*For My Son When He Can Read*" and "A Statement for Poetry," each of which attempts to arrive at as universal as possible a "definition of poetry."

Condensing brings with it difficulty for the reader. While the three "Objectivist" essays, as printed in 5 *Statements*, are ample, discursive, and peppered with illustrative passages, "An Objective" is dense, obdurate, and demands rereading: precisely, one suspects, as Zukofsky wanted it. The poet's "imbu[ing] criticism with something of the worth and method of his craft," as Zukofsky puts it in his "Prefatory Note," will necessarily result in a critical statement whose very brevity reflects the importance of its doctrine. As in Zukofsky's poetry, every word counts; its reader, in turn, must bring to it a concentration similar to that demanded by the poems. In the 5 *Statements* texts of these three essays, a reader can learn much about the literary climate in which Zukofsky forged his poetics, and can find the particular poetic examples from which he inductively arrived at his more general statements. But this information by no means provides a shortcut to understanding "An Objective"; and while the material Zukofsky omitted from the three essays is of compelling interest to any reader interested in his writing career, it perhaps in the end obscures the significance of the poetics "An Objective" most compactly adumbrates.

While Zukofsky incorporated the majority of the *5 Statements* texts of "Poetry/*For My Son When He Can Read*" and "A Statement for Poetry" into *Prepositions* largely unchanged, he also trimmed these two essays. Each essay includes, as something of a tailpiece to its primary discussion, a list (or lists) of various quotations, from his own work, from that of his friends and contemporaries, and from literary history in general, that he found talismanic. In *Prepositions* these quotations have been deleted from the two essays. Perhaps most strikingly, the *5 Statements for Poetry* text of "Poetry/*For My Son When He Can Read*" includes the entire text of Walt Whitman's "Respondez!," a poem which Zukofsky singles out as "Whitman's greatest poem." It was included (under various titles and in variously revised editions) in editions of *Leaves of Grass* between 1856 and 1876, but Whitman excluded it from "definitive" later editions. (In a revision-by-excision that looks forward to Zukofsky's own practice, Whitman retained six lines of "Respondez!" as "Reversals" and another three as "Transpositions.")

I have tried to produce here an edition that records as thoroughly and faithfully as possible the state of these five essays' texts in their 1958 *5 Statements for Poetry* publication, and the variations between that publication and their earlier appearances. My listing of variants might seem unduly pedantic, but one must never forget the extent to which Zukofsky's writing depends upon often minute, jeweller-like machinings of language. In his "Foreword" to *5 Statements*, Zukofsky refers to his essays as "stops in the excursion of a poet who wished to imbue criticism with something of the worth and method of his craft." Zukofsky liked these phrases, and repeated them in the "Prefatory Note" to *Prepositions*, but with a significant revision—"*steps* in the excursion of a poet who wished to imbue criticism with something of the worth and method of his craft" (my emphasis). This single-letter revision, which dramatically alters the sense of its sentence, can teach us much about Zukofsky's art.

The three further items included in this addendum to *Prepositions* are each of significant interest to Zukofsky's readers. Zukofsky's "Poet's Preface" to his and Celia Zukofsky's translation of Catullus fixes the method of that decidedly heterodox translation in a pair of memorable sentences. His foreword to the 1967 edition of *"A" 1-12* is a complex and lyrical commentary on the first half of the long poem on which he labored for almost half a century, and whose twenty-four-movement structure was nearing completion when he looked back on its first twelve movements. Zukofsky's 1968 interview with L. S. Dembo provides a fascinating commentary on a wide variety of aspects of his writing. Zukofsky elaborates at length on his critical terms "sincerity" and "objectification"; he discusses his views on epistemology and the theory of language; and, through detailed examinations of a number of his short poems, he gives what amounts to a description of his working poetics. It may seem odd to include an interview in a volume of critical *prose*—although Zukofsky's spoken discourse comes closer to formal "prose" than that of many other poets—but of course there is fine precedent in the expanded *Prepositions*'s inclusion of "For Wallace Stevens" and "About the Gas Age," both edited versions of largely impromptu "talks."

The editor extends thanks to Jennifer A. Low and Paul Zukofsky for reading and commenting on the introduction and annotations, to Bill Armstrong at the Interlibrary Loan Division of Florida Atlantic University's Wimberley Library for tracking down fugitive publications, and to Suzanne Deffendall for word-processing support.

5 Statements for Poetry

Editorial Note

This edition reproduces the 1958 text of 5 *Statements for Poetry*.

The first three essays included in 5 *Statements for Poetry* were first published in the early 1930s. "Program: 'Objectivists' 1931" appeared in *Poetry: A Magazine of Verse* 37.5 (February 1931): 268–272. "Sincerity and Objectification: *With Special Reference to the Work of Charles Reznikoff*" appeared in the same issue of *Poetry*, 272–285. "'Recencies' in Poetry" appeared as the preface to *An "Objectivists" Anthology*, edited by Louis Zukofsky (Le Beausset, Var, France, and New York: To, Publishers, 1932), 9–25. There are minor differences between the texts of these essays in their earliest published forms and in their 5 *Statements* form. This edition uses 5 *Statements for Poetry* as its copy-text, but in order to present as full a record as possible of the progressive states of these essays, I have included in footnotes the significant differences between the 5 *Statements* texts and their earlier publications.

The 1932 text of "'Recencies' in Poetry," which was typeset and printed in France, has a large number of typographical errors and is extremely inconsistent in its treatment of book, periodical, and poem titles. Most of these errors and inconsistencies are eliminated in the 5 *Statements* text; I have corrected a few others for this edition, always signalling such corrections in footnotes. I have retained Zukofsky's own quotations of others' poetry, including his few slight alterations.

"Poetry/*For My Son When He Can Read*" was first published in *Cronos* 2.4 (March 1948): 22–30, and was reprinted as an appendix to the first edition of *"A" 1–12* (Kyoto, Japan: Origin Press, 1959), 269–288; "A Statement for Poetry" appeared as "Poetry (1952)" in *Montevallo Review* 1.3 (Spring 1952): 49–54. The texts of the periodical publications of these essays are very close to the versions published in 5 *Statements,* and since the 5 *Statements* texts of these essays are in turn very close to those reprinted in *Prepositions,* this edition presents only the additional material that Zukofsky chose to omit when he edited them for *Prepositions.*

5 Statements for Poetry

FOREWORD

These five essays may be viewed as stops in the excursion of a poet who wished to imbue criticism with something of the worth and method of his craft—poetry. In this sense, four of the pieces are restatements of the constant theme first expressed as "Sincerity and Objectification" in 1930.

Louis Zukofsky
May 9, 1958

PROGRAM: "OBJECTIVISTS" 1931

An Objective: (Optics) — The lens bringing the rays from an object to a focus. (Military use) — That which is aimed at. (Use extended to poetry) — Desire for what is objectively perfect, inextricably the direction of historic and contemporary particulars.

It is understood that historic and contemporary particulars may mean a thing or things as well as an event or a chain of events: i.e., an Egyptian pulled-glass bottle in the shape of a fish or oak leaves, as well as the performance of Bach's *Matthew Passion* in Leipzig, or the Russian revolution and the rise of metallurgical plants in Siberia.

To avoid repetition: the visiting editor of this issue of POETRY has indicated his interests in American poetry of the last decade in an article published in the latest quarterly number of *The Symposium*. ("American Poetry 1920–1930", Vol. II, 1 Jan. 1931)[1]

The following list of works absolutely necessary to students of poetry is reprinted from this article:

Ezra Pound—*XXX Cantos* (Paris, 1930); William Carlos Williams— *Spring and All* (Dijon, 1923); Marianne Moore's *Observations* (New York, 1924); T. S. Eliot's *The Waste Land* (New York, 1922), and *Marina* (London, 1930); E. E. Cummings' *Is 5* (New York, 1926); references to earlier volumes of Cummings; Wallace Stevens' *Harmonium*; Robert McAlmon's *North America*; Charles Reznikoff; *The Exile Nos. 3* and *4*, edited by Ezra Pound (Chicago, 1928).

These poets seem to the present editor to have written in accordance with the principles heading this note. So do the contributors to

1. [The material within parentheses does not appear in the 1931 text.]

this number. (The contributors to the "Objectivists" February 1931 issue of *Poetry* were Carl Rakosi, Louis Zukofsky, Howard Weeks, Robert McAlmon, Charles Reznikoff, Norman Macleod, Kenneth Rexroth, S. Theodore Hecht, George A. Oppen, Harry Roskolenkier, Whittaker Chambers, Henry Zolinsky, Basil Bunting, Jesse Loewenthal, Emanuel Carnevali, John Wheelwright, Richard Johns, Martha Champion, Parker Tyler, Charles Henri Ford, Samuel Putnam, Joyce Hopkins, William Carlos Williams and René Taupin.)[2]

It has been especially pleasant to include work of Rimbaud as translated by Emanuel Carnevali. Of Carnevali, Mr. Ezra Pound writes:

Several years ago Professor Michaud expressed his view that Carnevali was one of the two poets in America whose work attained an international standard. Michaud was writing in a careless and popular manner, and his judgments do not carry any particular weight; however, that sort of thing is evidently good enough for the Sorbonne.

One has known of Carnevali's existence for a decade. The work has shown temperament, "fire," a refusal to be controlled, an intensity of feeling without which no poet is ever satisfactory, though this fury is not in itself a complete poetic equipment.

For a number of years one has recognized that Carnevali was one of the few who *might,* and one has speculated as to whether his handicap was too great. It seems to me that the time has now come when one can without reservation recognize his validity as a writer. (The reader is referred to Carnevali's *The Hurried Man*—Contact Press, Paris; to the files of the first four numbers of *Pagany;* and to many poems in POETRY since his introduction in March, 1918.)

Implied stricture of names generally cherished as famous, but not mentioned in this editor's *American Poetry 1920–1930* or included among the contributors to this issue, is prompted by the historical method of the Chinese sage who wrote, "Then for nine reigns there was no literary production."

None at all; because there was neither consciousness of the "Objectively perfect" nor an interest in clear or vital "particulars." Nothing—neither a new object nor the stripping of an old to the light —was "aimed" at. Strabismus may be a topic of interest between two strabismics; those who see straight look away.

2. [The material within parentheses does not appear in the 1931 text.]

Ernest Hemingway's *They All Made Peace—What Is Peace?* is as good
now as it was in *The Little Review* in 1922:

All of the turks are gentlemen and Ismet Pasha is a
Little deaf. But the Armenians. How about the
Armenians?
Well, the Armenians.

Lord Curzon likes young boys.
So does Chicherin.
So does Mustapha Kemal. He is good looking too. His eyes
Are too close together but he makes war. That is the way he is.

Lord Curzon does not love Chicherin. Not at all. His beard
Tickles and his hands are cold. He thinks all the time.

Lord Curzon thinks too. But he is much taller and goes to
St. Moritz.

Mr. Child does not wear a hat.
Baron Hayashi gets in and out of the automobile.
Monsieur Barrère gets telegrams. So does Marquis Garonni.
His telegrams come on motorcycles from MUSSOLINI.
MUSSOLINI has nigger eyes and a bodyguard, and has
His picture taken reading a book upside down. MUSSOLINI is
Wonderful. Read *The Daily Mail.*

I used to know MUSSOLINI. Nobody liked him then. Even I
Didn't like him. He was a bad character. Ask Monsieur Barrère.

We all drink cocktails. Is it too early to have a cocktail?
How about a drink, George? Come on and we'll have a cocktail,
Admiral. Just time before lunch. Well what if we do? Not too dry.

Well, what do you boys know this morning?

O they're shrewd. They're shrewd.

Who have we got in on the subcommission this morning, Admiral?

M. Stambulski walks up the hill and down the hill. Don't talk
About M. Venizelos. He is wicked. You can see it. His beard shows it.

Mr. Child is not wicked.
Mrs. Child has flat breasts and Mr. Child is an idealist and wrote
Harding's campaign speeches and calls Senator Beveridge Al.
You know me Al.
Lincoln Steffens is with Child. The big C makes the joke easy.

Then there is Mosul
And the Greek Patriarch.
What about the Greek Patriarch?

The materials of poetry:

The small magazines of today and the very recent past must be
praised for helping to keep up an interest in these matters.[3]

3. [The 1931 text continues as follows, without a paragraph break:]
    Mr. Pound has treated this subject in detail in an article in *The English Journal*
(Chicago) for November, 1930. The small magazines are to be praised for standing
on their own against the business of the publishing racket, the "pseudo-kulchuh" of
certain national liberal weeklies published in New York, and the guidance of the
American university.
    Pound, Williams, McAlmon, Cummings, Reznikoff, etc., have had to publish a
good deal of their work in privately printed editions. In every case the work was worth
publishing, a statement not applicable to 95% or more of the usual publishers' lists.
At least one American publisher could save his face, and add honor and intelligence
to publishing, by reprinting Ezra Pound's critical works—*Spirit of Romance, Pavannes
and Divisions, Instigations, How to Read,* etc.—all of the utmost importance to any discussion of the materials of poetry.
    Mr. Parker Tyler and Mr. Charles Henri Ford gladly offered their poems for a
symposium including the editor, and they are offered his thanks.
    Miss Harriet Monroe and Mr. Morton Dauwen Zabel deserve the sincerest appre-
ciation for giving over these pages to the contributors and the editor. Finally, parody-
ing a great writer (V. I. Ulianov—*The State and Revolution*) editing this number has
been too pleasant and too useful to permit further discourse about it.

SINCERITY AND OBJECTIFICATION

With Special Reference to the Work of Charles Reznikoff

I

In 1918, Reznikoff published twelve lines (*vide XII, Five Groups of Verse*) containing in their elements the atmosphere of Eliot's *Waste Land* and *Hollow Men*. The poem included the line,

> Smooth and white with loss of leaves and bark—

and since Eliot's *Poems* were first published in America in 1920, there can hardly be a question of the influence of method in a discussion of the line's value. Reznikoff reprinted this poem in the 1927 collection: one guesses, not for any care the author may have had for the particular dejection expressed, for since that state he has been concerned with other matters, but for the element of method already apparent in the clarity of image and word-tone.

Simultaneously, Reznikoff excluded, from his 1927 collection, certain early work. He denied himself *symboliste* semi-allegorical gleam, and anticipated a conviction that surrealism in 1928 was not essentially novel, and that for him at least, ten years earlier, it was not worth doing.

> Showing a torn sleeve, with stiff and shaking fingers the old
>   man
> Pulls off a bit of baked apple, shiny with sugar,
> Eating with reverence food, the great comforter.

> *IX — Third Group of Verse*

The verbal qualities of Reznikoff's shorter poems do not form mere pretty bits (American poetry, circa 1913) but suggest, as in the quotation heading this paragraph, entire aspects of thought: economics, beliefs, literary analytics, etc. The entire matter involves the process of active literary omission and a discussion of method finding its way in the acceptance of two criteria: sincerity and objectification.

II

In sincerity shapes appear concomitants of word combinations, precursors of (if there is continuance) completed sound or structure, melody or form. Writing occurs which is the detail, not mirage, of seeing, of thinking with the things as they exist, and of directing them along a line of melody. Shapes suggest themselves, and the mind senses and receives awareness. Parallels sought for in the other arts call up the perfect line of occasional drawing, the clear beginnings of sculpture not proceeded with.

Presented with sincerity, the mind even tends to supply, in further suggestion which does not attain rested totality, the totality not always found in sincerity and necessary only for perfect rest, complete appreciation. This rested totality may be called objectification—the apprehension satisfied completely as to the appearance of the art form as an object. That is: distinct from print which records action and existence and incites the mind to further suggestion, there exists, tho it may not be harbored as solidity in the crook of an elbow, writing (audibility in two-dimensional print) which is an object or affects the mind as such. The codifications of the rhetoric books may have something to do with an explanation of this attainment, but its character may be simply described as the arrangement, into one apprehended unit, of minor units of sincerity—in other words, the resolving of words and their ideation into structure. Granted that the word combination "minor unit of sincerity" is an ironic index of the degradation of the power of the individual word in a culture which seems hardly to know that each word in itself is an arrangement, it may be said that each word possesses objectification to a powerful degree; but that the facts carried by one word are, in view of the preponderance of facts carried by combinations of words, not sufficiently explicit to warrant a realization of

rested totality such as might be designated an art form. Yet the objectification which is a poem, or a unit of structural prose, may exist in a
very few lines. Three examples—one of sincerity, and two of objectification—are cited from Reznikoff:

I   *Aphrodite Urania*

The ceaseless weaving of the uneven water
                                                Third Group of Verse

II   *Hellenist*

As I, barbarian, at last, although slowly, could read Greek,
At "blue-eyed Athena"
I greeted her picture that had long been on the wall:
The head slightly bent forward under the heavy helmet,
As if to listen; the beautiful lips slightly scornful.
                                                Jerusalem the Golden

III

How shall we mourn you who are killed and wasted,
Sure that you would not die with your work unended—
As if the iron scythe in the grass stops for a flower.
                                                First Group of Verse

The first example illustrates sincerity, not objectification, each
word possessing remarkable energy as an image of water as action. The
title carries connotative and associative meaning in itself and in relation to the line; yet the line and title together, tho interdependent,
have not been arranged as a unit in the condition or relation of an
object. Instead, the mind is attracted to the veracity of the particular
craft, the validity of writing apprehending the most energetic con-
stituents of possible objectification.

The second and third examples are objectification. In the second,
the purposeful crudity of the first line as against the quantitative (not
necessarily classic) hexameter measures of the others, the use of words
of two syllables (*greeted, picture, slightly,* etc.) with suitable variations of
words of four and three (*barbarian, beautiful*); the majority of the words
accented on the first syllable, all resolve into a structure (which incidentally translates the Hellenic) to which the mind does not wish to

add; nor does it, any more than when it contemplates a definite object by itself. The mind may conceivably prefer one object to another - the energy of the heat which is Aten to the benignness of the light which is Athena. But this is a matter of preference rather than the invalidation of the object not preferred.[1]

The second example is so much an object that the title, *Hellenist*, is a mere tag not even necessary for designation. The third example needs no title and has none. The fact that it was originally an epitaph for Gaudier Brzeska may compel the attention of a few, but adds nothing to the poem as object. Objectification in this poem is attained in the balance of the first two lines; the third line adds the grace of ornament in a simile, as might the design painted around a simple bowl.

At any time, objectification in writing is rare. The poems or the prose structures of a generation are few. Properly no verse should be called a poem if it does not convey the totality of perfect rest. In contemporary writing, the poems of Ezra Pound alone possess objectification to a most constant degree; his objects are musical shapes. Objectification is to be found in Poems *VIII, X, XVIII, XXIII, XXVI* in William Carlos Williams' *Spring and All*. With the exception of Marianne Moore's poems *An Octopus* and *Like a Bulrush*, and T. S. Eliot's *Mr. Appollinax*, progressions of sincerity and not objectification are to be found in these poets. It is interesting that the work of Marianne Moore is largely a portrait of the author's character intent upon the presentation which is sincerity, rather than the revealed rest of objectification which is, for example, *An Octopus*. In the work of T. S. Eliot it is often the single quatrain (or whatever the unit of composition may be) which possessed objectification; together, his quatrains are a series rather than the entirety of a poem. Whatever objectification the writings of E. E. Cummings possess (i.e., *Him, Song III, Amores VII, Unrealities V* in *Tulips and Chimneys*; at least a half-dozen poems in *Is 5*) is an equilibrium between the extremely connotative speech of an energy of five senses which are vitally young, and an aptness of purposeful print, and musical rhetoric weaving this energy into an interlacing (sometimes, unfortunately, astray). To what extent objectification bearing the trade-mark of the Americas may be expected out of a geography and humanity constantly shifting, is indicated with ironic evenness in

1. It is assumed that epistemological problems do not affect existence, that a personal structure of relations might be a definite object, or *vice versa*. [Zukofsky's footnote, present in both 1931 and *5 Statements*.]

Robert McAlmon's *North America, Continent of Conjecture* (1929): mock historicalness, positing that "in the justness of her undertakings [America] had a strict resemblance to other countries and still has it," joins isolate attenuations—chorus blues of a possible *American Songbag*—and offers not merely North America's but the race's *Unfinished Poem.* More objectification cannot be expected from writing than from its subject matter—whatever exists. Still humans live alongside of objects, and those interested assume poems are such. The degree of objectification in the work of Charles Reznikoff is small.

It is questionable, however, whether the state of rest achieved by objectification is more pertinent to the mind than presentation in detail. Probably deferring to an ideal of perfection, Reznikoff has called his writings in cadence, not poems, but verse. They are actually almost constant examples of sincerity. For, of writing one may at least expect not the meretricious—a contact with concepts which does not result in, but misses, tangible rendition.

There is to be noted in Reznikoff's lines the isolation of each noun so that in itself it is an image, the grouping of nouns so that they partake of the quality of things being together without violence to their individual intact natures. The simple sensory adjectives are as necessary as the nouns. If Reznikoff has written elsewhere of the "imperious dawn," the single abstract adjective occurs without the pang of reverie. The metaphor, as in all good writing, has been presented with conciseness in a word. Another writer would have at least a distended clause on "Necessity with ruling arm."

The disadvantage of strained metaphor is not that it is necessarily sentimental (the sentimental may at times have its positive personal qualities) but that it carries the mind to a diffuse everywhere and leaves it nowhere. The belief that writing should not do the last is not assumed a moot point. A writer will not pile on metaphor, any more than a musician sensitive to declamation will destroy Shakespeare's line in an arrangement like "Co-ome away, co-ome away, death." One is brought back to the entirety of the single word which is in itself a relation, an implied metaphor, an arrangement and a harmony.[2]

2. The creation of new words, as in Joyce's *Work in Progress*, obviously does not violate the old; he is merely creating new arrangements and new harmonies. Incidentally, Gertrude Stein does the opposite; i.e., she uses old words for all the possible connotative and grammatical associations she can get out of them. [Zukofsky's footnote, present in both 1931 and *5 Statements*.]

> Ships dragged into the opaque green of the sea,
> Visible winds flinging houses apart—
> And here the poplar lifting the pavement an inch.
>
> *Third Group of Verse*

The economy of presentation in this writing is a reassertion of faith that the combined letters—the words—are absolute symbols for objects, states, acts, interrelations, thoughts about them. If not, why use words? The words, for example, render the equivalent of the sounds of things, sometimes of birds:

> The traveler
> Whom a bird's notes surprise
> His eyes
> Search the trees—
>
> *Jerusalem the Golden*[3]

In a work most indigenously of these States, and beginning perhaps a century of writing, as Wordsworth's preface of 1800 began it in England, in *Spring and All* (1923) William Carlos Williams writes:

Crude symbolism is to associate emotions with natural phenomena, such as anger with lightning, flowers with love; it goes further and associates certain textures with . . . It is typified by the use of the word "like" or that "evocation" of the "image" which served us for a time. Its abuse is apparent. The insignificant "image" may be "evoked" never so ably and still mean nothing.

An excellent specific for writers: yet the correction of the contemporary fault does not necessarily dictate the use of the bare catalog, tho the last may be used more effectively than in Whitman—Whitman himself did it; the simile can be not a wandering ornament, but a confirmation of the objects or acts which the writer is setting down. *Like*'s have often been seen together, or have been strongly felt together, as in Reznikoff's:

> From the bare twigs
> Rows of drops like shining buds are hanging.
>
> *First Group of Verse*

i.e., and each drop is close to where a bud may be.

3. [This passage is cited as *"Uncollected"* in the 1931 publication.]

That preoccupation with the accuracy of detail in writing—which is sincerity—is evident on a larger scale in Reznikoff's narrative verse, perhaps the most neglected contribution to writing in America in the last ten years. Avoiding the subterfuge of those who have "written narrative poems" with one eye on the glory that was Greece (Sophocles or the *Anthology*), or the glamour which was Arthurian romance, or the agility which was Chaucer, etc.—subterfuge which has tended to confirm a suspicion that narrative poetry is perhaps not easy to our age— Reznikoff, in his *Third* and *Fourth Groups of Verse*, again looked about him (in the boroughs of New York) and wrote verse which is definitely his own and thus *sincerely* contemporary. Among these poems there is this example of objectification from the *Fourth Group:*

> The shoemaker sat in the cellar's dusk beside his bench and
>   sewing-machine, his large blackened hands, finger-tips
>   flattened and broad, busy.
> Through the grating in the sidewalk over his window, papers
>   and dust were falling year by year.
>
> At evening Passover would begin. The sunny street was
>   crowded. The shoemaker could see the feet of those who
>   walked over the grating.
> He had one pair of shoes to finish and he would be through.
> His friend came in, a man with a long black beard, in shabby, dirty
>   clothes, but with shoes newly cobbled and blacked.
> "Beautiful outside, really the world is beautiful."
> A pot of fish was boiling on the stove. Sometimes the water
>   bubbled over and hissed. The smell of the fish filled the
>   cellar.
> "It must be beautiful in the park now. After our fish we'll take
>   a walk in the park." The shoemaker nodded.
> The shoemaker hurried his work on the last shoe. The pot on
>   the stove bubbled and hissed. His friend walked up and
>   down the cellar in shoes newly cobbled and blacked.

For the rest there is sincerity—in the rendering of character and speech; in the rendering of speech of our time singular enough to be recorded in a poem; in the tension of tragedy *XI, Third Group:*

> She sat by the window opening into the airshaft,
> And looked across the parapet
> At the new moon.

She would have taken the hairpins out of her carefully coiled
     hair,
And thrown herself on the bed in tears;
But he was coming and her mouth had to be pinned into a smile.

If he would have her, she would marry whatever he was,
She who, slim and gentle once, would soon become clumsy,
     talking harshly.

A knock. She lit the gas and opened her door.
Her aunt and the man—skin loose under his eyes, the face
     slashed with wrinkles.
"Come in," she said as gently as she could and smiled.

In the last quotation, melody has been stopped and monodies of
recurrent prose paragraphs have been substituted. (Cf. Pound's Cathay,
in which melody is continuous—even a line such as "Emotion is born
out of habit" is melodious in the context.) The total rhythm has been
lulled to emphasize each word's particular hush, with the result that
objectification, inevitably recognized as the complete satisfaction
derived from melody in a poem, is missed. Yet the lives of Reznikoff's
people slowly occur in the sincerity of the craft with which he has chosen to subdue them. One returns in the end not to the aging girl at the
window, nor to "her aunt and the man," but to the sincerity which has
seen, considered, and weighed the tone these things have when rendered in only necessary words.

Analogies sidetrack, but in an explanation of the elementary they
are convenient elements. To the vulgar utilitarian a bookcase rocks
perhaps, but a preponderance of verbal carelessness does not even
wobble. Moreover, one is fooled by the "vested interests" into the belief
that "everybody is writing." To attract these interests, the "purple passages" in Reznikoff might be quoted; from the *Fifth Group:*

> These inconsiderable seconds fill
> The basins of our lives to overflowing,
> And we are emptied
> Into the sink and pipes of death.

"I have a quarrel with the clock" and "How furiously it ticks this fine
morning" are even more worthy of notice.

Weaknesses in Reznikoff's verse may be pointed out. But when sincerity in writing is present the insincere may be cut out at will and information, not ignorance, remains. Sincerity among authors differs with the range of their sensations and apperceptions, but what is negative to sincerity remains negative to all who are sincere. So much that is vicious, as writing, is omitted from all of them, and of these there are probably no more than can be counted on the fingers of both hands in a generation. Reznikoff is included among these. One speaks of sincerity as of that ability necessary for existence if one is a writer. Naturally, the bubble does not know what a more actual body brushing past it may do to it, and in a minute it is not even a bubble.

III

Interested in craft, Reznikoff has not found it derogatory to his production to infuse his care for significant detail and precision into the excellent verbalisms of others. In *Editing and Glosses* he has given the main narrative and verbal substance of most of the Pentateuch and of the episodes connected with the life of David. For the most part, the *Glosses* are quotations out of the King James' Version, verified or altered by a study of the Hebrew. The narrative has been rendered concisely in emphasized cadence and given the condition of Reznikoff's mental bearings and literal art.

It is more important for the communal good that individual authors should spend their time recording and objectifying good writing wherever it is found (note the use of quotations in Marianne Moore from Government guide-books, Pound's translations and quotations in the *Cantos*, Carlos Williams' passages out of Spanish and early American sources in *In the American Grain*; cf. Reznikoff's *The English in Virginia* in *Pagany IV* 1930) than that a plenum of authors should found their fame on all sorts of personal vagueness—often called "sophistication."

Recording:

> I have run through a troop,
> And jumped over a wall.
> He teaches my hands war,
> To bend the bow;

He has given me my enemies:
I made them as dust before the wind,
I threw them away as dirt in the street.

Reznikoff has done better than improvising on *David and Michal.* Admitting in a conversation that he would now have this final passage of the *Glosses* omitted, Reznikoff's defense of his lapse may well be the continual strain of having to publish one's own work for a "literary market" not interested in sincerity as craft.[4] And yet, sincerity, even in isolation, persists.

4. In this connection it is necessary to note three exceptions: first, Malcom Cowley commented briefly but favorably on an early collection of Reznikoff's verse published in 1920, but since then revised. Second, Miss Monroe in February, 1921, called his brief free-verse poems "as incisive as a hokku." Third, Ezra Pound has expressed the opinion that Reznikoff's verse and prose are "good"; also, "after reading Reznikoff's work, suspicions as to whether the next wave of literature will be Jewish; and whether the lack of prose in German is due to drawing off the idiomatic energy into Yiddish."

Mr. Reznikoff's bibliography is as follows: *Five Groups of Verse,* 1927 (collections of 1918, '19, '20, '21, revised); *Nine Plays,* 1927; *By the Waters of Manhattan* (*Paper Books*), 1930; *An Annual,* 1929 (including *Editing and Glosses*): all privately printed, the author "set the type by hand and did the presswork" of the first two. Reference to Reznikoff's prose and *Nine Plays in Verse* is omitted in this article, which is an extract from an essay written a year ago. [Zukofsky's footnote, present in 1931 but omitted in *5 Statements.*]

"RECENCIES" IN POETRY

The intention of this is not to object in behalf of the February 1931 issue of *Poetry*[1] (Chicago) but to offer some explanations. No apologies—Except what is perhaps one: that had the editor managed to include two purposive statements in Feb. *Poetry*, his analysis of confusions might have agreed with the analyzed confusions of his readers and saved a quantity of subsequent correspondence. The absence of not seeing more than the nadir of the nose—the absence of a habit of reading 4 or 5 times for a meaning—in certain readers is probably regrettable. However that may be, these are the statements:

1—The quotes around "objectivists" distinguish between its popular meaning in the "Program" of Feb. *Poetry*, and the philosophical etiquette associated with objectivist.

2—The several definitions of *An Objective* and the use of this term extended to poetry—as slightly reworded in the Feb. issue—are from the sixth movement of the editor's partly published poem *"A"*[2] dated the early summer of 1930, almost a year before the "Objectivists" number. The lines referred to read:

> *The melody, the rest are accessory —*
> *. . . . my one voice; my other . . .*
> *An objective — rays of the object brought to a focus,*
> *An objective — nature as creator — desire for what is objectively perfect,*
> *Inextricably the direction of historic and contemporary particulars.*

Assuming the intention of these lines to be poetry, the implications notwithstanding the hurried conviction of certain hasty readers

1. [Both 1932 and 5 *Statements* read "Poetry" (without italics).]
2. [Both 1932 and 5 *Statements* read ""A"" (without italics).]

that analysis has no "organic relation" (quotes) to poetry, seem to be that as critic the editor of Feb. *Poetry* began as a poet, and that as a poet he had implicitly to be a critic. Wm. Carlos Williams had said before him, in *Spring and All*,—"I believe it possible, even essential, that when poetry fails it does not become prose but bad poetry."

A poet finds the continuously present analysis of his work preferable to criticism so-called. Yet what other criticism exclusive of his poem seems permissible? In preference to the brands of circumlocution requisite to ponderous journals and designated by Mr. Pound as *backsidebeforeness*, a "prose" criticism whose analysis follows without undue length of misinterpretation the more concise analysis of a considered poem seems permissible, if the general good demands such a prose. The direction of this prose, tho it will be definition, will also be poetry, arising from the same source or what to a third reader might seem the same source as the poetry—a poetically charged mentality. Tho perhaps gratifying to the poet whose poem is under observation —this prose, with all its poetic direction and right impetus, should, to the critic himself with his merely poetically charged mentality, seem secondary even tertiary and less; i.e. compared with that act which is a poem, not, of course, compared with "critical" backsidebeforeness.

An example of backsidebeforeness—Mr. Eliot in a recent preface to a volume containing Johnson's *London* and *The Vanity of Human Wishes*: "those who demand of poetry a day dream, or a metamorphosis of their feeble desires or lusts, or what they believe to be the 'intensity' of passion, will not find much in Johnson. He is like Pope and Dryden, Crabbe and Landor, a poet for those who want poetry and not something else, some stay for their own vanity. I sometimes think that our own time with its elaborate equipment of science and psychological analysis, is even less fitted than the Victorian age to appreciate poetry as poetry."

Two mistakes are evident in this quotation—justifying a certain important critic's statement that the editor of *The Criterion* is becoming more inelegant every day.

First, Mr. Eliot makes the graceless error of writing down to those who consciously want a something else from poetry—not poetry—as some stay for their own vanity. Secondly, he seems to "sometimes" think that minds elaborately equipped with specific information, like science, must always confuse it with other specific information, like poetry. That may be the case with unfortunates. The point, however, would be not to proffer solemnly or whiningly confusions to the confused, but to indicate by energetic mental behavior how certain information may be useful to other information*, and when the divisions which signalize them are necessary.

Such a process does not need to be accurately painful; rather it should be painlessly complete—as certain people are complete and ready to go anywhere but to the doctor.

Again, an example of what might be designated pigeonhole criticism from which the pigeon has escaped—

The critic, not Mr. Eliot this time, quotes Johnson:

> *Year chases year, decay pursues decay,*
> *Still drops some joy from with'ring life away;*
> *New forms arise, and different views engage,*
> *Superfous[3] lags the vet'ran on the stage,*
> *Till pitying nature signs the last release*
> *And bids afflicted worth retire to peace.*

His criticism of this passage follows:

"To write poetry so precise, lucid and pure, one must be what the Southern negro calls a settled person; one must be mature; one must live in a world that offers the least evidence of the ceaseless social change. One must not be distracted by too much speculation, or lost in the mutability of sensation. One's mind must be made up: such a poet will have taste. The more precise the writing the purer the poetry. I do not know what poetry is as an essence, but it is clear that Johnson, some of Pope, a great deal of Dryden and Landor, are pure poetry. Nor do I know what pure poetry is; (etc........ ending:) Our equivalent for taste is sensation. But that part of Johnson which is not poetry is nothing, nor does it pretend to be. This is what one should expect from him whose honesty and intelligence as well as whose precision of style we should do well to cultivate."

Discount the critic's fallacious assertion that the poetry quoted is precise—It does not seem precise and lucid, i.e. profoundly entire,— not a matter of something worn on a sleeve—, in anything but its versi-

*Mr. Eliot's poetic use of facts about ships, in *Marina*, is, it cannot be said an elementary but a good example. [Zukofsky's footnote, signalled by an asterisk and present in both 1932 and 5 *Statements*.]

3. [Johnson's poem reads "Superfluous"; Zukofsky's text reads "Superfous" in both the 1932 edition and 5 *Statements*.]

fication. And its versification to be pure would need to be working with a precise diction to offer more than the nicety of 18th century poetic. Discount that what the Southern Negro calls a settled person has nothing to do with it; that Johnson must, in spite of or because of his maturity have been aware of the ceaseless social change around him or at some time, for where else *could* the armful sweep of perorated obsequy have come from?—"And bids afflicted worth retire to peace"—(*Worth:* cultural involved with economic standing? *afflicted* implying at least an impress if not an oppressor and obviously an oppressed?) Discount that Johnson did not need to be *lost* in the mutability of sensation, there was on authority a good deal of him that could not exactly escape sensation. Discount that Johnson's mind was many times made up most accurately and explosively, if even at times pigheadly—his critic does not in the least indicate where the taste which such a poet (assertively) will have, could have come from.

Certainly the more precise the writing, the purer the poetry. But this has already been considered. And it will not do to say "that part of Johnson which is not poetry is nothing", one cannot speak of a part of a poem any more than of a part of a flow.—"Words, writes Mr. Pound, do not function in this manner. They are like the roots of plants: they are organic, they interpenetrate and tangle with life, you cannot detach them as pieces of an anatomical figure. The dissection of capillaries and vein is at a certain stage no longer possible."

Leaving for the moment, Mr. Pound's classicism—or what else is it —and going back to the critic: let alone that he may have never met an essence, he should if he is engaged by it to the extent of written assertion know what pure poetry is. Or we shall never know how to dispose of our sensations before we begin to read poetry, or how to raise them to honesty and intelligence—as well as—those of us who are precisely afflicted—to that precision of style, we should do well to cultivate.

Criticism is then secondary or tertiary as it may be. So is perhaps an "interest in books."

"Thass a funny lookin' buk . . . Ah . . . Wu . . . Wu . . . Wu . . . Wot you goin' eh to do with ah . . . ah read-it?"—Parenthesis, Mr. Pound.

But a critic-poet-analyst is interested in growing degrees of intelligence. He has an economic bias. He has been doing a job. It will perhaps as soon not as[4] be his salvation. He does not pretend it to be

4. [The 1932 text of "'Recencies'" reads "not as"; the typescript of *5 Statements* reads "as not," but a manuscript marking restores the earlier reading.]

more than a job. Guillaume de Poitiers had several jobs. He was a poet. He went to war. Obviously he divided his energy, perhaps, perhaps not, to the hindrance of his poetry. At any rate—poetry defined as a job, a piece of work.

A desk as an object. "The contingent organism is incurably transitive," says Mr. Kenneth Rexroth, "to demand of it the same kind of completeness revealed in self-consciousness is to attempt to permit the observer identification with the observed as it is for itself. Only God," concludes Mr. Rexroth with theological and poetic explicitness, "is thus "inside" (quotes) things."

For even a desk has something to do with the capillaries and veins the dissection of which at a certain stage is no longer possible—The desk then as a piece of work, the parts, the process of making it—"We cannot", says the critic of Mr. Eliot's criticism of Johnson, "have a classical attitude in perfection without a classical society."

Yet—The classicism of desk-making—The taking over of classical principles of desk-making—The preoccupation with such principles which controlled the early and devout religiosity of desk-making—The taking over of the deep observation of past time so that a desk made to-day may yet be a desk today and to-morrow—Scrap the analogy, battleships—[5]

A poem. A poem as object—And yet certainly it arose in the veins and capillaries, if only in the intelligence—Experienced—parenthesis—(every word can't be overdefined) experienced as an object—Perfect rest—Or nature as creator, existing perfect, experience perfecting activity of existence, making it—theologically, perhaps—like the Ineffable—

A poem. Also the materials which are outside (?) the veins and capillaries—The context—The context necessarily dealing with a world outside of it—The desire for what is objectively perfect, inextricably the direction of historic and contemporary particulars—A desire to place everything—everything aptly, perfectly, belonging within, one with, a context,—

A poem. The context based on a world—Idle metaphor—a lime base—a fibre—not merely a charged vacuum tube—an aerie of personation—The desire for inclusiveness—The desire for an inclusive object.

5. [The 1932 text reads "Scrap the analogy—Battleships—," as does the 5 *Statements* typescript, but a manuscript marking indicates a revision to "Scrap the analogy, battleships—"]

A poem. This object in process—The poem as a job—A classic[6]—

Homer's *the wet waves* not our *the wet waves*[7] but enough association in the three words to make a context capable of extension from its
time into the present. Because, there is, tho meanings change, a linguistic etiquette, a record possibly clear to us as the usage of a past context—The context as it first meant—or if this may not be believed—an
arrived at equilibrium—or at least the past not even guessed by us
arrived at an equilibrium of meaning determined by new meanings of
word against word contemporarily read.

A poem: a context associated with "musical" shape, musical with
quotation marks since it is not of notes as music, but of words more
variable than variables, and used outside as well as within the context
with communicative reference.

Impossible to communicate anything but particulars—historic and
contemporary—things, human beings as things their instrumentalities
of capillaries and veins binding up and bound up with events and contingencies. The revolutionary word if it must revolve cannot escape
having a reference. It is not infinite. Even the infinite is a term.

The subject of this: "Recencies" in Poetry. Quotes around "recencies" because only good poetry—good an unnecessary adjective—is
contemporary or classical. A standard of taste can be characterized
only by acceptances of particular communication and concerned, so
to speak, whenever the intelligence is in danger of being cluttered with
exclusions—not with books but with poetic invention. The nothing,
not pure nothing, left over is not a matter of "recencies", but a matter
of *pasts*, maybe *pasties*.

It would be just as well then dealing with "recencies" to deal with
Donne or Shakespeare, if one knew them as well as a linguistic usage
not their own can know them. And yet contexts and inventions seem to
have been derived from them.

In fact it is pertinent that historians exist, if certain language
structures are to be recognized—i.e. Pound from the Troubadours,
Eliot from Webster, etc.

However—where there is no invention, no poem, no object which
communicated and which is—where there is an impure nothing—
permit to enter EXCLUSION.

6. ["classic" reads "Classic" in the 1932 text.]
7. ["*the wet waves*" reads "*The Wet Waves*" in both instances in the 1932 text.]

The history of EXCLUSION in poetry as recorded by an American, and in a sense for the first time in poetic criticism, since much
research would have to be accomplished before its concise poetical
and critical parallel can be found,—is brief. Three statements of Ezra
Pound as now recorded in "A retrospect", *Pavannes and Divisions*, and
dated 1912—

1—Direct treatment of the "thing"[8] whether subjective or objective.

2—To use absolutely no word that does not contribute to the
presentation.

3—As regarding rhythm: to compose in the sequence of the musical phrase not in the sequence of a metronome.

With those 3 statements as a basis, Pound could write five years
later: "No man ever writes much poetry that matters. In bulk, that is, no
one produces much that is final, and when a man is not doing this
highest thing, this saying the thing once for all and perfectly; when he
is not matching Homer, or "Hist-said Kate the Queen," he had much
better be making the sorts of experiments which may be of use to him
in his later work, or to his successors."

(Not much more than Mr. Pound's sort of experiment which will
be of use to a poet in his later work, or to his successors was claimed for
the sincerity of poets in the "Objectivists" number of *Poetry*—sincerity
defined in the critical section of that issue. A careful reading should
show this.)

The history of the principles of poetic invention as recorded by an
American poet is also brief—Mr. Ezra Pound—"In the Vortex"—
Instigations dated 1920—"It is possible, as I have written or intended to
write elsewhere to divide poetry into three sorts (1) melopoeia, to wit,
poetry which moves by its music, whether it be music in words or an
aptitude for, or suggestion of, accompanying music (2) imagism. . . .
(certain men move. . . . the images of their gods, whole countrysides,
stretches of hill and forest[9] travel with them); and there is thirdly,
logopoeia, or poetry that is akin to nothing but language which is a
dance of the intelligence among words and ideas and modifications of
ideas and characters."

Adding to Mr. Pound's statement, one can speak of an *attained*
emotion fusing these three principles of poetic invention. There is no

8. [The 1932 text reads "the "thing" (quotes) whether . . ."]
9. [The 1932 text reads "hillland and forest . . ."

use in a surplus of distinctions. Obviously there can be only that emotion which in its movement, in its verbal existence, sensuously and intelligently manifests poetry—i.e. speaking of poetry—The desk, not the lumber.

Mr. Pound again—Emotion is the organizer of poetic form. The image is at the basis of poetic form. Elsewhere, Pound had defined the image as that which presents an intellectual and emotional complex in an instant of time. One can go further, try to dissect capillaries or intelligent nerves—and speak of the image felt as duration or perhaps of the image as the existence of the shape and movement of the poetic object. It is known now as it was known previous to 1913 when certain American writers perpetrated a great many errors and to a great extent sabotaged poetry—Mr. Pound was the only exception—that the poet's image is not dissociable from the movement or the cadenced shape of the poem.

A new cadence is a new idea—again Pound.

An idea—not an empty concept. An idea—its value including its meaning. The desk, i.e. as object including its value—The object unrelated to palpable or predatory intent—Also the meaning, or what should be the meaning of science in modern civilization as pointed out in Thorstein Veblen's masterly essay.

The protagonist of Pound's poem—

> *He made no immediate application*
> *Of this to relation of the state*
> *To the individual —*

No predatory manifestation—Yet a manifestation making the mind more temperate because the poem exists and has perhaps recorded both state and individual—

By all means a literature of the proletariat—which will be only literature after all—if there are writers. They will never get across to the proletariat if they are not. As writers, most proletarians are too idle to permit themselves the necessary communication of analysis. "A poet" said Keats, "is the least poetical of anything in existence: it is for ever, in, for, and fulfilling some other object."

There are several kinds of poetic objects, i.e. poems; many particulars. Two examples of movement directing an image are Williams' *Full Moon* and the opening of Pound's XXXth Canto:

Compleynt, compleynt I hearde upon a day,
Artemis singing, Artemis, Artemis
Agaynst Pity lifted her wail:
Pity causeth the forests to fail,
Pity slayeth my nymphs
Pity spareth so many an evil thing.
Pity befouleth April,
Pity is the root and the spring.
Now if no fayre creature followeth me
It is on account of Pity,
It is on account that Pity forbideth them slaye.
All things are made foul in this season,
This is the reason, none may seek purity
Having for foulnesse pity
And things growne awry;
No more do my shaftes fly
To slay. Nothing is now clean slayne.
But rotteth away.

Continuing with the components of the poetic object—Diction—
The diction of Pound's song just quoted, of his epistolary passages in
the *Cantos,* of Marianne Moore's quotations serving only to sharpen
her own meanings in *Observations,* the diction of Cummings' colloquial
chanting . . . recently not showing as much growth as Helen Kane's.

The components of the poetic object continued: the sound and
pitch emphasis of a word are never apart from its meaning.

In this sense each poem has its own laws, since no criticism can
take care of all the differences which each new composition in words
is. Yet criticism would hardly be different if musical notations or signs
were used instead of words. Example: any piece of original music and
the special criticism it produces.

The components of the poetic object continued:

Typography—certainly—if print and the arrangement of it will
help tell how the voice should sound. It is questionable on the other
hand whether the letters of the alphabet can be felt as the Chinese feel
their written characters. Yet most western poets of consequence seem
constantly to communicate the letters of their alphabets as graphic
representations of thoughts—no doubt the thought of the word influences the letters but the letters are there and seem to exude thought.

The value of such discussion:

The value of Tzara's attempt to rehabilitate the mind—
The value of Aragon's humor—
"The only human value of anything, writing included", says Wm. Carlos Williams, "is the intense vision of the facts, add to that by saying the truth and action upon them—clear into the machine of absurdity into a core that is covered."—

Add—the core that covers the work of poets who see with their ears, hear with their eyes, move with their noses and speak and breathe with their feet. And yet lunatics are sometimes profitably observed: the core that is covered, the valuable sceptic knows, may in itself be the intense vision of a fact.

Intention must, however, be distinguished from accomplishment which resolves the complexity of detail into a single object. Emphasize detail 130 times over—or there will be no poetic object.

The complexity of "the stream of consciousness"—that phrase has been heard before.

Mr. Pound says—"The stream of consciousness in *Ulysses* is as different from any stream of consciousness that has actually occurred, as a plot of Racine's. It is equally a composition and condensation. After the principle of conscious "flow" has been manifested the relative value of presentations of such imagined streams will depend as writing in the past has depended, on the richness of content and on the author's skill in arranging it. There is no formula that can by merely getting itself adapted, enable a man to exceed his own capacity."

Or not following Mr. Pound in this case, one might just as well not mention the streaming consciousness.

Or put the job of explanation up to cabinet-making again: certain joints show the carpentry not to advantage, certain joints are a fine evidence; some are with necessary craftsmanship in the object. The first type—showing the carpentry not to advantage—is always present in a great deal of unnecessary writing; the second and third are rare, the second—which is a fine evidence—is rare to this time, the third— which with necessary craftsmanship is hid in the object—is whenever craftsmanship is present characteristic of this time. Against obvious transitions, Pound, Williams, Rakosi, Bunting, Miss Moore, oppose condensation. The transitions cut are implicit in the work, 3 or 4 things occur at a time making the difference between Aristotelian expansive unities and the concentrated locus which is the mind acting creatively upon the facts.

"Recencies"? No more modern than a Shakespearian conceit which manages to carry at least two ideas at a time. Or Dante's literal, anagogical and theological threefold meaning referred to in a letter to Can Grande.

The institutions which prepare pedagogs have never really taught to read the classics. Outside these institutions, and sometimes in them, certain mentalities are no longer interested in the forms of discursiveness. Because writing is a swiftly cleansing process some minds act as if they washed everyday and do not wait for the weekly review. The "objectivists" number of *Poetry*[10] appeared in February. Since then there have been March, April, May, June, July and we are now past the middle of August. Don't write, telegraph.

In contemporary poetry 3 types of complexity are discernable. 1 —the swift concentration of multiple references usually lyrical in movement—almost any poem by Donne, for example. 2—the conceit —Shakespeare's "when to the sessions", his working out of love as bookkeeping, or Donne's "Valediction", his "two twin compasses"—3 —the complexity of the epic—Byron's *Don Juan,* or most of it.

Or extending the word *contemporary* to include the present —as an example of the first type of complexity there is L. Z.'s "Madison, Wis., Remembering the bloom of Monticello (1931)"[11]—to be spoken with an accent on every syllable—like vaudeville recitative, (1). (2) The most perfect recent example of the conceit—which might be defined as that formally integrated structure building up two ideas concurrently—seems to be Williams' "Botticellian Trees", printed in the "Objectivists" number of *Poetry.* (L. Z.'s "Prop XLI" in defense of the conceit is curious—since it contradicts on the face of it all his critical values opposed to the confusion of the senses. Still, as has already been pointed out, the digression of mentality is perhaps only another fact for the poet to record.)[12] Finally (3) the complexity of the epic. M. Taupin's accurate statement regarding Salmon's *Prikaz* was included in the Feb. issue of *Poetry* as indicative of what poets should ultimately attempt. "—give to the epic its rightful qualities, to find again the essential distinction of the epic, which is neither love nor hate but the restitution of these sentiments to a chain of facts which exist, and the

10. [Both 1932 and *5 Statements* read "Poetry" (without italics).]

11. [There are no quotation marks around this poem title in either 1932 or *5 Statements.*]

12. [In the 1932 publication these two sentences are not enclosed in parentheses.]

existence of which confers upon them the marvellous indispensable to all poetry."

"It is a living coral" by Williams may perhaps be too descriptive— it is it can be seen a description of the Capitol frieze in Washington— but the events the description deals with have been left to their integrality. The past and continuous actions of a people have been recorded. Williams has also his poem "To Elsie"—"The pure products of America go crazy."

Other examples of the complexity of the epic not limiting their content to the USA are few: Eliot's *Waste Land,* McAlmon's *Portrait of a Generation* and *North America,* L. Z.'s *"The"* and unfinished *"A",* and the greatest poem of our time Pound's *Cantos.*

The word complexity used several times now is perhaps misleading. Ultimately, the matter of the poetic object and its simple entirety must not be forgotten. The *Cantos'* meaning is the *Cantos:* in spite of all the complexities they deal with. Restituting love and hate to a chain of poetic fact they have for instance devoted the duration of one canto to Confucius.

I.e. order and the facts as order. The order of the *Cantos* as the order of all poetry is to approach a state of music wherein the ideas present themselves sensuously and intelligently and are of no predatory intention. A hard job, as poets have found reconciling contrasting principles or facts. In poetry the poet is continually encountering the facts which in the making seem to want to disturb the music and yet the music or the movement cannot exist without the facts, without its facts. The base matter, to speak hurriedly, which must receive the signet of the form. The troubles and resolution of Keats' *Ode to a Grecian Urn,* for instance. There is also the expression of this trouble in the 7th movement of *"A"* which attempted to resolve the writer's criticism of poetry into the movement of the poem. The problem presents (assumably) to a poet of the order of the *Cantos* the adequate difficulty necessary for continued interest in his work.

Summarising:

The "Objectivists" number of *Poetry*—"Objectivists" in quotes: no infringement, i.e. of philosophical etiquette, intended.

The interest of the issue was in the few recent lines of poetry which could be found, and in the craft of poetry, NOT in a movement. The contributors did not get up one morning all over the land and say "objectivists" between tooth-brushes. Somewhere the so-called program of the number implied that a "poet" who is not conscious of Lenin's statement that it is better to have lived thru a revolution than to write about it is not worth his salt. This may seem pigheaded—but the interest of poets is after all in particulars. Poems are only acts upon particulars, outside of them. Only thru such activity do they become particulars themselves—i.e. poems.

The mind may construct its world—this is hardly philosophy—if the mind does construct its world there is always that world immanent or imminently outside which at least as a term has become an entity. Linguistic usage has somehow preserved these acts which were poems in other times and have transferred structures now. Fake, mere word-mongering, the lack of a process of words acting on particulars, show up as rot in all times. Maybe there are more botchers today than ever. The good poems of today are—as jobs—not far from the good poems of yesterday.[13]

13. [The 1932 text continues as follows, without a paragraph break:]
    Stalin has been spending some of his time in his one or two rooms not destroying Shakespeare, but has been reading the not really predacious Englishmen on his vacation.

LOUIS ZUKOFSKY.
The Gotham Book Mart, New York, Aug. 1931

POETRY

For My Son When He Can Read

[The *5 Statements* text of "Poetry/*For My Son When He Can Read*" is identical to that which appears in *Prepositions,* except for the last five typescript pages of the *5 Statements* version, which Zukofsky has omitted. The first two paragraphs below correspond to the last two paragraphs of the essay in *Prepositions* (pp. 10–11)—where they have been slightly revised—and the essay then continues as below. The text of Walt Whitman's "Respondez!" and Zukofsky's sentence introducing it (pp. 218–221 below) were not included in the 1948 *Cronos* publication of this essay.]

Poetry never grows sentimental. It never exaggerates or destroys the thing it is. It may border on the perilous or record the sentimental among other events and remain poetry.

Writing this, Paul, for a time when you can read, I do not presume that you will read "me." That "me" will be lost today when he says good night on your third birthday, and not missed tomorrow when he says good morning as you begin your fourth year. It took all human time to nurse those greetings. And how else can the poet speak them but as poet.

I will speak no other way to friends, for friendship cannot exaggerate, and is not tacit. To my friends, this good night and good morning should encompass my intention as quickly as whatever lines I have written that at this moment I remember:

Sum, you are constructed, as of the tides, of your voice, . . .

And of labor:
Light lights in air, . . .

To be moved comes of want, tho want be complete
as understanding.

    . . . history does not begin again
When a thought trains on the fact that begins again.

And lest the impersonal quantities intended by these examples seem to be blown up, as we say of a photograph, to proportions that make the detailed qualities imprecise, I turn to the work of friends, whose names—whatever has happened or may happen to them as persons—are but fiat for the worth of their work to any time:

to Bunting—

    always mobile and at home everywhere
where there is salt water . . .

to Pound—

Hast' ou fashioned so airy a mood
To draw up the leaf from the root?

    . . .

And the rest as time has cleft it

to Williams—

    . . . all gentleness and its
enduring . . .

to Lorine Niedecker—

    Think what's got away in my life!

to Reznikoff—

    Despite this and despite this, . . .

Knowing he has made or recognized a thing apart from himself, the poet is most the poet. Because of the needs of this "piece" I have turned, it may appear with the stubbornness of a father, as much to my own lines as to those of my friends. But to stress what has been said before, poetry, like friendship, does not exaggerate and is not tacit: this is after all a piece for you, and as such the lines of friends find only a precise place in it. My intention should appear even more complete to you if I say that I shall be most the poet when Celia finishes her music to the words of "Pericles." For the work she has put into them has often made us hear "Shakespeare" speak. And in this, which we shared together, poetry without which life would have little present has been everywhere with a sense for everything.

Were the three of us not subsumed in the form of these notes, Whitman's greatest poem (interring the years 1856 thru 1870) could more easily have served the definition of poetry we anticipate:

RESPONDEZ!

Respondez! Respondez!
(The war is completed—the price is paid—the title is settled
     beyond recall;)
Let every one answer! let those who sleep be waked! let none
     evade!
Must we still go on with our affectations and sneaking?
Let me bring this to a close—I pronounce openly for a new
     distribution of roles;
Let that which stood in front go behind! and let that which
     was behind advance to the front and speak;
Let murderers, bigots, fools, unclean persons, offer new
     propositions!
Let the old propositions be postponed!
Let faces and theories be turn'd inside out! let meanings be
     freely criminal, as well as results!
Let there be no suggestion above the suggestion of drudgery!
Let none be pointed toward his destination! (Say! do you
     know your destination?)
Let men and women be mock'd with bodies and mock'd with
     Souls!
Let the love that waits in them, wait! let it die, or pass still-
     born to the other spheres!

Let the sympathy that waits in every man, wait! or let it also
    pass, a dwarf, to other spheres!
Let contradictions prevail! let one thing contradict another!
    and let one line of my poems contradict another!
Let the people sprawl with yearning, aimless hands! let their
    tongues be broken! let their eyes be discouraged! let none
    descend into their hearts with the fresh lusciousness of
    love!
(Stifled, O days! O lands! in every public and private corrup-
    tion!
Smother'd in thievery, impotence, shamelessness, mountain-
    high;
Brazen effrontery, scheming, rolling like ocean's waves
    around and upon you, O my days! my lands!
For not even those thunderstorms, nor fiercest lightnings of
    the war, have purified the atmosphere;)
—Let the theory of America still be management, caste, com-
    parison! (Say! what other theory would you?)
Let them that distrust birth and death still lead the rest! (Say!
    why shall they not lead you?)
Let the crust of hell be neared and trod on! let the days be
    darker than the nights! let slumber bring less slumber than
    waking time brings!
Let the world never appear to him or her for whom it was all
    made!
Let the heart of the young man still exile itself from the heart
    of the old man! and let the heart of the old man be exiled
    from that of the young man!
Let the sun and moon go! let scenery take the applause of the
    audience! let there be apathy under the stars!
Let freedom prove no man's inalienable right! every one who
    can tyrannize, let him tyrannize to his satisfaction!
Let none but infidels be countenanced!
Let the eminence of meanness, treachery, sarcasm, hate,
    greed, indecency, impotence, lust, be taken for granted
    above all! let writers, judges, governments, households,
    religions, philosophies, take such for granted above all!
Let the worst men beget children out of the worst women!
Let the priest still play at immortality!
Let death be inaugurated!
Let nothing remain but the ashes of teachers, artists, moral-
    ists, lawyers, and learn'd and polite persons!
Let him who is without my poems be assassinated!

Let the cow, the horse, the camel, the garden-bee—let the
  mud-fish, the lobster, the mussel, eel, the sting-ray, and the
  grunting pig-fish—let these, and the like of these, be put
  on a perfect equality with man and woman!
Let churches accommodate serpents, vermin, and the
  corpses of those who have died of the most filthy of dis-
  eases!
Let marriage slip down among fools, and be for none but fools!
Let men among themselves talk and think forever obscenely
  of women! and let women among themselves talk and
  think obscenely of men!
Let us all, without missing one, be exposed in public, naked,
  monthly, at the peril of our lives! let our bodies be freely
  handled and examined by whoever chooses!
Let nothing but copies at second hand be permitted to exist
  upon the earth!
Let the earth desert God, nor let there ever henceforth be
  mention'd the name of God!
Let there be no God!
Let there be money, business, imports, exports, custom,
  authority, precedents, pallor, dyspepsia, smut, ignorance,
  unbelief!
Let judges and criminals be transposed! let the prison-keepers be put in prison! let those that were prisoners take the
  keys! (Say! why might they not just as well be transposed?)
Let the slaves be masters! let the masters become slaves!
Let the reformers descend from the stands where they are
  forever bawling! let an idiot or insane person appear on
  each of the stands!
Let the Asiatic, the African, the European, the American, and
  the Australian, go armed against the murderous stealthi-
  ness of each other! let them sleep armed! let none believe
  in good will!
Let there be no unfashionable wisdom! let such be scorn'd
  and derided off from the earth!
Let a floating cloud in the sky—let a wave of the sea—let
  growing mint, spinach, onions, tomatoes—let those be
  exhibited at shows, at a great price for admission!
Let all the men of These States stand aside for a few smouch-
  ers! let the few seize on what they choose! let the rest gawk,
  giggle, starve, obey!
Let shadows be furnish'd with genitals! let substances be
  deprived of their genitals!

Let there be wealthy and immense cities—but still through
  any of them, not a single poet, savior, knower, lover!
Let the infidels of These States laugh all faith away!
If one man be found who has faith, let the rest set upon him!
Let them affright faith! let them destroy the power of breed-
  ing faith!
Let the she-harlots and the he-harlots be prudent! let them
  dance on, while seeming lasts! (O seeming! seeming! seem-
  ing!)
Let the preachers recite creeds! let them still teach only what
  they have been taught!
Let insanity still have charge of sanity!
Let books take the place of trees, animals, rivers, clouds!
Let the daub'd portraits of heroes supercede heroes!
Let the manhood of man never take steps after itself!
Let it take steps after eunuchs, and after consumptive and
  genteel persons!
Let the white person again tread the black person under his
  heel! (Say! which is trodden under heel, after all?)
Let the reflections of the things of the world be studied in
  mirrors! let the things themselves still continue unstudied!
Let a man seek pleasure everywhere except in himself!
Let a woman seek happiness everywhere except in herself!
(What real happiness have you had one single hour through
  your whole life?)
Let the limited years of life do nothing for the limitless years
  of death? (What do you suppose death will do, then?) [1]

---

1. [Zukofsky's text of "Respondez!" follows that of the 1876 edition of *Leaves of Grass*.
Whitman retained nine lines of the poem in later editions of *Leaves of Grass* under the
titles "Reversals" and "Transpositions":

REVERSALS

  Let that which stood in front go behind,
  Let that which was behind advance to the front,
  Let bigots, fools, unclean persons, offer new propositions,
  Let the old propositions be postponed,
  Let a man seek pleasure everywhere except in himself,
  Let a woman seek happiness everywhere except in herself.

(Note 1, continued)

TRANSPOSITIONS

Let the reformers descend from the stands where they are forever bawling
    —let an idiot or insane person appear on each of the stands;
Let judges and criminals be transposed—let the prison-keepers be put in
    prison—let those that were prisoners take the keys;
Let them that distrust birth and death lead the rest.

See the Editor's Introduction, above.]

A STATEMENT FOR POETRY (1950)

[*Prepositions* presents a text of "A Statement for Poetry" which is identical to that of *5 Statements,* except for its formatting—indentation and section divisions—which has been simplified in *Prepositions,* and its last two type-script pages, which arrange ten "Other Comments" on the art of poetry. These comments, reproduced below, are not included in *Prepositions.* They come at the end of the essay, separated from it by a ruled line.]

Other Comments

I. Chronicles 15. (time described ca. 1000 BC) ". . . singers with instruments of musick . . . lifting up the voice . . . and Chenaniah
   was for song: he instructed about the song, because he was
   skilful."

Homer (ca. 800 BC) "one who serves the public . . . a heavenly singer at
   a feast"

Confucius (*Analects* ca. 500 BC) "Education begins with poetry, is
   strengthened through proper conduct, and consummated
   through music."

Plato (*The Symposium* ca. 389 BC) "Poetry . . . complex and manifold.
   All creation or passage of non-being into being is poetry or
   making, and the processes of all art are creative. Still
   . . . only that portion of the art which is separated off from

the rest, and is concerned with music and metre, is termed poetry."

Aristotle (*Poetics*, 4th c. BC) "The poet's aim . . . to combine every element of interest, if possible, or else the more important and the major part of them (16). The poet should say very little *in propria persona*, as he is no imitator when doing that (24) (and cf. 2) . . . the objects the imitator represents are actions . . ."

Dante (*De Vulgari Eloquentia* ca. 1300) ". . . poetry seems to remain a pattern to prose writers, and not the converse (Bk. 2, i) . . . in works of art, that is noblest which embraces the whole art (Bk. 2, iii) . . . poetry, which is nothing else but a rhetorical composition set to music (Bk. 2, iv) . . . the exercise of discernment as to words involves by no means the smallest labour of our reason (Bk. 2, vii) . . . a canzone appears to be nothing else but the completed action of one writing words to be set to music (Bk. 2, viii)"

Sidney (*An Apology for Poetry*, 1595) ". . . that cannot be praiseless which doth most polish that blessing of speech; which considers each word . . . by his forcible quality, . . . by his measured quantity, carrying even in themselves a harmony (without, perchance, number, measure, order, proportion be in our time grown odious)."

Shakespeare (*Hamlet*, II, ii, 1603) ". . . the lady shall say her mind freely, or the blank verse shall halt for 't."

A. N. Whitehead (*Science and the Modern World*, 1925) "Value is the word I use for the intrinsic reality of an event. Value is an element which permeates through and through the poetic view of nature."

W. C. Williams (*Paterson III*, 1949) "The province of the poem is the world."

Louis and Celia Zukofsky:
Translating Catullus

[Louis and Celia Zukofsky worked at their translation of the complete Catullus from 1958 to 1966. It was published in 1969 as *Catullus (Gai Valeri Catulli Veronensis Liber)*, by Cape Goliard in London and Grossman in New York. In spring 1962 the journal *Kulchur* (issue 5) printed the Latin texts of three of the Catullus poems—XLI, XLII, and LXIII—with the Zukofskys' translations *en face*, as "3 Carmina & 3 Cats." "Translating Catullus" is the Zukofskys' pair of brief "prefaces" to that selection. The 1969 *Catullus*, as well as the text of the Zukofskys' translation included in the *Complete Short Poetry* (Baltimore: Johns Hopkins University Press, 1993), omits the "Poet's Preface" and the final sentence of the "Translators' Preface ("The Latin text printed here . . .").]

Two ways of looking at it:

Poet's Preface

This version of Catullus aims at the rendition of his sound. By reading his lips, that is while pronouncing the Latin words, the translation—as his lips shape—tries to breathe with him.

L. Z.

Translators' Preface

This translation of Catullus follows the sound, rhythm, and syntax of his Latin—tries, as it is said, to breathe the "literal" meaning with him.

The skip from 17 to 20 in the sequence of poems is traditional, after the earliest codices, Codex Oxoniensis (late 14c.) and Codex Sanger-manensis or Parisiensis (c. 1375). Modern scholars usually include car-men 18 (fragment 2 in our book) with the *fragmenta* of the canon, but omit carmina 19 and 20 as spurious. The Latin text printed here is that of the Loeb Classics edition (London, 1913, revised 1924) of Francis Warre Cornish. "Passages omitted" from it have been restored as they appear in Elmer Truesdell Merrill's edition (Boston, 1893).

C. Z.

L. Z.

foreword to "A" 1-12

[The first twelve movements of Zukofsky's *"A"* were first published in book form in 1959 by Cid Corman's Origin Press in Kyoto, Japan, in an edition of 200 copies. *"A" 1-12* was reprinted in 1966 by Jonathan Cape (London) and in 1967 by Doubleday & Company (New York) in its "Paris Review Editions" series. Zukofsky added the "foreword" for the Doubleday edition; its italicized third paragraph rephrases and rearranges some sentences from his 1941 short story *"It Was."* The "foreword" does not appear in the 1978 University of California Press and 1993 Johns Hopkins University Press editions of the complete *"A".*]

FOREWORD

"A"

a poem of a life

—and a time. The poem will continue thru 24 movements, its last words still to be lived. Bach is a theme all thru it, the music first heard in 1928 affecting the recurrences or changes as may be of the story or history.

After 40 years of the writing and still with it, it is easier to say *here it is* than explain what seems to me to be clear. It comes to as I have said elsewhere (somewhat differently):

not to fathom time but literally to sound it as on an instrument and so to hear again as much of what was and is together, as one breathes without pointing to it before and after. The story must exist in each word or it cannot go on. The words written down — or even inferred as written over, crossed out — must live, not seem merely to glance at a watch.

L. Z.
2/25/67

Interview

[This interview was conducted by L. S. Dembo on May 16, 1968, in Madison, Wisconsin, and was published in *Contemporary Literature* 10.2 (Spring 1969): 203–219, as part of "The 'Objectivist' Poet: Four Interviews." I have changed page references for Zukofsky's poems from *ALL: The Collected Short Poems* to the more recent *Complete Short Poetry* (Baltimore: Johns Hopkins University Press, 1993).]

Q. I know that "objectivism" was short-lived as a movement, if it ever existed at all, but your essay in the February 1931 issue of *Poetry* does seem to suggest a particular way of looking at reality. In fact, you actually use the term nominalism in connection with André Salmon. Wouldn't you say that your own poems from the beginning attempted to get away from normal generalization and theme to present an experience of the object or of nature directly?

A. Well, I don't want to get involved in philosophy. I might as well say that *Bottom: on Shakespeare* was written to do away with all philosophy. Naturally you can't do it without getting involved in their blasted terminology. In the first place, objectivism . . . I never used the word; I used the word "objectivist," and the only reason for using it was Harriet Monroe's insistence when I edited the "Objectivist" number of *Poetry*. Pound was after her; he thought the old rag, as he called it, was senile, and so on. He had had his fights with her; he couldn't get across the people he wanted, and in one of his vituperative letters he told old Harriet the magazine would come to nothing, that there was this youngster who was one of the best critics in America . . . well, I'm reminiscing. In any case, Harriet was fond of Pound and after all she was enterprising. Well, she told me, "You must have a movement." I said, "No, some of us are writing to say things simply so that they will affect us as new again." "Well, give it a name." Well, there were pre-Raphael-itism, and dadaism, and expressionism, and futurism—I don't like any of those *isms*. I mean, as soon as you do that, you start becoming a bal-loon instead of a person. And it swells and a lot of mad people go chas-ing it. Another word I don't want to use is "reality." I try to avoid it; I use it in *Bottom*, I think, only because I had to quote some text. Occasionally, a really profound man—a Cardinal Newman, for exam-ple—can use the word; there isn't any word you can't use if you have enough body to make something of it. Anyway, I told Harriet, "All right, let's call it 'Objectivists,'" and I wrote the essay on sincerity and objectification. I wouldn't do it today. (I've sworn off criticism after *Bottom*, after nineteen years of going through all that.) In any case I wouldn't use the same terminology anymore. But looking back at that essay, and as it was revised in *Prepositions* . . . what I did in this volume of criticism was to get it down to the bare bone. Granted that there are certain infelicities of style in the original. Actually, I don't think I changed ten words in editing the collected criticism. I omitted a great deal though, and that made all the difference.

But let me explain what I meant by "sincerity" and "objectifica-tion." Any artist lives with the things as they exist. I won't go into the theory of knowledge. I don't care how you think about things, whether you think they are there outside of you, even if you disappear, or if they exist only because you think of them. In either case you live with things as they exist. Berkeley's table that exists only in the mind, Plato's table that couldn't exist without the idea of a table, or Aristotle's table that was a table because you started with wood and had a purpose to make something for the good of society—you're still talking about a table. The theory of knowledge becomes terribly dull to me unless somebody like Wittgenstein, who really saw what the word game was, writes about it. Then it becomes very moving, because of the life, the fact, that goes on in your head no matter how evaporated the body becomes, no mat-ter how much "gravity" you have (what Laurence Sterne defined as the mysterious carriage of the body to betray the defects of the mind).

But getting back to sincerity and objectification: thinking with the things as they exist. I come into a room and I see a table. Obviously, I can't make it eat grass. I have delimited this thing, in a sense. I call it a table and I want to keep the word for its denotative sense—as solid as possible. The only way it will define itself further will be in a context. In a way it's like grammar; only grammar is more abstract. In traditional grammar, you start with a *subject*. "I'm going to talk about *that*," says Aristotle. "What are you going to say about *it*?" "Well, what *can* I say about *it*?" says Aristotle: "*It* is, *it* exists, or *it* acts, or sometimes you hit *it* on the head and *it* seeks an action, a change in voices as we call it. Grammar is that kind of *thing*. The object *is*. Now what objects *aren't*?"

To the human being with five senses . . . . (How many more is he going to get when he goes up there beyond gravity? Probably lose them all.) Some senses are more important to some people than to others. To the cook, I suppose taste and smell are the most important; to the musician, hearing (the ear); to the poet, all the senses, but chiefly, sight (the eye)—Pound said we live with certain landscapes. And because of the eye's movement, something is imparted to or through the physical movement of your body and you express yourself as a voice.

Let's say you start with a body, the way a kid does when it's born, and it cries almost immediately. It takes a long time for its eyes to focus, a month I suppose. But anyway, the eye concerns the poet; the ear concerns the poet because he hears noises, and like the kid he's affected. And you can do all sorts of things with the noises. You can imitate natural things, and so forth. I like to keep the noises as close to the body as possible, so that (I don't know how you'd express it mathematically) the eye is a function of the ear and the ear of the eye; maybe with that you might feel a sense of smell, of taste even. So much of the word is a physiological thing. I know all of the linguists will say I'm crazy. In fact I think there's a close relationship between families of languages, in this physiological sense. Something must have led the Greeks to say *hudor* and for us to say *water*.

But the word is so much of a physiological thing that its articulation, as against that of other words, will make an "object." Now you can make an object that is in a sense purely image and, unless you're a great poet, it can get too heavy. You will become one of those painter-poets who are, really, too frivolous; they exist in every generation. You know, they look at something and immediately want to write a poem. That's not the way to make an image; it ought to be involved in the cadence—something very few people realize. What I mean is the kind of thing you get in Chapman's "the unspeakable good liquor there."

Obviously, the man who wrote that knew what it was to gargle something down his throat. So body, voice, in handling words—*that* concerns the poet.

The last thing would be, since we're dealing with organs, the brain or intellect. That's very abstract. The parallel in physics would be the gaseous state. Now gas exists, but it is awfully hard to write the gas-stuff unless you have a very clear mind.

The objectivist, then, is one person, not a group, and as I define him he is interested in living with things as they exist, and as a "words-man," he is a craftsman who puts words together into an object.

I tried in *A Test of Poetry* to show what I meant by giving examples of different poets writing—colloquially, not philosophically speaking —on the same subject. People are free to construct whatever table they want, but if it's going to be art, you had better have some standards. I at least want a table that I can write on and put to whatever use a table usually has. Well, this is all the answer to one question, and I don't really like to discuss these things . . . .

Q. Please go on.

A. Well, I'd prefer a poem that embodied all I have said here, a poem which said them for me, rather than the criticism. They say my poetry is difficult. I don't know—I try to be as simple as possible. Anyway, I have a poem that shows what I've been talking about, "The Old Poet Moves to a New Apartment 14 Times" [*Complete Short Poetry*, pp. 222–224]. Let me read some of it:

> The old poet
> moves
> to a new apartment
> 14 times

1

> "The old radical"
> or surd—

2

I's (pronounced eyes)
the title of his last

followed by *After I's.*
"After"—*later* or
chasing?

3

All the questions are answered with their own words . . .

[Interrupting:] What was your question?

Q. "All the questions are answered with their own words." Why don't you continue?

A. All you have to do is say "yes" or "no." That's about all we have ever done as far as action is concerned. The trouble is most people just won't be that definite. [Continues reading:]

> All the questions are answered with their own words
> intellect the way of a body a degree "before"
> soughed into them

[Commenting:] I'm thinking of boiling off water so that it becomes vapor.

> if the words say silence suffers less
> they suffer silence
> or the toy of a paradox
> a worth less worth
> than that *shall* will be said
> as it is

[Commenting:] There is something that exits and the "shall," well, I don't know; it's up to the scheme that seems to be running everything, God, whatever you want to call it.

4

Aleatorical indeterminate

[Commenting:] Are we determined or not determined?

> to be lucky and free and original
> we might well be afraid to think
> we know beforehand exactly
> what we're doing

[Commenting:] It sometimes helps not to know "exactly," and no one knows exactly. How can he know "exactly"? I think we might as well be honest about that.

> rather let it happen

> but the 'illogical' anticipation,

> music, has always been explicit
> as silence and sound have

[Commenting:] What have you? What does this art consist of? Well, with poetry as with music, I go on, with silence and sound, "how long is a rest to rest." All right, according to John Cage, sometimes it's all silence. You want it that way? Doesn't make very much *sense* to me. I don't see why you should call it music. Maybe it is. That's the intellect part of it. John Cage is an intellect; I think that's the trouble with him. Otherwise, he's very wonderful, does some marvelous "things" to evoke silence.

> in the question
> how long is a rest to rest.

> In the 'old' metered poetry
> the Augustan proud of himself
> jingle poet as he says it

> freedom also happens
> tho a tradition precounts

[Commenting:] He may think he's writing a line in iambic pentameter, but is he? Does he control every bit of it? It's a question: are you going to write by chance? Are you going to be absolutely rational about it? All conventional poetry . . . poets have the idea that they're in complete control of what they're doing. Sometimes it happens that the jingle poet has a marvelously metrical line that somebody else may do consciously for that effect. Or he can't help himself; it's in the language that two stressed syllables will come together. He's already determined by the speech that exists. It's one of the functions that the poet, if he's entirely honest, will realize.

> freedom also happens
> tho a tradition precounts
>
> but someone before him
> is counting for him
> unless it happens
>
> that the instant has him
> completely absorbed in that someone:

[Commenting:] Sometimes you may like Shakespeare so much you may, as Emerson says, turn out to be as good as Shakespeare for a minute.

> a voice not a meter

[Commenting:] That's what I'm emphasizing.

> a voice not a meter
> but sometimes a meter's a voice.

[Commenting:] Sometimes you discover what you think is a measure and it's the same as that objectivist voice. And it's nothing "new"— that is, hankering for the *new* in the sense of *novelty*. I'd say this of Chaucer, of Wyatt at his best. You can't carry the poetic object away or put it in your pocket, but there is a use of words where one word in context defines the other and it enriches so that what is put over is somebody's reaction to existence. That's all I was going to say.

Q. What about the relation between "sincerity" and "objectification"?

A. Sincerity is the care for the detail. Before the legs of the table are made, you can see a nice top or a nice grain in the wood, its potential, anyway, to be the complete table. Objectification is the structure. I like to think of it as rest, but you can call it movement. I cut out things from the original essay because I wanted to avoid all the philosophical jargon. Actually, looking back at it, it wasn't bad for a guy of twenty-five or twenty-six; it's certainly clearer than parts of Whitehead. I don't mean the mathematical Whitehead; I couldn't even kiss his toe there. I don't know whether it was as good as Peirce . . . .

Q. Concerning the phrase, "thinking with the things as they exist," doesn't one man make them different from another, or doesn't what existence means to one man differ from what it means to another?

A. That's true. But I'm thinking of only one person, the poet. Anyway, there's a certain amount you've got to get across to the next man or there's no sense in talking about art—we'll have bedlam. If you're talking about art, you want to give it to at least one person— that's your audience. Otherwise, unless you're talking to yourself, you probably set up a person. I mean, if we can't agree that this is a table, then, all right, you can use it to sleep on, but you're messing up uses. I'd say the business of writing is to see as much as you can, to hear as much as you can, and if you think at all to think without clutter; then as you put the things together, try to be concise.

Q. Well, what is involved in thinking without clutter? I don't think it's as simple as it seems to be.

A. It depends on how long or how deeply you've lived; after all, it's thinking or, if you wish, sensing with the things as they exist. I said in the essay—perhaps it isn't explicit—that it depends on the depth of the person. Everybody, some time in his life, wants to write poetry for reasons that have nothing to do with poetry. A kid falls in love and he wants to write a poem; it might turn out to be a good one simply because he's so innocent. But it's not likely. That is, if you want to be a good carpenter, you either know something about your craft or you don't. Each poem is in a sense its own law; I mean the good poem always is and there's no other like it. But if you're talking about at least a minimum of human value, humane value, you better have some kind of standard, especially if you're going to be true to your language, if you really want to affect people, and so on.

Q. Still, doesn't the "clear physical eye" see in a different way from the eye working with the brain or influenced by abstractions? For example, there's a poem in *All* that goes:

> Not much more than being,
> Thoughts of isolate, beautiful
> Being at evening, to expect
>   at a river-front:
>
> A shaft dims
> With a turning wheel;
>
> Men work on a jetty
> By a broken wagon;
>
> Leopard, glowing-spotted,
>   The summer river—
> Under: The Dragon:
>
>   [*Complete Short Poetry,* p. 22]

It seemed to me the poet here was seeing as an objectivist, in terms of particularities rather than wholes. He seems to be literally thinking with the things as they exist and not making abstractions out of them.

A. But the abstract idea is particular, too. Every general word is particular, *as against another*—glass, table, shoe, arm, head . . . "reality," if you wish. Individually they're all, apart from their sound, abstract words. I'd like to keep them so that you don't clutter them with extra adjectives, extra adverbs; the rest is just good speaking. It might turn out to be crabbed rather than being glib, but if you're good, maybe you'll be blessed by some grace. But this poem is an example of what happens if you deal mostly with sight and a bit of intellect.

Q. Yes, that's what I meant. And doesn't this mean that the poet sees in terms of individual details—with "sincerity," in your sense?

A. But it all mounts up. I suppose there's a general statement: "Not much more than being," whatever that is. The opposite would be non-being. And then I go ahead and say a little more about it; that being becomes isolate being, a beautiful being. These are all assertions. Where is this? That's the first tangible thing, a river-front; the one I saw was probably the Hudson or the East River. But the point is that the river-front becomes more solid as against the general flow of intellect in the beginning. The first part is intellective, "gaseous"; the second part would resemble the "solid" state.

Now what kind of being? There is a shaft with a turning wheel; there are men on the jetty, and a broken wagon. It could have been a good wagon, but I wanted it to be broken. And above this, the sky. So actually I suppose the guy who was doing this was trying to get the whole picture, instead of saying as a "romantic" poet, "Now I'm seeing, now I'm being; I see the jetty; this wagon was once pretty."

What really concerned me in these early poems was trying to get away from that kind of thing—trying to get away from sounding like everybody else. We are all dealing with the same things. Someone makes a table, a bad one; someone makes one that is new and hopefully not to be thrown out the next day.

Q. Where do the leopard and the dragon fit in?

A. That's the contellation. "Leopard, glowing-spotted, / The summer river— / Under: The Dragon:"

Q. Why do you refer to the constellation?

A. There I'm . . . I'm not for metaphor, unless, as Aristotle says, you bring together unlikes that have never existed before. But they're in words; they're in verbs: "the sun rises." My statements are often very, very clipped.

Q. Well, the colon in the last line after "Under" would seem to imply that the dragon is under the river.

A. "Summer river— / Under: . . . . ." There is a question of movement and enough rest; notice the space after "Under." The dragon is
also reflected in the river—inverted. Of course, that kind of thing has
already been done by Mallarmé—not that I knew as much Mallarmé
then as I do now.

Q. Well, to continue this matter of seeing, it seems that many of
your poems—for example, "Immature Pebbles"—are based on "the
unsealing of the eyes bare," as you put it in "her soil's birth." Isn't this
kind of vision associated with what you have called the "spontaneous
idea," which seems to be the mental activity that corresponds to "thinking with the things as they exist"?

A. Yes. I would hope so. All poetry is that. Suddenly you see some
thing. But what was I doing in "Immature Pebbles"? [Thumbing to the
page and looking at it (*Complete Short Poetry*, pp. 41–42):] I start with a
quote from Veblen. *"An Imponderable is an article of make-believe which
has become axiomatic by force of settled habit. It can accordingly cease to be
an Imponderable by a course of unsettling habit."* Well, this was Veblen's
way of writing; it amuses me sometimes. But it was always very difficult.
Actually, Veblen was the kind of man who'd give you a bag of bees and
walk off. All right, I started out with that: an imponderable is an article
of make-believe and it's associated with settled habit, the ordinary, the
mundane, and so on. The only thing is to unsettle it. This particular
spring, in the poem, happens to be the kind of thing that you see on
any beach, but I observed very particular things. Notice that the spring
is still too brisk for water suds, and I've even defined it, "bathers' dirt."
    (All you can say about this poem is . . . it doesn't even have to be
me, but the person will result from the poem. That's why I think it's
useless to try to explain one's poetry. Better that it explain itself after
the poet is gone. One way of its explaining itself is by your reading
what's there: $2+2=4$ does not say $2+2=5$. Now where the difficulty may
come in is that sometimes you get an equation that is so condensed, it
is good only for the finer mathematician. I don't say that to compli-
ment myself, but, you know, mathematicians have standards of fineness; the more condensed the equation, the "nicer" it is.)
    Well to go on, "ripples / make for . . . An observer's irrelevancy of
April." May follows. Obviously, he's not very happy about it because it is
"objectless / of inconsequence" and brings "the expected to the accus-

tomed / in this place." How happy can it be? Obviously, this man who is looking at the "shivering" bathing suits and "the mandrill's blue and crimson / secret parts" is looking at things the "wrong" way and he wants to get away from the scene. But at the same time he has rendered it, "In our day, impatience / handles such matters of photography / more pertinently from a train window." I think you can gather that the man who wrote this poem isn't interested in photographing people bathing on a beach. That's it.

All right, is it as good as Seurat's painting? It may have rendered as much as Seurat in words. Obviously, Seurat was happier with his points of paint than I was with my words. But I've certainly rendered much of these "immature pebbles," in the sense that one may give another the (perhaps undesirable) gift of a *table*. These kids are pebbles; they're a part of nature, they're "nice," but I'd rather see them through a train window. I didn't want to make a photograph and yet I did. It's an ironic poem, but irony is one of the ways of saying things. I prefer singing to this type of thing, but there it is.

Q. I wonder whether you'd mind also commenting on "'Mantis,'" and the poem interpreting it [*Complete Short Poetry*, pp. 65–73]. You seem to be concerned here with the sestina as the ideal expression of the "battle of diverse thoughts" or associations arising in the poet's mind upon his encounter with a mantis.

A. I never said it was the *ideal* form of expression. You have to be careful with this sapless guy, you know. Actually, I was trying to explain why I use the sestina, and there are a lot of old forms used. I suppose there are two types of natures. One is aware of the two-hundred-year-old oak, and it's still alive and it's going to have some use to him; the other one is going to say cut it down and build a supermarket. I'm not inclined to be the latter, nor do I want to imitate a traditional form, but if that thing has lasted for two hundred years and has some merit in it, it is possible I can use it and somehow in transferring it into words—as I said in *"Aleatorical indeterminate"*—make something new of it. And the same for the form of the sestina. Musicians have done that with fugues; there are some today who try to do counterpoint or traditional harmony, but most won't even talk in that terminology. Ultimately it'll come down to silence or sound, words or no words. And where are you going to get them? Where does language come from? Are you just going to make it out of a mouthful of air? Sometimes, but most of the time you don't; there's a world already there; it might be a poetic form that is still useful.

Now the so-called "modern" will say you cannot write a sestina anymore, that Dante did it and it's dead and gone. But every time I read Dante, it's not dead. The poet is dead, but if the work is good, it's contemporary. There's no use in writing the same sestina as Dante, because in the first place, you couldn't do it, except by copying it word for word and believing it's yours—an extreme case. What is possible is that L. Z. or somebody else could write something as good as it. Well, Williams came along and said, "No, we've got to get a new poetic foot," and while he did some wonderful things instinctively, I wish he had omitted some of the theory. Pound was more sensible. What kind of meters can you have? Well, what you've had throughout the history of poetry: you can count syllables, or your language is stressed and so you will count accents, or else you have a musical ear and know when so much sound approximates so much sound and there's a regularity of time. You want to vary the time or have no time signatures . . . whatever the case, it'll have to hold together. So there's no reason why I shouldn't use this "old" form if I thought I could make something new.

"'Mantis,' An Interpretation" is an argument against people who are dogmatic. On the other hand, I point out that as it was written in the nineteenth century (and some "contemporaries" are nineteenth century), the sestina was absolutely useless. It was just a facility—like that of Sunday painters, who learn to smear a bit of oil on canvas. They're not Picasso; Picasso has used every form you can think of, whether it came from Greece, Crete, or Africa. But what I'm saying in "'Mantis,' An Interpretation" is not that the sestina is the ideal form; rather that it's still possible. Williams said it was impossible to write sonnets. I don't know whether anybody has been careful about it. I wrote five hundred sonnets when I was young and threw them away. Then I wrote "A"-7 and a canzone, which is quite different from the sonnet, as Pound pointed out. A very intricate form.

Q. I didn't mean to imply that the sestina was the ideal form of expression *per se*. I thought that for the particular experience that the poet was having with the mantis on a subway, his undergoing a process of "thought's torsion," the sestina was most appropriate.

A. Someone else might have done it differently, but for me that's what it led to. I have that kind of mind. Somehow, you know, the thing can become kind of horrible—to connect a thing with everything. But how can you avoid it? And it's not that I want to be long-winded; I want to be very concise. And when I've done it the long way, as in *Bottom: on Shakespeare* or *"A"*, which is unfinished, then I want to make it very short. For anybody who is interested in the theory of knowledge, which is done away with in *Bottom*, here is the short way of doing it:

I's (pronounced eyes)

Hi, Kuh,

those
gold'n bees
are I's

eyes,

skyscrapers.

[*Complete Short Poetry*, p. 214]

A man can't help himself, any more than Shakespeare could help himself, from saying the same things over and over. The idea is to say them so that people always think you're saying something new. Not that I'm always conscious that I'm doing it. It isn't that I have this concept in my head, that I must say *this*. God knows, when I was through with doing away with epistemology in *Bottom* . . . . (And I don't see why Wallace Stevens ruined a great deal of his work by speaking vaguely about the imagination and reality and so on. He can be a wonderful poet, but so much of it is a bore, bad philosophy.) I was trying to do away with all the things the Hindus avoid by saying, as in *"A"*-12: "Before the void there was neither / Being nor non-being / Desire, came warmth, / Or which first? / Until the sages looked in their hearts / For the kinship of what is in what is not." They had no trouble with non-being, you see.

I said solid state, liquid, gas; as a matter of fact you can word it sense, essence, non-sense. As to the handling of words, there are the words of *sense*. Then, there are words that generalize and say "without this that thing can't be essence." So you have words like truth and reality. The "real" is bad enough, but at least it's a voice, a kid saying, "For real?" But then the philosopher adds the "i-t-y" and you start playing all kinds of word games and that's non-sense. You can get lost, really lost. But the Hindu knew that all these things existed. They do exist and sometimes you want to record it. So much for epistemology. When I'm sick of it, thoroughly sick of it, I handle it in this way. It was *enough* that I wrote five hundred pages of *Bottom.*

Q. What do you mean, you got rid of epistemology in *Bottom?* The work seems to me to be all epistemology.

A. "The questions are their own answers." You want to say "yes," say "yes"; you want to say "no," say "no." It's a useless argument. Well Wittgenstein . . . he was the kind that wondered why anybody should bother to read him. As at the beginning of "I's (pronounced *eyes*)" . . . the *haiku*—everybody's writing *haiku.* You remember Elsie, Borden's cow? That's what I meant, and I greeted her up on the sign there: "Hi, Kuh." "Those / gold'n bees / are I's." Obviously some apparition or vision. She's up there anyway and the golden bees . . . I don't know, she makes honey. The bees are also "eyes." You were wondering which "eyes" see. On the other hand, suppose, without my glasses, I look out at the tower—"those / gold'n bees / are I's, / eyes, / skyscrapers": all I see is Christmas crystallography. It's wonderful, but absolutely astigmatic.

All right, the epistemological question? *I* see this? Yes. The eyes see it? But there's also an object out there. All right, whichever way you want.

Q. Where does the idea of love fit in? It seems to be the chief theme of *Bottom.*

A. Well, it's like my horses. If you're good enough to run or feel like running, you run. If you want to live, you love; if you don't want to live, you hate, that's all. It's as simple as that. It's like being and non-being again—just different words for states of existence.

Q. The horses in "A"-7 don't have any manes.

A. Oh, those particular horses are sawhorses. They don't have any manes. Oh, I see what you're after. I don't think that way, though.

When I say they don't have any manes, that's all I mean. It's like the old song, "Yes, We Have No Bananas."

Q. But you say these sawhorses are also words—so they're not just sawhorses.

A. Then if I say that, they are words. I use words for them; how can I get them across except in words? I say "sawhorse"; otherwise they'd better speak for themselves. That's a case of objectification. There are the sawhorses. All right, somebody can look at them and not bother with them. They interested me. But I wanted to get them into movement because I'm interested in the sound of words. So I got them into movement. Of course, in "A"-7 I have also talked about words, what to do with words.

"A" is written at various times in my life when the life compels it. That also means that my eye is compelling something or my ear is compelling something; the intellect is always working with words. Being a certain creature with my own bloodstream, etc., I will probably, unless I discover something new to interest me or something worthwhile to write about, probably repeat many things. All art is made, I think, out of recurrence. The point is to have recurrence so that it isn't mere repetition, like Poe's "Bells, bells, bells, bells." The idea is to have these recurrences so that they will always turn up as new, "just" different. Something has happened to the movement or you see the thing "differently." Now this business of words occurs in the first movement, "A"-1, and though I'd like to forget it, I must say this: I think that too much of our literature is about the craft of literature. Two great faults I'd like to avoid, but unfortunately I'm among men—I live in my times . . . . The other fault is pretension to learning. How can they all know so many things? By the time I'm eighty I hope to be very simple, if I haven't shut up.

Q. Yet there is a great deal of erudition in *Bottom*, isn't there?

A. I never looked at it as erudition. These were the things I read, and I've probably read very little compared to most people. I don't consider myself a scholar. These are the things I've read, the things I've loved. You've asked about love before. I suppose love means if you do something, that's love; otherwise you don't do anything. There can be, I suppose, a purely passive kind of love. I'm certainly not proud of the erudition. On the other hand, notice that much of the citation of Shakespeare is edited, not because of presumption, but because I wanted to show off the good things.

Q. [Student:] I've been reading the French poet, Ponge, who's extremely interested in words and objects, too. And Sartre, in a little essay on Ponge called "Les Mots et les choses,"[1] mentions that he feels Ponge participated in a kind of crisis of language between 1918 and 1930, and that he was trying to make a word an object like the objects he saw. I was wondering whether you felt that you also participated in a crisis of language, a kind of devaluation of words.

A. Well, things happen, you know, in one's time. I've read some of Ponge and recently Cid Corman printed a good deal of him, at any rate a notebook. He's trying to write a poem in the old-fashioned style about pines, so that it will turn out to be like something by Valéry or Hérédia —the Parnassians or the post-Parnassians, something like that. And no, he felt these *things;* they were, of course, botanical things. (Incidentally, I wish that instead of studying philosophy I had studied some botany.) One of the nice statements that Ponge makes is that the poet who falsifies the object is an assassin; instead of calling the object what it is, this kind of poet develops grand metaphors and all the "baroque" curlicues. Well, I suppose you get to a time where worlds apart two people might be doing similar things. The work itself, of course, is different. Ponge is consistently concerned with botanical objects, just to describe pine needles, for instance. On the other hand, will they—the pine needles—help him? The one line about pine needles in the *Cantos*—the feeling of the redness of the pine needle in the sun— does what Ponge doesn't succeed in doing in that notebook at all, though I admire what he is after. It's certainly more worthwhile than attempting another imitation of Baudelaire. I mean either you show that you're alive in this world, in making something, or you're not.

Q. Would you mind commenting on *"A"*? Do you conceive of the poem as having an overall structure?

1. [The student has misremembered the title of Jean-Paul Sartre's 1945 essay "L'Homme et les choses," collected in *Situations I* (Paris: Gallimard, 1947) 226–270. *Les Mots et les choses* is the title of a 1966 book by Michel Foucault (translated as *The Order of Things*).]

A. I don't know about the structure of *"A"*. I don't care how you consider it, whether as a suite of musical movements, or as something by a man who said I want to write *this* as I thought I saw the "curve" of it in twenty-four movements, and lived long enough to do so. I don't know, how would you consider Mahler's *Song of the Earth* or something like that? No, I didn't think of Mahler. I simply want the reader to find the poem not dull. As I said on another occasion, not anxious to say it then: "Written in one's time or place and referring to other times and places, as one grows, whatever ways one grows, takes in, and hopes to survive them, say like Bach's music." Maybe you get that out of it; maybe it will make its music. I feel a curve or something like that. But in working it out . . . it's the detail that should interest you all the time.

I feel that life makes the curve. That's why Williams kept adding to *Paterson;* he found he had more and more to say and that it was all part of the poem. (You know, the poet is insatiable. I could go on talking forever.) Otherwise, you get down to the old argument, there is no such thing as a long poem; there are some good lines, and so forth. Maybe, I don't know. A long *poem* is merely more of a good thing, shall I put it that way? So the nice thing is, for instance, that Pound's *Cantos* are still coming out. I hope he isn't crazy devoting so much time to the idea that they charged six-percent interest in Pisa, and how wonderful it was. No—rather "Imperial power is / and to us what is it? / The fourth; the dimension of stillness." That's the great Pound. Or in a very late canto, "When one's friends hate each other / how can there be peace in the world?" And with that I leave you.

ABOUT THE AUTHOR

Louis Zukofsky (1904–1978) was born on the Lower East Side of Manhattan. His early work, including his first important published poem, "Poem beginning 'The'," strove to establish the poem as object by employing syntactic fragmentation and line breaks that disrupt normal speech rhythm. Zukofsky invented the term "objectivist" and is widely considered one of the primary forerunners of contemporary avant-garde writing. His many books include *"A"*, *Prepositions*, *Bottom: on Shakespeare*, *Complete Short Poetry*, and *Collected Fiction*.

Library of Congress Cataloging-in-Publication Data

Zukofsky, Louis, 1904–1978.
  Prepositions + : the collected critical essays / foreword by Charles Bernstein ; additional prose edited and introduced by Mark Scroggins. — Rev. and expanded ed.
    p.   cm. — (The Wesleyan centennial edition of the complete critical writings of Louis Zukofsky ; v. 2)
  Rev. ed. of: Prepositions. c1981.
  ISBN 0-8195-6428-1 (pbk. : alk. paper)
    I. Title: Prepositions plus. II. Scroggins, Mark, 1964–   . III. Zukofsky, Louis, 1904–1978. Prepositions. IV. Title.

PS3549.U47 A16 2000
814'.52—dc21   00-035169